PHOTOS   6
EFFECTS MAGIC

By Rhoda Grossman and Sherry London

Contributions by Michel Bohbot, Aren Howell, Scott Kelby,
Gary Kubicek, Kelly Loomis, Felix Nelson, Sharon Steuer,
Cher Threinen-Pendarvis, and David Xenakis

New Riders

201 West 103rd Street, Indianapolis, Indiana 46290

PHOTOSHOP 6 EFFECTS MAGIC

International Standard Book Number: 0-7357-1035-X

Library of Congress Catalog Card Number: 00-104522

Printed in the United States of America

First Printing: February 2001

05 04 03 02 01   7 6 5 4 3 2 1

Interpretation of the printing code: The rightmost double-digit number is the year of the book's printing; the rightmost single-digit number is the number of the book's printing. For example, the printing code 01-1 shows that the first printing of the book occurred in 2001.

Trademarks

Warning and Disclaimer

Publisher
David Dwyer

Associate Publisher
Al Valvano

Executive Editor
Steve Weiss

Product Marketing Manager
Kathy Malmloff

Managing Editor
Sarah Kearns

Acquisitions Editor
Linda Anne Bump

Development Editors
Linda Laflamme

Project Editor
Michael Thurston

Copy Editors
Keith Cline
Stephanie Holmes

Technical Editors
Robert Barnes
Wil Cruz
Ryan Frank
Brad Stone
Lorrie Wehr

Cover Designer
Aren Howell

Interior Designer
Steve Gifford

Project Opener Images
Wil Cruz

Compositor
Ron Wise

Indexer
Lisa Stumpf

Software Development Specialist
Jay Payne

ABOUT THE AUTHORS

Rhoda Grossman

With a background in traditional fine art, illustration, and cartooning, Rhoda began to transfer her skills to the Macintosh in 1989. She demonstrated digital caricature at numerous computer graphics trade shows in the early '90s, and contributed step-by-step artwork to books on Photoshop and Painter. She wrote *Photoshop Effects Magic* (1997, Hayden Books) and more recently co-authored (with Sherry London) books on Painter techniques. This is the third collaboration for Rhoda and Sherry. Rhoda teaches digital art and graphic design at the Center for Electronic Art in San Francisco and Foothill College in Los Altos Hills, California. Her portfolios and a cartoon autobiography can be seen at **www.digitalpainting.com**.

Sherry London

Sherry London is an artist, a writer, and a teacher—which is exactly what a going-into-college aptitude test predicted. (It also predicted that she would make a rotten housekeeper!) She was a Contributing Editor for *Computer Artist* magazine (before that publication's untimely death) and has written for *Electronic Publishing, Pre, MacWeek, MacUser, Digital Vision,* and the combined *MacWorld/MacUser* magazine. She currently writes for *Photoshop User Magazine*. She has taught Photoshop, pre-press, and QuarkXPress at Moore College of Art and Design and at Gloucester County College. She has spoken at a number of conferences, including the Thunder Lizard Photoshop Conference and the Professional Photographers of America convention. She has written a number of books on Photoshop, Painter, Illustrator, and After Effects. She teaches an online Photoshop class at **www.educationtogo.com** and is also working on a Photoshop special effects online course for **www.ehandson.com**. You can reach her at **sherry_london@yahoo.com** or visit her Web site at **www.sherrylondon.com**.

Michel Bohbot

Michel is an award-winning illustrator who combines digital with traditional rendering skills. Michel is a recent president of the San Francisco Society of Illustrators. He has taught courses in Illustration and Business Practices at the Academy of Art College in San Francisco. His current project is an illustrated novella. See more of Michel's work at **www.portfolios.com/ michelbohbot**.

Aren Howell

Aren earned degrees in Graphic Design and Photography from Ball State University in Muncie, Indiana. She has been a graphic designer for 10 years, and has spent the last seven of them designing for various imprints within Macmillan USA, including Adobe Press, Hayden, Sams, and Que. She currently works for New Riders Publishing designing book covers and product marketing materials. Aren's work has been recognized in *Print's Regional Design Annual*, the American Advertising Awards, and the American Graphic Design Awards. If she's not playing golf, she can be reached at **aren.howell@pearsonptr.com**.

Scott Kelby

Scott is President and CEO of KW Media Group, Inc., a software training and publishing company. He is Editor-in-Chief of *Photoshop User Magazine* and *Mac Today* magazine for graphic designers using the Macintosh. One of his more recent books is *Photoshop 6 Down and Dirty Tricks*. Scott is training director for the Adobe Photoshop Seminar Tour and the Technical Chair and Educational Director of PhotoshopWorld (the annual convention for Photoshop users). He's also featured in a series of Photoshop, Illustrator, and Web design video training tapes. An Adobe Certified Expert in Photoshop and one of the leading trainers in the country, Scott teaches Photoshop to thousands of users every year. Visit his Web site at **www.scottkelby.com**.

Gary Kubicek

A professional photographer for more than 20 years, Gary installed Photoshop 2.5 onto his new computer in 1993 and within a month converted his traditional darkroom into a digital darkroom. He is a contributing author for eight books on Photoshop and a technical editor for ten books. Gary is also a digital imaging consultant and teaches Photoshop at Manlius Pebble Hill School in DeWitt, New York. He can be reached at **gary@kubicek.com**.

Kelly Loomis

Kelly is a freelance designer and artist based in northern California. Her traditional work includes stained glass art, for which she does business as *Paine in the Glass*. Her styles and skills range from sketching and painting to jewelry design and clay. She left the corporate world in 1998 to immerse herself in digital graphic design. One of Kelly's favorite features of working digitally: "Clean up is a breeze!"

Felix Nelson

Felix is a traditional illustrator who took a "digital u-turn" in 1988 when he was first introduced to a Mac II cx. He is the Senior Art Director of *Photoshop User* and the Art Director of *Mac Today*, a graphics magazine for Macintosh users. Felix is also the Creative Director of The National Association of Photoshop Professionals. He served as a technical consultant for *Photoshop 6 Down and Dirty Tricks* (Scott Kelby, NAPP Publishing).

Sharon Steuer

Sharon is an artist and illustrator whose work has appeared in numerous books and magazines. Her work has been widely exhibited since the early '80s, and she's taught computer imaging in art schools and training centers throughout the country. Sharon is a recipient of the national Faber Birren Color Award and a Windsor Newton Painting award. Her *Illustrator WOW!* book received the Benjamin Franklin Award as the most outstanding computer book of 1997.

Cher Threinen-Pendarvis

Cher is the author/editor of the highly successful *Painter WOW!* series of books (Peachpit Press). She has won awards for design and fine art, and her digital paintings have been exhibited worldwide. She teaches workshops in computer art in California and Illinois, and is a frequent speaker at national graphics conferences. Both hyphenated and multi-talented, Cher has influenced thousands of digital artists in her many years of teaching and writing about electronic design tools. Did anyone mention that she is an active surfer?

David Xenakis

David Xenakis is the owner of Xenakis Design Services, a corporate high-end color print preparation firm that also offers digital pre-press training. He presents Photoshop and pre-press seminars nationwide. He is also the president of XRX, Inc., a corporation that produces *Knitter's Magazine,* Stitches Fair, and consumer shows. *Knitter's Magazine* (**www.knittinguniverse.com**) was the first nationally distributed publication to be done entirely in QuarkXPress. His interest in pattern comes from his experience as a knitter and weaver. David is the author of *Photoshop 6 In Depth* and has co-authored previous editions of that book with Sherry London.

DEDICATION

Rhoda Grossman

To my students past, present, and future: It's thrilling to watch your creativity find expression on the computer and gratifying to play a small part in the process.

Sherry London

To diversity and peace: Just as this book proves that so many different styles and artistic approaches can join harmoniously into one, so do I dedicate this book in the hope that our world, too, can learn to live together in peace.

ACKNOWLEDGMENTS

Sherry London

I would like to thank the staff at New Riders for their care in putting this book together. I especially want to thank Linda Bump for her very warm friendship.

I want to express my appreciation of and admiration for all of the contributing authors. Their work adds so much to this book. Being able to work with this select group has been a golden experience.

I hope that co-author Rhoda enjoyed the experience enough to team up again! Working with you is always fun!

Margot Maley-Hutchinson, our agent at Waterside, deserves both thanks and good night's sleep (after having just brought little Sammy into the world).

My husband Norm, as always, is the rock of my life. His patience as I write these books is inexhaustible.

Rhoda Grossman

Many thanks to the contributing artists who took time from their busy lives to help create this book.

I'm very grateful to John Webster for providing such wonderful source photos for several projects.

Special thanks go to WACOM Technologies for all the tablets given to me over the years.

Thank you, Sherry, for the opportunity to work together again. Collaborating with you is such a pleasure. How can I say "no"?

A Message from New Riders

As the reader of this book, you are our most important critic and commentator. We value your opinion and want to know what we're doing right, what we could do better, in what areas you'd like to see us publish, and any other words of wisdom you're willing to pass our way.

As Executive Editor at New Riders, I welcome your comments. You can fax, email, or write me directly to let me know what you did or didn't like about this book—as well as what we can do to make our books better. When you write, please be sure to include this book's title, ISBN, and author, as well as your name and phone or fax number. I will carefully review your comments and share them with the authors and editors who worked on the book.

Please note that I cannot help you with technical problems related to the topic of this book, and that due to the high volume of email I receive, I might not be able to reply to every message. If you run into a technical problem, it's best to contact our Customer Support department, as listed later in this section. Thanks.

Email: steve.weiss@newriders.com

Mail: Steve Weiss
            Executive Editor
            New Riders Publishing
            201 West 103rd Street
            Indianapolis, IN 46290 USA

Visit Our Web Site: www.newriders.com

On our Web site, you'll find information about our other books, the authors we partner with, book updates and file downloads, promotions, discussion boards for online interaction with other users and with technology experts, and a calendar of trade shows and other professional events with which we'll be involved. We hope to see you around.

Email Us from Our Web Site

Go to www.newriders.com and click on the Contact link if you

- Have comments or questions about this book.
- Want to report errors that you have found in this book.
- Have a book proposal or are interested in writing for New Riders.
- Would like us to send you one of our author kits.
- Are an expert in a computer topic or technology and are interested in being a reviewer or technical editor.
- Want to find a distributor for our titles in your area.
- Are an educator/instructor who wants to preview New Riders books for classroom use. In the body/comments area, include your name, school, department, address, phone number, office days/hours, text currently in use, and enrollment in your department, along with your request for either desk/examination copies or additional information.

Call Us or Fax Us

You can reach us toll-free at (800) 571-5840 + 9 + 3567 (ask for New Riders). If outside the U.S., please call 1-317-581-3500 and ask for New Riders. If you prefer, you can fax us at 1-317-581-4663, Attention: New Riders.

Technical Support and Customer Support for This Book   Although we encourage entry-level users to get as much as they can out of our books, keep in mind that our books are written assuming a non-beginner level of user-knowledge of the technology. This assumption is reflected in the brevity and shorthand nature of some of the tutorials.

New Riders will continually work to create clearly written, thoroughly tested and reviewed technology books of the highest educational caliber and creative design. We value our customers more than anything—that's why we're in this business—but we cannot guarantee to each of the thousands of you who buy and use our books that we will be able to work individually with you through tutorials or content with which you may have questions. We urge readers who need help in working through exercises or other material in our books—and who need this assistance immediately—to use as many of the resources that our technology and technical communities can provide, especially the many online user groups and list servers available.

■ If you have a physical problem with one of our books or accompanying CD-ROMs, please contact our Customer Support department.

■ If you have questions about the content of the book—needing clarification about something as it is written or note of a possible error—please contact our Customer Support department.

■ If you have comments of a general nature about this or other books by New Riders, please contact the Executive Editor.

To contact our Customer Support department, call 1-317-581-3833, from 10:00 a.m. to 3:00 p.m. U.S. EST (CST from April through October of each year—unlike the majority of the United States, Indiana doesn't change to Daylight Savings Time each April). You can also access our tech support Web site at http://www.mcp.com.

INTRODUCTION

Photoshop has been the standard for pixel-based image editing and manipulation for generations (a generation being about 18 months in this industry). Version 6 contributes significantly to the powerful set of tools you have come to expect from Photoshop.

Photoshop 6 Effects Magic lets you learn from some of the top innovative professionals in computer art and take your skills to the next level. Its purpose is to facilitate your exploration of new features and deepen your understanding of more familiar tools.

Sherry and Rhoda were joined by several very talented contributors, including Michel Bohbot, Aren Howell, Scott Kelby, Gary Kubicek, Kelly Loomis, Felix Nelson, Joni Ruethling, Sharon Steuer, Cher Threinen-Pendarvis, Patricia Uffelman, and David Xenakis.

Everyone on the writing team of *Photoshop 6 Effects Magic* does more than just write. We are all working artists. We share not only the technical savvy we have developed using Photoshop in real-world assignments, but our creative process as well.

WHO WE ARE

The two main authors of this book are Sherry London and Rhoda Grossman, who have co-authored *Painter 5 f/x* and *Painter 6 f/x & Design* (Coriolis). Sherry has also written numerous books on a wide variety of CG applications. Sherry's background in fiber art makes her a "whiz-kid" with patterns and textures. Rhoda is the author of *Photoshop 4 Effects Magic*. She brings her experience in traditional fine art and illustration to the computer.

WHO YOU ARE

This book is intended for intermediate to advanced users of Photoshop and assumes you have a familiarity with the program's fundamentals. You're reading this because you want to get a deeper understanding of those fundamentals, as well as a solid grasp of new features.

We are aware that there is no such thing as a "generic" user of Photoshop. You might be advanced in the tools and features you use everyday, but intermediate on others. You might even be a beginner in a few areas. For that reason, we have included some basics where needed. As a result, advanced users and beginners with a sense of adventure can all benefit from this book.

WHAT'S IN THIS BOOK

Every project in *Photoshop 6 Effects Magic* is a step-by-step project showing you how to create realistic and fantastic effects, ranging from a watercolor rendering of a rose to an extraterrestrial environment. While flipping through these pages, you'll see images developing for each project. You can work a project from start to finish, even if all you do is read the captions on the figures! We do, of course, give you more complete instructions in the text, including notes and tips, that will make you an insider in short order.

We've divided the book into sections based on the methods described: Painting Techniques, Photographic Techniques, Image Manipulation Techniques, and Compositing Techniques.

THE COMPANION CD

Included on the CD that comes with this book are all the files and images necessary to complete the projects. Please note that the project files are for learning purposes only. Copyrights for the images are held by the artists who created them and you may not republish them in any form without written permission from the authors.

OUR ASSUMPTIONS AS WE WROTE THE BOOK

We had four assumptions when we wrote this book, based on our collective experience learning and working with software.

You Like to Learn Visually

A picture used to be worth a thousand words. Even at today's exchange rate, it's still a lot more valuable to see an image rather than have it described to you. You won't have to guess whether you've done a step correctly. We've included a figure adjacent to as many steps as necessary to make sure you stay on track.

Your Time is Valuable

You don't want to spend forever learning one effect, and you don't want to wade through a lot of incidental material before you get to the good stuff. The projects in this book are focused and self-contained. Each project begins with a short paragraph explaining what you will be doing, as well as a brief summary of what tools and techniques will be used to achieve the effect. Find a project that fascinates you and plunge right in.

You Want a Deeper Understanding of Photoshop

It's not enough to learn a recipe for an effect. You need to know how a command or feature works. One of the goals of this book is not only to take you through the steps toward an end result, but also to make sure you understand how you got there. Most steps include a short explanation about why you are using a given tool or setting.

You Want to Learn Techniques You Can Really Use

We want to help you apply these techniques in your own work. To that end, each project includes a number of variations. Try them and then come up with a few of your own. This will allow you to master the techniques and not just the specific images presented here.

CONVENTIONS USED IN THIS BOOK

Every computer book has its own style of presenting information. We begin each project by showing you the end result in all its glory. Next, you'll find the step-by-step instructions for completing the project, including succinct and extremely valuable explanations. That text is in the left column. In the corresponding column to the right are the screen captures and stages of the image as they develop.

We include the complete path for a command the first time it is used in a project, and then just refer to the command itself. For example, Image/Adjust/Levels becomes Levels the next time it's mentioned. Keyboard shortcuts are given as PC/Macintosh equivalents. For example, Ctrl(Cmd)+L will bring up the Levels dialog.

JOIN THE REVOLUTION

How can we refer to the industry's most widely used and established 2D graphics program as revolutionary? This upgrade, Adobe Photoshop 6, represents a quantum leap in overall features and possibilities. When you learn what Text Warp, Liquify, and Art History can do, you'll understand why we're so excited. Try a few projects, and see for yourself.

AIRBRUSH TECHNIQUES

"Everything I've ever done was out

of fear of being mediocre."

—CHET ATKINS

TRADITIONAL AIRBRUSH RENDERING WITH DIGITAL TOOLS

In Photoshop, you can achieve the look of

traditional airbrush painting with the aid of

paths, selections, and layers. Here's a great

way to use a low-resolution source photo

for a high-resolution work of art.

Airbrush Techniques

by Rhoda Grossman

GETTING STARTED

Traditional airbrush painting is done with a tool that sprays tiny droplets of color under varying amounts of air pressure. To prepare the surface before painting, the artist cuts a series of masks to protect or reveal sections of the work.

You'll create an airbrush rendering of a rose. The rose photo you'll work with is also the source image for Watercolor effects in Project 5.

PREPARING THE PATHS

To prepare for painting, you'll make a set of paths and convert them to selections. The saved selections are loaded later, and used as masks for the airbrush rendering.

Just as the traditional airbrush artist must spend considerable time preparing masks before beginning to paint, you will find that this stage of the work is detail-oriented and possibly even tedious. But taking extra time to ensure accuracy, at this stage, pays off when you apply color.

1   Open **rose.tif** from the CD-ROM. Increase size or resolution if you want.

Save the image with another name and keep the original on your desktop to use for color reference throughout the project.

2   Use the Freeform Pen tool from the Pen tool pop-up menu to draw paths around several petals, making sure they are not touching each other. Save the working path by double clicking its name in the Path list. Name it petals 1.

> **Tip:** You might prefer the standard Pen tool if you have skill controlling anchor points and curves, or you want to practice those skills. If you are using a mouse, you can get more control using the Magnetic option for the Freeform Pen tool (the Magnetic feature has been moved to the Options strip.
>
> After you have made a rough shape around one of the petals, hold the Ctrl (Cmd) key down to access the Direct Selection tool for moving anchor points and changing direction lines. Photoshop 6 makes it easy to fine tune paths with the Auto Add/Delete option. When you click on a point, it is deleted; when you click anywhere else on the path, a point is added!

Make a path by drawing around non-touching petals with the Pen tool.

3 Create a new layer, and use the Paths/Fill Path comand in the Paths pop-up menu with 100% Normal color.

Choose any color, as this just keeps track of which shapes belong to which path.

Tip: The Paths palette shares a space with the Layers and Channels palettes. Switch among them by clicking on the file tab for the feature you want to work with. The arrow button on the upper-right gives menu choices for the active palette.

4 Create additional sets of paths for non-contiguous shapes until you have included the entire flower. Name them petals 2, petals 3, and so on. Fill each with a contrasting color. Use the same layer for all color fills.

In this example, everything fits into four paths.

5 Delete the color fill layer. Fill the background with black. Make another transparent layer and name it petals 1.

The color fill layer has served its purpose. You don't really need the background layer with the original image anymore, as long as you have a copy of it open. The copy can be a smaller version to minimize demands on your computer. You'll use the new transparent layer for painting.

Make a new layer and fill the path with a solid color.

Make a new path for each set of non-touching petals and fill each one with a different color.

Fill the background with black and make a new transparent layer for painting.

BEGIN PAINTING

The first transparent layer is ready to paint. You'll make a new layer for each set of petals, convert the path to a selection, and use the Airbrush tool with colors sampled from the rose photograph.

1 Use the Paths/Make Selection command in the Paths pop-up menu to load the petals 1 path into a selection. Use Select/Save Selection to save the selection into a channel.

Tip: Saving the selections is not absolutely necessary, and it adds considerably to the file size. If your scratch disk space is limited, don't bother saving the selections. Paths, like any vector-based data, take up very little space. You can convert paths into selections as they are needed. Just make sure you don't delete the paths until your painting is finished.

2 Choose the Airbrush tool, and use it in Normal mode set at 100% pressure. Press the Alt (Opt) key to sample color from the photo. Spray on the basic color of each shape, adding some shading as you go, but don't get into much shading or detail at this stage.

Note: You can use the keyboard to change brush size and pressure, and to toggle visibility of the "marching ants" as needed. The left bracket key makes your brush smaller, and the right bracket key makes it larger. The numeric keys set the pressure: 1 for 10%, 2 for 20%, and so on. More pressure means more paint is applied as you spray. Ctrl(Cmd)+H hides or reveals the selection's edges.

You'll probably find larger sizes and maximum pressure are suitable for establishing the basic color of a petal. Lower pressure is suggested for shading and smooth transitions. Smaller brushes are useful for adding detail later.

Convert a path to a selection and paint with the Airbrush tool, sampling color from the source photo.

3 Make a new transparent layer named petals 2 and
load the petals 2 path as a selection. Paint with the
Airbrush tool, as before. Repeat for each path.

Be sure to match the layer and path names to avoid
confusion as you work.

Paint the basic colors for each group of
shapes on its own layer.

FINE TUNING

There might be some black background showing between some of the petals,
as a result of your paths not being perfectly fitted together. This problem can be
solved with one or more of the following techniques.

- Select an existing path and rework it with the
  Direct Selection tool, tweaking the anchor points
  and curves so they are flush against adjoining paths
  for a different layer. Add anchor points as needed.
  Then load the corrected path as a selection and
  paint with the Airbrush tool. Be sure to paint on
  the correct layer.

- Load a path as a selection and use Quick Mask
  mode to paint portions of the mask that don't
  conform exactly to the petal shape. It is easier to see
  how you're doing if the black background is made
  invisible. You can also use a different mask color if
  the default 50% red is too similar to the pink petals.
  Then switch from Quick Mask to Normal mode to
  paint corrections with the Airbrush tool.

Repair an imperfect selection in
Quick Mask mode.

> **Tip:** If you repair a selection instead of a path, it's a good idea to save that selection. Avoid having more than one selection saved for a single path by overwriting the previously saved selection. The dialog box for Save Selection lets you choose a destination. Instead of the default NEW channel, choose the channel that you loaded. The improved selection replaces it.

- If the black lines showing through are fairly thin and even, all you need to do is enlarge each selection with the Select/Modify/Expand command. A setting of one or two pixels should be enough if you kept the same size and resolution as this source image. Then paint or fill the new selection edges.

- With all or most of the black spaces repaired, develop the forms of the petals by adding lighter and darker colors. Continue as before to sample color from the source image, and also use Dodge and Burn when appropriate.

- If all else fails, you could always resort to painting a medium brown on the black background under all the "cracks." Whatever works!

You don't need to rely on loading selections at this stage because each group of petals is on its own layer. Click the Lock Transparency check box (formerly Preserve Transparency) if you want to constrain your color to areas that have already been painted.

Expand the selection by one or two pixels. Repaint to the new edges.

ADDING TEXT

The finished image can become a card or poster. Add more space below the rose and create some airbrushed type. By using type selections and shifting them a few pixels between painted strokes, you'll achieve a layered look without actually using layers.

1   Choose Image/Canvas Size, with the anchor point found at the top of the dialog box. Add about two inches vertically. The extra canvas extends through the black background below the rose.

2   Click the Type Mask tool. Click the "T" Type tool and then click the Create a Mask or Selection tool. Find the font and designate the size you want. Type **Rose** or **A Rose is a Rose**, or whatever you prefer.

   A mask in the shape of letters is created as you type. Unlike the standard Type tool, a new layer does not appear. The font used here is "Sand," a casual-looking typeface with irregular edges.

Use the Type Mask tool to create selections in the shapes of the letters you type.

3   Choose the Transform Selection command in the Select menu to change the size of the type masks vertically and/or horizontally, or to change its angle. When you are satisfied with the type mask, save the selection.

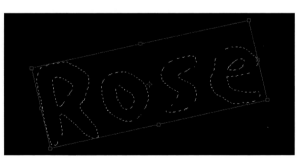

Use Transform Selection to adjust the size, position, and angle of the type masks.

Note: The Transform Selection command behaves exactly like the Free Transform command, except it operates on selection edges instead of the content of a selection. Press the Shift key if you want to constrain proportions as you enlarge or reduce the selection. Move the cursor until it is curved in order to change the angle of the type. If the bounding box extends beyond the image window, zoom out and drag a corner of the image window out to enlarge it. Photoshop's "big data" feature keeps anything larger than the image from being lost, and you now have access to the anchor points of the transform bounding box.

4 Use the Eyedropper tool to sample color from a shadow region of the rose. Paint the type selections with the Airbrush tool, using broad horizontal strokes with low or uneven pressure. Allow some of the background to remain untouched by color.

Although airbrush effects are generally used to create smooth and even color, this time you are deliberately using rough techniques in order to emphasize the casual style of type.

Apply airbrush strokes roughly and unevenly, using a color from the shadow areas of the flower.

5 Move the entire type mask a few pixels up and to the right. Be sure you have a selection tool active, so only the "marching ants" shifts, and not the contents of the selection. Use the keyboard arrow keys to nudge the type selection one pixel at a time.

6 Sample a medium yellow from the rose and use rough uneven strokes to paint the type in its new position.

Offset the type selections and apply similar strokes with yellow.

7 Nudge the type mask once again to offset it from both of the previous positions. This time paint with the brightest pink sampled from the rose.

Apply the third layer of airbrush strokes with light pink.

MODIFICATIONS

As long as you've got those paths you worked so hard to create, use them again to add effects quickly. The Stroke Path command in the Paths menu lets you choose from all the painting and toning tools as well as the Rubber Stamp, Pattern Stamp, and History states. Here's the result of stroking paths with the Burn tool. The edges of the petals are emphasized by a richer tone.

> **Note:** To combine two or more paths into a single path, load each one as a selection, holding down the Shift key for each additional item. Or choose the Make Selection command in the Paths menu and the Add to Selection radio button for each additional path. Then convert the compound selection back into a path. It automatically becomes a new entry in the Paths list. In this project, if your paths are tightly fitted, combining them all into a single selection should give you an outline of the entire rose.

Use the Stroke Path command with the Burn tool.

The original rose photo was designated as the History state, and this is the result of stroking all the paths with the Art History Brush at these settings: Normal mode, 100% Opacity, Tight Short style, 100% Fidelity, 50-pixel area, and 0 spacing. It's a much softer look with delicate wrinkles, which would have been impossible to produce with the air-brush. If you find the effect is too strong, use the Fade command in the Edit menu, or use the History Brush to restore some areas back into a previous state.

Before using the Stroke Path command, you'll need to enter a color, size, opacity, and other settings, or trust that the current settings produce a pleasing result.

Use the Stroke Path command with the Art History Brush.

Tip: Suppose you have two or more versions of the rose image open and you want to use the Stroke Paths command on a version that has had its paths deleted. It could happen! Fortunately, Photoshop enables you to use Alpha channels from any open image with the same pixel dimensions. Just convert the paths of "Image A" to selections (Alpha channels). When you activate "Image B," the Load Selection command gives you access to the saved selections for "Image A."

Note: The final image (shown at the beginning of this project) stops just short of photographic realism. If you want to re-create every wrinkle and striation, do so. You can even add the fly! As with most artwork, knowing when to quit is important. Don't overwork it.

Here's another text effect that uses airbrush techniques. The font is Stencil, and it has been stretched vertically with the Transform Selection feature. Against a gradient of black to green, the word "camouflage" blends into the background just enough to demonstrate its meaning. The random patches of greens, blues, and browns in the lettering are painted with some variation in brush size, pressure, and Blending mode. You can use the Multiply mode to darken the color and Screen mode to lighten it.

Airbrush random patches of color to provide a camouflage effect.

13

COLORIZING

GRAYSCALE IMAGES

"There's no place like home."

—DOROTHY, IN *THE WIZARD OF OZ*

COLOR MODE FILLS USING SELECTIONS BASED ON VALUE RANGE

Whether you need realistic or fantastic effects,

here are techniques for adding color to

grayscale images. You can use similar methods

to alter and enhance color images.

Project 2
Colorizing Grayscale Images

by Rhoda Grossman

GETTING STARTED

You can begin either with a grayscale photo or desaturate a color image. The image you'll use is a still life with a cow skull surrounded by rusting metal bits, broken glass, and rotting vegetation. Use the Info palette and Magic Wand to make selections of midtones, highlights, and shadows, filling each with a different color tint. Then add realistic variation "by hand."

REALISTIC COLOR: SELECTING RANGES

The first stage of the project is to make selections of highlight, midtone, and shadow areas. By saving the selections to the Channels palette, you can use them later to add color to the image.

1 Open **SKULL.tif** from the accompanying CD-ROM. Convert from grayscale to RGB mode.

2 Choose the Magic Wand tool and enter the following:

Tolerance: **24**

Anti-aliased: **Checked**

Contiguous: **Unchecked**

Note: Disable the Contiguous option so you can automatically select all pixels in the image, which meet the selection criteria. Lower Tolerance values result in fewer pixels selected and Higher Tolerance increases the number of pixels selected. You will probably need to use some trial-and-error to determine the appropriate pixel tolerance for other images.

3 Open the Info palette. Hold the Magic Wand over the medium gray area to the left of the skull above the eye-socket. Move the cursor around until Info shows about 200 for R, G, and B. Click to select all pixels within a 24-pixel range above or below that value. Save the selection (Select/Save Selection) and name it midtones.

Save the midtones selection in a channel.

4 Using the settings from Step 2, hold the Magic Wand over the lightest area of the skull, and click when Info shows about 250 for R, G, and B. Save the selection as highlights.

5 Use the Magic Wand again until Info shows about 90 for R, G, and B. Save the selection as Shadows.

Note: Why not choose the very darkest black with RGB at 0 for selecting shadow pixels? In the next section, you will fill each range of grays using the Color mode. Color mode replaces the gray pixels with color at the same value, but has no effect on pure black (or pure white).

Save the highlights selection in a channel.

Save the Shadows selection in a channel.

REALISTIC COLOR FILLS

Using Color mode, you can fill each saved selection with color.

1 Load the midtones selection. Use a blue foreground color with the RGB values of 141, 161, 198. Apply Edit/Fill with the settings:

Contents: **Foreground color**

Blending Mode: **Color**

Opacity: **50%**

Fill the midtones with blue in Color mode.

2 Load the highlights selection. Change the foreground color to a pale yellow (R241, G235, B191). Apply a fill with the same settings as in Step 1.

3 Load the Shadows selection and fill in Color mode, this time with a burnt sienna color (R171, G94, B60).

Fill the highlights with pale yellow in Color mode.   Fill the shadows with burnt sienna in Color mode.

INCREASING REALISM

It's unlikely that a still life like this would actually have single hues restricted to one of three value ranges. This artificial uniformity needs to be broken up. Some touching up "by hand" creates more convincing variations within the color. Some of the pixels, for example, in the skull are too blue because they fell into the midtone range.

1 Enter the RGB values for pale yellow (R241, G235, B191). Use the paintbrush in Color mode at 50% Opacity and paint over those blue regions.

   This should result in toning down the blue enough to produce more realistic effects.

Tone down the blues in the skull with yellow in Color mode.

2   In Color mode, use the blue foreground color
    (R141, G161, B198) to paint some of the bits in
    the orange-brown shadows. Vary the opacity of the
    brush as you work.

    About 50% Opacity gives the pixels a noticeable
    bluish cast while 30% appears to simply reduce the
    saturation of the rust color. The finished art is
    shown at the top of this project.

Note: Traditional artists know that complementary colors
opposite each other on the color wheel can be used to
neutralize each other. You are taking advantage of that
when you combine low opacity tints of blue with yellow
or orange.

EXPRESSIVE COLOR

Begin with the same source image, but this time create color effects that are not
meant to be realistic. You'll use gradient fills with a variety of blending modes
and learn to "massage" color with Hue/Saturation settings.

Note: You can reduce the size and/or resolution of the image if you have
a pokey computer and want to try variations more quickly. The following
settings work regardless of the size or resolution of your image.

1   Open **SKULL.tif** and convert it to RGB.

2   Activate the Gradient tool. Open the presets palette
    in the Options strip by clicking the arrow to the right
    of the gradient swatch. Choose the Violet, Orange
    preset. Use the Linear style and Color Burn mode at
    about 50% Opacity. Drag vertically from the top of
    the image to the bottom.

    Some detail at the dark end of the value range is lost.
    The result seems more dramatic than using Color
    mode, which always keeps values intact.

Apply the Violet, Orange gradient in
Color Burn mode at 50% Opacity.

Tip: Hold down the Shift key to constrain your gradient
and drag it to a perfect vertical angle.

3   Undo the gradient.

    Prior to clicking Undo, you can use the History
    palette to save a snapshot of the image at this stage.

4   Keep the same violet, orange preset, and change to
    Difference mode and 100% Opacity. Drag vertically
    from top to bottom.

    Difference mode can usually be counted on to
    produce some wild color effects, and you won't
    be disappointed this time. Some of the color is so
    wild it is outside the CMYK gamut, so it can't be
    shown here.

5   Turn on the Gamut Warning in the View menu.
    Choose Select/Color Range and pick Out of Gamut
    from the Select menu. Click OK. Hide the selection
    edges [Ctrl(Cmd)+H] to make the "marching ants"
    invisible without deselecting any pixels.

    The Gamut Warning enables you to see which pixels
    are too saturated to print accurately. They appear as
    dull gray areas. You'll fix the problem in the next
    step. Be sure to leave the Gamut Warning on.

6   Use Image/Adjust/Hue/Saturation [Ctrl(Cmd)+U] to
    edit the Master instead of separating ranges of color.
    Reduce Saturation until the gray Gamut Warning
    disappears.

    You can make a snapshot of this state if you like it
    well enough to save.

Turn on Gamut Warning
in the View menu.

Reduce saturation until all colors
are within the CMYK gamut.

7   Use Hue/Saturation once again, this time working
    with Hue (H) and Lightness (L) as well as Saturation
    (S) in separate color ranges. You can try your own
    settings or use these:

    Reds: **S −82, L +14**

    Magentas: **H +101**

    Greens: **S −76, L +49**

    Cyans: **S −82**

    Blues: **S −72, L +61**

    The result here is a rather ghostly effect with the
    skull looking as if it were made of crumbling ashes.
    The foreground now appears to be sandy soil.

    Severely reducing saturation in all or most of the
    color ranges results in some subtle effects. You can
    see the image update as you manipulate each slider,
    so you can make decisions about Lightness and Hue
    before you click OK.

Massage Hue, Saturation,
and Lightness in separate
color ranges.

GRADIENT MAPPING

A new way to add or alter color is by using the Gradient Map found in the
Adjust menu in Photoshop 6. It applies your choice of gradient by mapping
the lightness values of the image to the colors along a gradient ramp. Many
presets are available. You can create your own custom gradients as well.

1   Begin with the original skull still life, converted to
    RGB or CMYK mode.

2   Use Image/Adjust/Gradient Map. A dialog box
    appears with the current "Gradient Used for
    Grayscale Mapping" displayed and applied to
    the image.

Note: The Gradient Editor enables you to change the colors and their positions
(color stops) along the gradient ramp. This is an efficient way to apply specific
color to each value range in the image without having to make selections for
highlight, midtones, and shadows. You are not restricted to just three value ranges
and you can customize any gradient in numerous ways—change one or more
colors, move color stops or transition midpoints, and add or delete color stops.

Choose the gradient you want by clicking the arrow to the right of the gradient ramp. This opens the Gradient Picker along with a pop-up menu giving you access to all the gradient presets. The Color Harmonies 2 presets are shown with the Orange, Purple, Red gradient selected and applied to the image.

Now you'll create a custom gradient to produce the same results you achieved earlier with selections and Color mode fills.

3   Undo the Gradient Map you just applied, or return to the previous state of the image through the History palette.

4   Choose the Gradient tool and click once on the current gradient in the Options strip. This brings up the Gradient Editor.

5   Make a new Gradient Map with the colors used earlier: Pale yellow, grayish blue, rust, and add black at the extreme right of the ramp.

You can preview the effect in the image before you commit to it. Add your custom gradient to the current library by naming it and clicking the New button.

Note: The colors in a gradient are mapped to the tonality of your image from left to right, the lightest areas receiving the leftmost color, and the darkest tones getting the color at the extreme right. If the gradient gets darker smoothly from left to right, the original grayscale tones are maintained. If other types of variation in lightness appear along the gradient, the lightness values in the image change accordingly. The result can resemble the effect of using Image/Adjust/Curves creatively.

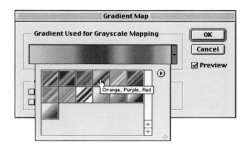

Select a gradient in the Gradient Map dialog box.

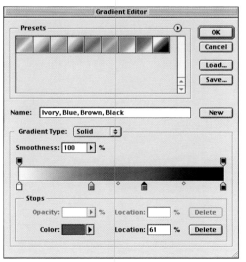

Make a new Gradient Map and save it.

6 Click OK to apply the Gradient Map to the skull image. The result should be quite similar to the version you made earlier, but this time no selections were required.

> **Note:** Users of Corel (or MetaCreations, or Fractal Design) Painter might recognize a similarity between Photoshop's Gradient Map and Painter's "Express in Image" command. Painter provides a bias slider for altering color mapping much like the Curves command in Photoshop.

Apply your custom Gradient Map to the image.

MODIFICATIONS

If you're getting tired of the skull still life, another image is available for this project on the *Photoshop 6 Effects Magic* CD-ROM. It's **OPARADIS.tif**, a grayscale photo of a Bird of Paradise plant.

This image has three distinct regions to be colored—leaves, flowers, and background. More accurate selections are required than for the skull still life.

> **Note:** For a quick and dirty solution, you can simply pick a green and orange and use the paintbrush in Color mode for leaves and flowers, respectively. Background color is up to you. But accuracy and realism will be better if you take the trouble to create selections for each area and then apply fills.

Use the Magic Wand tool to make the basic selection of the leaves. Improve the selection in Quick Mask mode. Toggle Quick Mask mode on or off by pressing **Q**. Use the Paintbrush or Airbrush to add to the selection/mask by painting with white. Subtract pixels from the selection/mask by painting with black. Return to Standard mode. The changes you made now show as marching ants. Save it to a channel. Do the same with the flowers and the background.

To have more options later, make a new layer for color. Load each selection in turn, filling it with your choice of color in Normal mode set at 100% Opacity. Use a simple gradient for the background.

Switch the Blending mode for the layer to Color, so the values of the original show. Reduce the opacity of the color layer as needed. This one is set to 75%.

Use Quick Mask mode to perfect the Magic Wand selection of leaves.

On a new layer, add color fills to each selection.

Change the layer to Color mode and reduce its opacity.

Make a cast shadow from combined and transformed selections.

It's useful to have saved channels for each section of the image. You could modify them later in a number of ways. Feather them, for example, for a softer color fill. Or use the Transform Selection feature to distort and reduce the combined leaves and flowers selections to make a cast shadow. You'll need to subtract the original leaves and flowers selections before you fill with the shadow color.

Practical uses for Color mode fills or painting with Color mode include altering the existing color in a portion of an RGB or CMYK file. Change the color of an article of clothing in a fashion layout, for example, without having to arrange for another photo shoot. Emphasize one item in a photograph by coloring it and leaving the rest in grayscale. If the photo is in full color to begin with, desaturate everything except the item you want to attract the viewer's attention. This photo at the entrance to an estate is more dramatic when color is restricted to what you see beyond the gate.

Desaturate a portion of a photo to emphasize the areas with color.

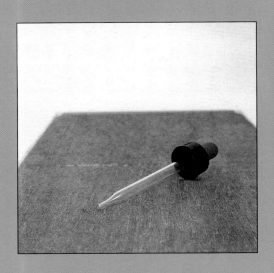

BRUSH TECHNIQUES

"Start every day off with a smile

and get it over with."

—W.C. FIELDS

PAINTERLY EFFECTS WITH CUSTOM BRUSHES AND ART HISTORY

Photoshop's painting tools aren't just for

retouching photographs. You can use them to

create an entire painting or illustration from

scratch. It's useful to know how to control

brush behavior, and how to make new brushes

that have the qualities you want.

Brush Techniques

by Rhoda Grossman

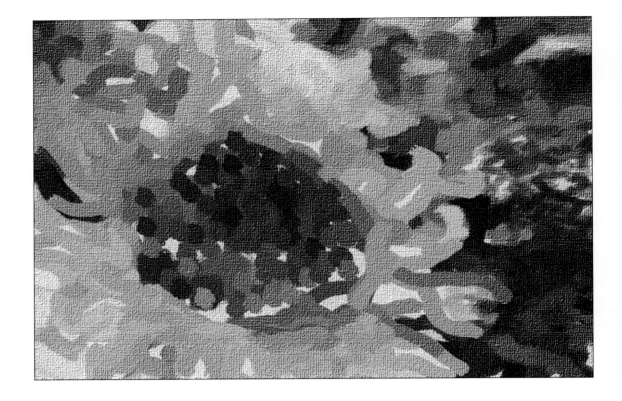

GETTING STARTED

In this project, you'll create your own custom brushes and re-create exciting abstract
paintings from ordinary source images with the new Art History feature. Later, you'll
have the opportunity to work with a source image in ways that bear no resemblance
to retouching whatsoever!

Note: Many brush effects are difficult to produce without a
WACOM tablet, and this project assumes you are using one.

BRUSH CONTROLS

Warm up by making a few test strokes with different kinds of brushes and variations in the Brush Controls on the Options strip.

1 Open a new white image in RGB mode at 72ppi. Make it big enough to allow some practice scribbling.

2 Activate the Paintbrush tool and choose the Hard Round 19-pixel brush from the default brushes. Using the following settings in the Options strip:

Mode: **Normal**

Opacity: **100%**

Wet Edges: **Off**

Use the Brush Dynamics controls (found at the extreme right of the Options Strip) to specify Stylus pressure for variation in Size and Opacity.

Turn on Wet Edges and make a similar stroke.

3 Switch to the Soft Round 27-pixel brush and use the same settings as in Step 2. Make two strokes as before, one with and one without Wet Edges.

Examine the qualities of a hard-edged and soft-edged brush stroke, with and without Wet Edges. The Wet Edges effect forces pigment to pool at the outer edges of the stroke. The effect appears more pronounced when you use a soft brush. This is useful for emulating traditional watercolor. See Project 5, "Photoshop Watercolors," for an in-depth exploration of watercolor techniques.

Use stylus pressure to control the size and opacity of brush strokes.

Compare two similar strokes with and without Wet Edges.

Note: The third variable in Brush Dynamics/Color refers to the interaction of foreground and background color. Variation in stylus pressure creates variation between those two colors. If you're working on a white surface and the background color is white, the Color Dynamic will appear to be the same as opacity.

Mouse users can produce a gradual reduction of size or opacity by choosing Fade from the Brush Dynamics pull-down menu and specifying the number of steps in pixels over which the fade will occur.

4 Find the Spatter 39-pixel brush from a list view of brushes and make some test strokes with your choice of Brush Dynamics settings.

By default, brushes are shown as small thumbnails. You can locate a brush by name if you choose "text only" or one of the list views from the flyout menu available when the Brush library is open. Shown here is the large list view, including both the name of the brush and a look at its thumbnail.

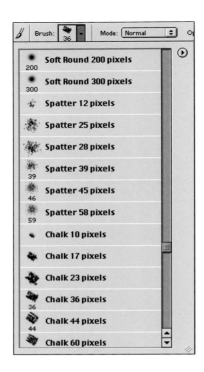

Select the Spatter 39-pixel brush from a list view of brushes.

5 Switch to the Chalk 36-pixel brush. Use a complementary color for the background color and make some strokes.

The example uses stylus pressure for all three Brush Dynamics variables. Notice that the thumbnails for the Spatter and Chalk brushes are not based on an ellipse. They each began as a group of pixels that were defined as a brush. You'll create some custom brushes using the Define Brush command in the next section.

Paint with a Spatter brush and a Chalk brush.

CREATING A CUSTOM BRUSH

You can create a brush from a spatter, a scribble, or a small portion of an existing image by selecting it and using the Define Brush command in the Edit menu. In this section, you'll make a Bristle brush from scratch.

1   Choose the Hard Round 1-pixel brush, the smallest brush in the Default Brush palette.

2   Using black, make a small scribble, similar to the one in the figure.

3   Drag a rectangular selection marquee to fit around your scribble.

4   Choose Edit/Define Brush.

The location of the Define Brush command is a bit illogical, as the New Brush command is in the brush flyout menu. "New" brushes can only be round or elliptical.

5   Give your new "sampled" brush a descriptive name when prompted and choose its default spacing.

> **Note:** The Spacing slider shows up when you click the Brush preview box in the left part of the Options palette. To save your setting, click the New Preset button.

Spacing is an important variable. The lower the spacing, the smoother the resulting brush stroke. You might want the decorative look that results when spacing is at 25% or higher. Use around 5% spacing for a smooth stroke that imitates the look of a real-life Bristle brush. Shown here (from the top) is 50%, 25%, and 5% spacing.

Make a tight scribble with the Hard Round 1-pixel brush and select it with the rectangular marquee.

Designate the spacing for your sampled brush.

Here are two items created with the sampled brush you just made. The lacy border was created by pressing the Shift key to constrain the strokes to straight lines. Spacing was set to 50% and all Brush Dynamics variables were turned off. This is a great way to make the edges for a certificate, your official "artistic license" perhaps? Add hand lettering with calligraphy—Photoshop provides a complete set of Calligraphic brushes.

The little kiwi bird has feathers made with blue foreground and violet background colors. The Brush Dynamics were set to Fade: Size and Opacity by 25 pixels and Color by 10 pixels. Fading color more quickly than the other variables gave the secondary color more prominence. The beak, legs, and feet were painted with a thin Calligraphic brush using a longer Fade (60 to 100 pixels).

With short fades and a soft round brush, you can make decorative scales on a fish. More variations in fade and color combinations put an entire flower garden within your reach. And you can do it all with a mouse!

Tip: To make your own collection of custom brushes, find the Brushes folder in the Presets folder. Copy one of the alternative brush families to another location. Rename it My Brushes or whatever you like, keeping the .abr extension on the file name. Then return it to the Brushes folder. Quit Photoshop and then relaunch it. Now, My Brushes is available for loading. Delete the brushes you don't want from the original presets, and add your own as you create them.

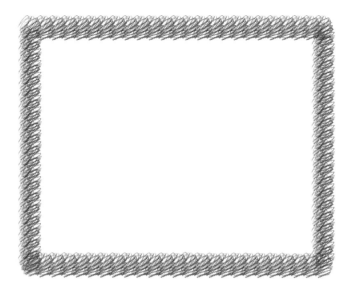

Make a variety of effects with variations in spacing and Fade amount.

ART HISTORY

Sharing space on the toolbox with the History Brush is the new Art History Brush. As does the History Brush, the new brush uses a previous state of the image as the source of color and value input. Art History, however, applies those colors and values with brush strokes that introduce an abstract quality. In this project, you will start with an image of sunflowers as your source and create a much more abstract version of it.

1   Open the file **SUNFLOWR.tif** from the CD-ROM. Fill it with white in Normal mode at about 85%.

    This results in a faint image of the original to use as a guide.

2   Choose the Art History Brush.

    Unless you made changes to History options, Photoshop automatically creates a snapshot of your image's original state to serve as the History source.

3   Select the Chalk 44-pixel brush from the Brush palette.

    Other good choices include the Spatter group in the Default palette and the sampled items in Natural brushes. You can, of course, create your own brushes to use with Art History.

Fill the source image with 85% white in Normal mode.

4 Choose Loose Long from the Style menu. Paint the petals of the large flower in the foreground.

> **Note:** Be sure you have the desired settings for Brush Dynamics. Only size and opacity are available, of course, as color is literally drawn from the original state of the image. It's unlikely you'll want your strokes to fade out as you paint them, so check to see that either Stylus is enabled or that Size and Opacity variations are turned off.

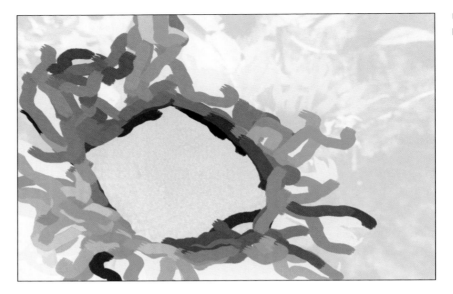

Use the Loose Long style to paint the larger petals.

5 Use the Spatter 39-pixel brush and the Tight Curl style to paint the center of the flower. Decrease the Fidelity to about 25%, so you can get more variation in color than is provided in the original image.

6 Select the unpainted area on the right with the Magic Wand, to protect the sections already painted. Replace default brushes with Natural Brushes 2 and use the Chalk-Dark 50-pixel brush with Tight Long style. Reduce Fidelity to about 35%.

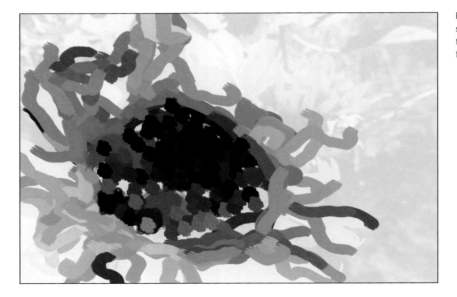

Reduce Fidelity to the source colors and paint the center of the sunflower with Tight Curls.

7 To paint areas remaining on the left, select them with the Magic Wand, and use the sampled brush you made earlier.

The example shows the Loose Long style and 72% Fidelity.

8 To create the look of paint on canvas, use the Texturizer in the Filter/Texture menu. The settings used for the image shown at the beginning of this chapter are as follows:

Texture: **Canvas**

Scaling: **125%**

Relief: **10%**

Light Direction: **Bottom Right**

Fill in remaining areas with your sampled brush.

Note: Even if you used all the settings recommended in the steps, your finished painting can't possibly look exactly like the example. There appears to be some randomness built into Art History. Embrace that element of unpredictability, if you can. If you must have complete control and perfectly reproducible results, you'll probably need to rely on filter effects.

MODIFICATIONS

You can use Art History effects sparingly to enhance parts of a photograph rather than completely repainting it. Find the photo **GONDOLAS.tif** on the CD-ROM. The challenge is to keep the foreground silhouette and create a painterly background.

Open GONDOLAS.tif.

Select all black areas, including windows, with the Magic Wand (Contiguous turned off) and Inverse the selection. Fill the background with a dark color. Brown is used in the example. Traditional oil paintings are often begun on a canvas covered with a thin wash of dark paint.

Use Art History with a Stipple brush from the Natural brushes presets. I used the 30-pixel size with a Tight style, switching from Long to Medium to Short as the painting developed. Fidelity to color is at 100%.

Select the background, and fill it with a dark color.

Working on a dark surface makes Lighten mode or Luminosity mode an effective alternative to the default Normal. When you work light over dark, the blank areas don't look quite as "naked," so don't fill the image completely. Instead, leave some rough variations to show the edges of strokes. The finished art looks fresh.

Paint with a Stipple brush in the Tight style with variations in length.

This photo of the Capitol building is more dramatic with a softer background to set it off. Several brushes in the Faux Finish presets were used, with reduced Fidelity (about 75%) to create more color variation in the sky. A similar approach is useful with portrait photography.

There are so many variables and choices to be made in the process of creating a painting with Art History Brushes. Different artists will certainly produce divergent results. Even one artist repeating this project will make different choices each time and end up with another variation. No wonder Monet painted those haystacks over and over at different times of day and seasons of the year.

Apply Art History painting to the background only,
to enhance the primary subject.

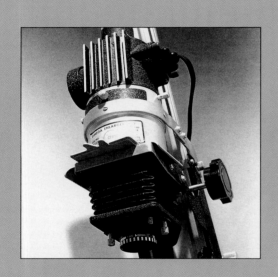

PAINTING WITH LIGHT

"Drinking and driving don't mix.

That's why I ride a bike."

—DUCKIE DALE, IN *PRETTY IN PINK*

CREATING AN OUTER SPACE ENVIRONMENT

By using a combination of filters, you can make

compelling extraterrestrial images of planets

and solar systems with clouds of "space gas."

Just tighten your asteroid belt, and get ready

to play with some radial gradients, Lens Flares,

and cloud fills.

Project 4
Painting with Light

by Rhoda Grossman

GETTING STARTED

Beginning with a blank white "canvas," you can create
an image using Gradient fills, Lighting Effects, and other
commands found in the Filter/Render menu. While using
the Fade command in the Edit menu, choose an alternative-
Blending mode to gain control over this combination of effects.

40

BUILD A PLANET

In this section, you'll begin with a white canvas (5 inches square at 200 ppi) in
RGB mode. A close-up of a planet can be created with a radial gradient, a color
inversion, and Hue/Saturation adjustments.

1 Click the Gradient tool. From the Options strip,
choose the Radial style and the Chrome preset. Drag
the pointer from the upper-left corner to the center
of the canvas.

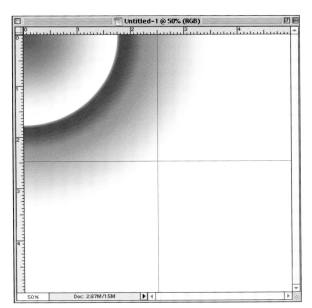

Drag a Radial Chrome gradient.

2 Use Image/Adjust/Invert (Ctrl[Cmd]+I) to reverse
the colors and values. Now your image has a black
background and the planet has a rich blue halo.

Invert colors of the Chrome gradient.

3 Use Image/Adjust/Hue/Saturation (Ctrl[Cmd]+U) to reduce saturation and lightness, and to adjust the hues of the image, using these settings:

Edit: **Blues**

Hue: **+180**

Saturation: **−45**

Lightness: **−30**

Notice only the Blue range is adjusted.

Edit the Blue range with Hue/Saturation settings.

Note: Editing the Blues leaves the planet's color unchanged, and only alters the glow. Drag the Hue slider completely to the right to give the planet and its glow the same general warm, orange color. An additional and unexpected benefit is the appearance of a pinkish ring around the planet. I chose to reduce saturation and lightness to make the glow more subtle. Higher values might suggest a much hotter celestial body, like a sun.

ADD SPACE GAS

To produce the effect of random areas of gaseous material, you'll fill the image with clouds and fade them until they are barely visible. This adds atmosphere and also helps to create the illusion of depth.

1 Choose a dark brown (such as R94, G80, B76) for the foreground color.

2 Apply Filter/Render/Clouds. The clouds will completely fill the image and obliterate the planet and its glow. Don't panic or do anything else either; the next step will fix the problem.

3 Use Edit/Fade and reduce the cloud fill to 25%. The result is a subtle variation of luminosity in the planet's glow.

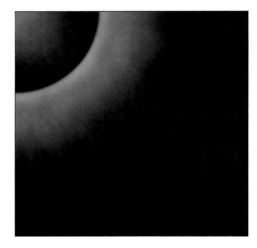

Fade the cloud fill.

Note: Using the Edit/Fade command provides an opportunity to change the Blending mode, as well as reduce the intensity of the effect. As alternatives to the 25% fade in Normal mode recommended in Step 3, set the Opacity to 40% and Mode to Exclusion. This combination results in a few clumpy clouds of gas over the dark areas with a noticeable reduction in brightness and contrast throughout the image. (Opacity: **45%**, Mode: **Hard Light**.) Clumpy clouds again, but no effect on brightness and contrast.

DESIGN A SPIRAL NEBULA

One of the more dramatic objects in space is a galaxy in spiral form. You'll use the cloud fill on a new layer, apply the Twirl filter, and trim away excess pixels. The Shear filter skews the nebula and, finally, a layer mask gradient will be used to create more depth.

1 Create a new layer. Use white and a gray-blue (R144, G169, B197) to make a cloud fill. You can use Ctrl(Cmd)+F because Render Clouds was the last filter applied.

2 Change the Blending mode for the cloud layer to Soft Light. Keep Opacity at 100%.

3 Apply the Distort/Twirl filter to the cloud layer with the angle you want.

The example used 569 degrees. If you would prefer a tighter or looser spiral, increase or decrease the angle setting.

Next you'll apply the Twirl filter.

Create a new layer with a gray-blue fill and Render Clouds.

4 Make an elliptical selection with the center of the twirl at the center of the selection and Feather set to 25 pixels.

5 Invert the selection and press Backspace/Delete to eliminate the outer area of the layer. Be sure to deselect the image before you start the next step.

Note: For easier selection centering, hold down the Alt (Opt) key and drag from the center.

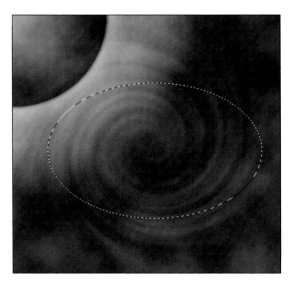

Select an elliptical shape around the spiral.

6 Use Filter/Distort/Shear with the settings shown.

This step creates the illusion that the nebula is seen at an angle along its edge. For a better composition, you might want to move the nebula over toward the right. Assuming the nebula is several hundred light years across, you'd expect the far edge to be dimmer than the edge closer to your point of view. You'll create this illusion in the next steps.

7 Change the Blending mode to Hard Light. Turn the layer's Opacity down to about 72%. The Hard Light Blending mode strengthens the spiral layer while 72% Opacity keeps it from being too strong.

8 Make a layer mask for the spiral layer.

9 Choose the Linear Gradient tool with the Black/White preset. Drag the gradient diagonally from the upper-left of the spiral and through the center to the lower-right. Flatten the image.

If the effect is too strong, press the Edit/Fade command, or simply repeat the gradient drag, making it end closer to the center of the nebula.

Note: Here's how a black-to-white gradient in a layer mask works. Pure black makes the pixels of the image layer 100% invisible. Pure white leaves the pixels unchanged. Shades of gray create partial visibility. So, a gradient from black to white makes the nebula, in this case, gradually fade into visibility. To determine the most pleasing fade-in, you might need to experiment with the angle or distance of the drag. Just be aware that the point where you begin to drag is pure black, and the point where you finish is pure white.

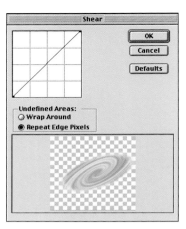

Shear the spiral.

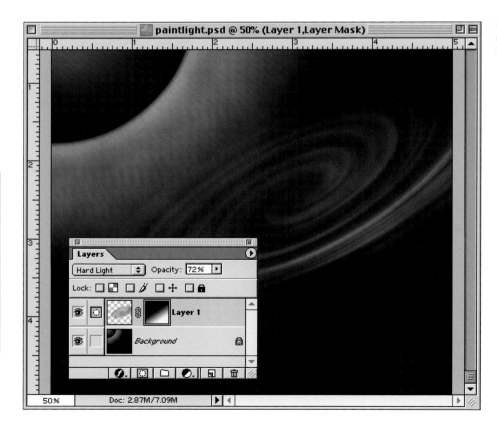

Create depth with a gradient in the layer mask.

BRIGHT DETAILS

You'll need a flashy bit to suggest that a star is beginning to show at the edge of the planet. To add it, you will use a Lens Flare and some selective reversion with the History Brush. Finishing touches are achieved with a custom Lighting Effect.

1   Use Filter/Render/Lens Flare with the Brightness set to 121% and the Lens Type set to 35mm Prime. Be sure to place the center point of the flare on the edge of the planet disk, about one-third of the distance from the top of the image.

2   Establish the previous state of the image as the source by clicking the button to the left of that state in the History palette. The History Brush icon appears to indicate that this state will be painted back into the current image.

3   With the History Brush, carefully paint over the rather large disk near the lower-right of the image.

You just finished an illustration that would look respectable in *Scientific American*. But if you'd rather approach the editors of *UFO Digest* or *Alien Invaders Weekly*, proceed. The next steps show how to create a custom Lighting Effect.

Note: The Lighting Effects dialog box has an unusually large number of controls. You can begin with almost any preset and alter it by adding or deleting lights, changing the color, position, direction, intensity, and focus of each light. Ambience is an important control, determining how much of the current image will still be visible.

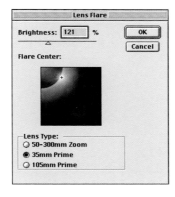

Place a Lens Flare at the edge of the planet.

Choose the previous state in the History palette for the History Brush to paint back. The disk is a side effect of the Lens Flare filter.

Erase unwanted Lens Flare elements with the History Brush.

4 Use Filter/Render/Lighting Effects and choose the Five Lights Down preset. Eliminate one of the lights by clicking on its icon in the preview box and pressing Backspace (Delete).

Change the colors of each of the remaining four lights by selecting it and clicking in the white swatch for Light Type to access the color picker. Choose a pink, a yellow, and a blue for the lights (from left to right), and allow the fourth light to remain white.

5 Increase Ambience in the Lighting Effects dialog box to about 53.

6 Use the preview on the left to select and alter the position, angle, and spread of each light. When you click on a light to select it, you'll see an ellipse with anchor points and the color indicator at its center. Move the light by dragging it from the center point. Change the angle by dragging the anchor point that is connected to the center by a line segment. Drag any of the anchor points to widen or narrow the spread.

There are no numerical settings, so use the figure as a guide. After you've gone to all that trouble, why not save your configuration as a new style? The result of adding color to the dark foreground is not only visually pleasing, but adds some mystery to the image. Are those luminous colors emanating from space ships, alien beings, or what?

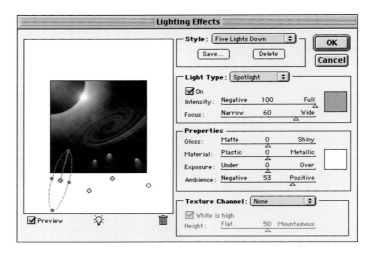

Add colored lights at the bottom by customizing the Five Lights Down preset.

46

MODIFICATIONS

Say you want to create just planets, moons, and other spherical objects in space. Skip the steps for creating the spiral nebula, and use the following recipe based on gradients and fades.

Replace the default gradients with the Special Effects gradients. You'll need to click the triangle in the Gradient indicator to get the Gradient palette, and then click another triangle to get the Gradient menu. Alternative libraries of presets are listed at the bottom of this menu.

With the Special Effects gradients loaded, choose the preset named Shiny Sphere. Change the Blending mode for the Gradient tool to Lighten and drag in the image. Don't save, because you'll need to fade this fill. Use Edit/Fade to soften the effect by 50%, and change the Blending mode to Exclusion. Now you've got a pale sphere in a hazy green mist.

Use the Shiny Sphere gradient to make a glowing green planet. The brighter moon within the planet's corona is made in a similar way. This time use the Matte Sphere preset (also in the Special Effects Gradient palette) in Lighten mode like you did before. Choose Edit/Fade once again, this time using the Color Dodge mode, reducing Opacity to taste. You might not want to fade this gradient at all. It looked pretty cool.

Use the Shiny Sphere gradient to make a glowing green planet.

Use the Matte Sphere gradient and then Fade with Color Dodge mode.

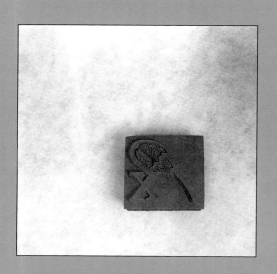

PHOTOSHOP WATERCOLORS

"A cynic is a man who, when he smells

flowers, looks around for a coffin."

—H.L. MENCKEN (1880-1956)

PAINTING A WATERCOLOR

Beginning with the same reference photo

of a rose used in Project 1, "Airbrush

Techniques," you can use two totally different

techniques to reach the same goal—

a watercolor rendering of the image. Painting

a watercolor relies on the Wet Edges feature

of the Paintbrush tool, but you can create a

watercolor image algorithmically. The variations

are endless, and results range from slightly

distorted reality to wildly fanciful.

Project 5

Photoshop Watercolors

by Rhoda Grossman and Sherry London

GETTING STARTED: PAINTING WITH WATERCOLOR

For Rhoda's technique, you'll use the painting skills you already have, or learn some of them here. Many variables are involved in both traditional and digital painting:

- Color, opacity, and texture of the paint
- Size and shape of your brush
- Pressure and direction of your brush strokes

In addition, you have some options not usually available to the conventional watercolor painter:

- Blending mode for applying strokes
- Fading the opacity of your last stroke
- Use of toning and smudging tools on previously painted areas

You'll use a photo for reference, make a rough sketch on a new layer, and build up color on another layer with brushes using Wet Edges.

> **Tip:** Use of a WACOM tablet is strongly recommended for this project, or any work that requires drawing and painting. The control and natural feel afforded by a pressure sensitive stylus simply cannot be achieved with a mouse.

WATERCOLOR PAINTING: THE PRELIMINARY SKETCH

The first phase in creating the painting is tracing an outline of the basic forms of the subject.

1 Open **ROSE.tif** from the accompanying CD-ROM. Duplicate the image.

By duplicating the image, you can have one copy to work on and another to remain on your screen for reference throughout the project.

2 Using either the original or a copy, make a new layer and fill it with white. Turn the Opacity of the layer down to about 60%.

Make sure you can see the flower enough to guide you through the next step.

Open the source image.

Note: If you'd rather skip this section, use the Sketch layer in **ROSE.psd** from the *Photoshop 6 Effects Magic* CD-ROM.

3 With the white layer active, sketch the outline of the rose petals using a small brush and a medium-dark color.

The example uses a brown composed of R169, G141, B131.

Tip: The sketch should be loose and casual. Don't even try to get much detail at this point.

Sketch the outlines of the rose on a white layer with 60% Opacity.

WATERCOLOR PAINTING:
PREPARE TO PAINT

You won't need many colors to paint the flower. Instead of using the Eyedropper tool every time you want to sample a color from the original image, it's handy to use a custom set of swatches derived from the rose. You can use the color table **Rose.act** provided in the resources on the *Photoshop 6 Effects Magic* CD-ROM, or create a similar set of swatches from scratch with the following steps:

1   Use Image/Adjust/Posterize to reduce the full range of color in the image to between six and eight levels.

Posterizing is not only the first step in creating a set of custom color swatches, it also serves another important function. It reduces the number of colors, so you can see highlights, shadows, and midtones much more clearly. Six to eight levels are recommended for this image. Choosing fewer levels tends to distort the colors. However, increasing the number of levels begins to reduce the functionality of this maneuver.

2   Use Image/Mode/Indexed Color with Palette set to Exact and Forced to None. Click OK, and open the Color Table now available in the same menu. Save it.

Use Exact to limit the colors to those actually in the image. In the example, eight levels were used to posterize and 92 colors appear in the Color Table. This is because all three color channels (R, G, and B) were reduced to eight levels of gray.

3   Open Swatches and enter the Replace Swatches command in the pop-up menu to load your custom Color Table.

Posterize the image to reduce the number of colors.

Load the Color Table derived from the source image.

WATERCOLOR PAINTING: PAINT

With the original Rose visible at about 33.3% magnification and the custom color swatches open, you are ready to paint. You'll use the paintbrush with Wet Edges on, and vary the size and opacity of your strokes. The painting begins with a thin wash of color. You'll gradually develop the forms with more saturated color and darker tones in the shadows. Large brushes are useful early in the painting, giving way to smaller sizes for details.

1 Choose a soft round brush about 65 pixels wide. Use Darken mode and set Opacity to 25%. Click Wet Edges.

Darken mode ensures the sketched outlines are unchanged. An important key to painting with a watercolor effect is using the Wet Edges option for your painting tool. Wet Edges imitates the look of pigment pooling toward the outside of the brush stroke as in traditional watercolor.

2 Specify the Brush Dynamics you prefer for Size, Opacity, and Color. The Brush Dynamics controls are found at the extreme right of the options strip when a painting tool is active.

Choose Stylus in Brush Dynamics in order to set the pressure of your stroke and to determine Size, Opacity, and/or Color. If you are using a mouse instead of a graphics tablet, use the Fade option for Opacity, which makes the brush dry out as you apply a stroke. You might need to experiment with the settings to get the fade-out effects you want.

Tip: Remember that Opacity can be manipulated quickly with numeric keys: Pressing **5**, for example, changes Opacity to 50%.

Tip: Use either Fade or Stylus in the Brush Dynamics to change between the foreground and background colors. With a pink foreground and a yellow background color, for example, you can make a gradient within a single brush stroke.

3 Paint the lightest colors first. Just a couple of pinks and yellows chosen from your custom swatches are enough at this stage. Apply light tints to the entire rose with large (65px to 100px) brushes.

Large brushes establish the basic colors quickly and avoid too many overlapping brush strokes. Overlapping strokes are desirable a bit later in the painting.

Tip: You can change brush size quickly with the bracket keys. The left bracket makes the brush smaller and the right bracket makes it larger.

4 Build up color while developing the forms of the flower.

This stage can be split into a number of stages, depending on your experience and how you prefer to work. It might include several overlapping strokes with the same color in certain areas. Darker shades should be added in shadow areas, and more saturated colors applied to midtones. A great way to "wipe up" too much color is with the Dodge tool.

Paint light tints on the entire rose.

Build up color and develop the forms of the petals.

Tip: Work the entire image to about the same degree of development, rather than concentrating on just one section. This assures that the painting remains balanced. Also, as your skill increases, the whole painting improves. It's also easier and more efficient, to apply the same color to all the areas that need it.

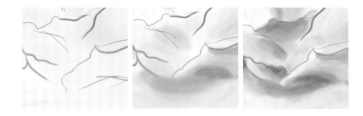

Work the whole image to the same level of development. (Detail of one area at three stages.)

5 Continue layering more color and adding detail with smaller brushes. Try some alternatives to the round brushes in the default palette.

You might want to change to a chisel-shape brush to paint in the crevices between petals. For the example, Rhoda used the Pencil-Thick brush in the Natural Brushes 2 palette.

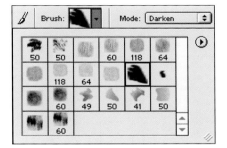

Use an alternative to the round brushes, such as the Pencil-Thick brush in the Natural Brushes 2 group.

6 Add a dark background with overlapping black strokes at about 50% Opacity.

As you apply the finishing touches, use the toning tools (Dodge, Burn, and Sponge) to lighten, darken, or change the saturation of painted areas. Use the Smudge tool for smoothing rough spots, but use it sparingly, because an authentic looking watercolor should have some variations due to brushstrokes overlapping. Take advantage of the Fade command when you want to reduce the strength of your last stroke.

Continue developing the rose and add a dark background.

In the before-and-after detail shown, shadows were intensified with the Burn tool. The Sponge tool was used in Desaturation mode to reduce the harshness of some burn strokes without changing the new (darker) value. On the right side of this portion of the image, the Smudge tool was used to soften and blend some watercolor strokes.

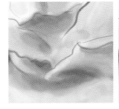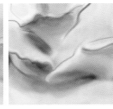

Use toning tools and the Smudge tool for finishing touches.

Add finishing touches. Use toning tools as needed.

MODIFICATIONS: WATERCOLOR PAINTING

Finishing touches can include emphasizing the crinkled edges of a few petals, using a small brush and a dark color from your swatches. Avoid using black or any completely desaturated gray in the painting. Ideally any white highlights should be the result of no paint applied. But you can recreate the look of pure white paper with white paint, the Dodge tool, or the Eraser at less than 100% Opacity.

You can eliminate the sketchy outline after rendering the rose in watercolor by creating a new white layer over the sketch before you begin to paint. Use Multiply mode for the layer so you can see the sketch while you're painting. This would be a good way to proceed even if you're not sure what you want to do with the sketch layer. You might end up merging the painted layer with the sketch, or reducing the opacity of the sketch without harming the painted layer.

Often, the most difficult stage of this project is knowing when you are finished. This is entirely a matter of your own style and preference. If you want a tight, realistic rendering, you might have to work longer to develop the details. If you believe "less is more" or "enough is enough," you will be satisfied when the rose is still a little rough in spots. See Project 1 for a step-by-step airbrush painting of the same subject.

Try watercolor techniques with portrait sketches or architectural renderings. Use Wet Edges for a quick and casual looking pattern with overlapping horizontal and vertical strokes.

A soft round brush with Wet Edges and a bright color makes glowing neon tubing in a single stroke.

Although you wouldn't know it from their name, the Spatter brushes in the default group produce strokes with the look of stiff bristles. They are an excellent choice for rough sketches or a dry brush effect. Use them with Wet Edges to produce partial transparency when layering strokes.

Note: "Dry brush" refers to the look of a brush running out of paint or loaded with a small amount of thick paint. The texture of bristles is made prominent with this technique. If you agree the Spatter brushes should be called Bristle brushes, use the Rename Brush command in the Brush Palette menu.

Paint patterns with Wet Edges.

Make neon tubing with a single stroke.

Use Spatter brushes for a dry brush effect.

ALGORITHMIC PAINTING: GETTING STARTED

Sherry's watercolor technique uses a number of Photoshop features to work its magic. You'll use the High Pass filter to create a mask that helps to retain image detail. You'll adjust the colors of the original image so they are fanciful (or you could leave them alone for a more realistic look). You'll learn how to use the Difference Clouds and Crystallize filters, as well as Difference mode, to produce a stylized watercolor of the original image.

ALGORITHMIC PAINTING: CREATING A DETAIL MASK

When you create the watercolor algorithmically, your first step is to create a mask. You will use this mask later to put detail back into your image.

1   Open the image **ROSE.tif** from the accompanying CD-ROM.

2   Create a duplicate of the Green channel of the image by dragging the Green channel to the New Channel icon in the Channels palette. Name the new channel Detail Mask. leave this channel active as you work the next few steps.

You need to build a Detail Mask channel now, even though you won't actually use it until much later in the technique. The Detail Mask channel will enable you to put back some of the features of the original rose after you have manipulated the image almost out of recognition. The Green channel usually contains the most contrast among the channels, so it will make the best Detail Mask for this image.

Choose an image, such as a flower, that would make a good subject for a watercolor.

3 Choose Filter/Other/High Pass with a setting of 2.0.

The High Pass filter reduces the contrast in the image. At a low setting, it reduces the contrast so much that you can use other filters or commands to easily create detailed black and white images from the High Pass image.

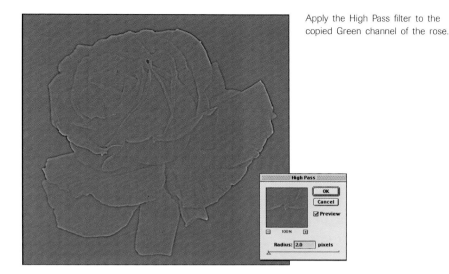

Apply the High Pass filter to the copied Green channel of the rose.

4 Open the Image/Adjust/Levels dialog box. Into the Input Levels boxes, enter the following settings:

Black Point: **134**

Gamma: **3.70**

White Point: **160**

The High Pass filter removed all the white and black from the channel. These values condense the range of values in the Detail Mask channel and set values that force the channel to mostly black or white, which is very good for a mask. All of the image detail is forced to white.

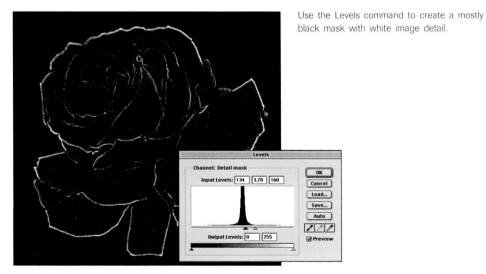

Use the Levels command to create a mostly black mask with white image detail.

5 Choose Filter/Blur/Blur More.

The Blur filter smoothes some of the jaggies left when you changed the image to sharp blacks and whites. If you want more control, you can always use the Gaussian Blur filter, but the small amount of automatic blur created by the Blur More filter is really quite adequate here.

Apply the Blur More filter to finish creating the Detail Mask.

ALGORITHMIC PAINTING: CHANGING THE IMAGE COLORS

You can change the colors in your image to make them more saturated and vary the tonal range. You don't have to work this section, but it can make your ultimate result more exciting, and you should know how to do it. Therefore, in this section, you'll push the colors of the rose around a bit.

1 Set your focus back to the RGB channel.

2 Choose Filter/Noise/Median with a setting of 4 pixels .

The Median filter blurs colors together to find an average color at a given spot. It keeps the colors more pure than using the Gaussian Blur filter. You can vary this setting, but the higher the Median value, the less texture your final image has. However, that could be just what you want.

Apply the Median filter to blur the rose.

3 Choose Image/Adjust/Hue/Saturation. Increase the image Saturation to 70.

You can increase the Saturation as much or as little as you like. Intense color here results in more intense color in the finished image.

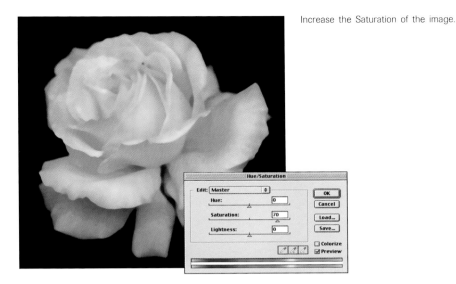

Increase the Saturation of the image.

4 Choose Filter/Sharpen/Unsharp Mask, and enter the following settings:

Amount: **150%**

Radius: **1 pixel**

Threshold: **0 levels**

This step restores some of the sharpness lost during manipulation with the Median filter.

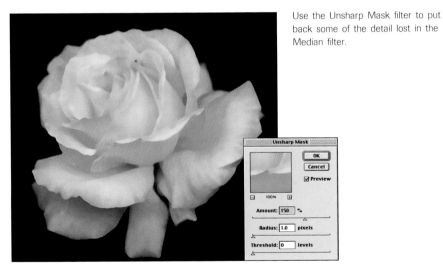

Use the Unsharp Mask filter to put back some of the detail lost in the Median filter.

5 Choose Image/Adjust/Levels. Pull down the Channel drop-down that says RGB when you first enter the dialog box. Choose the Red, followed by the Green, and finally, the Blue channel and enter the following settings:

Red Channel: White Point = **200**

Green Channel: White Point = **223**

                          Gamma = **.68**

Blue Channel: White Point = **157**

(You can also use the settings stored in **ROSE.alv** on the accompanying CD-ROM.)

This step expands the color range in the image by squeezing the white point closer to the black point. Don't change the black point in any of the channels. Each image requires different settings, so experiment with these on your own. If you move the Gamma point in a channel, you alter the image, tinting it toward either the color of the channel or its complement. Moving the Gamma slider left in the Red channel tints toward red, whereas moving it to the right tints toward cyan. The opposite of green is magenta, and the opposite of blue is yellow.

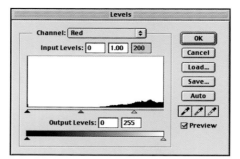

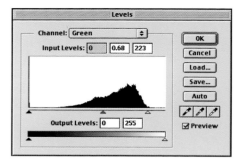

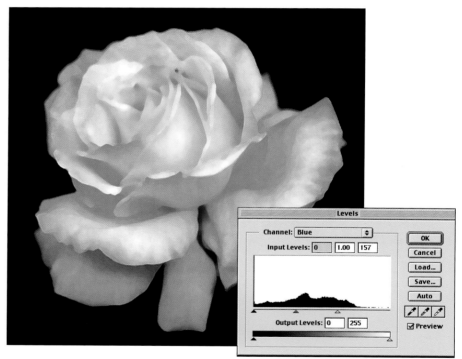

Use the Levels command to expand the tonal range of the flower for more intensity.

ALGORITHMIC PAINTING: ADDING TEXTURE

In this phase of the project, you'll add several filters to the flower to give it texture. The Emboss filter helps you choose the color tones for the image. The Crystallize filter breaks up the colors, and Layer modes provide the rest of the technique.

1 Duplicate the Background layer (as Background copy).

This enables you to preserve the original for later use or start over.

2 Choose Filter/Stylize/Emboss. Enter these settings:

Angle: **−17°**

Height: **3 pixels**

Amount: **100%**

The exact settings aren't important. The key determining factor is locating the setting that enables you to see the most vivid or contrasting edge or trace colors in the image. You need to pick two of these trace colors for the next step.

3 Using the Eyedropper tool, select a pink from the edge of the rose for the foreground color. Press the Alt (Opt) key and select a strong blue for the background color. To duplicate the colors shown here, enter these settings:

Foreground: **R255, G185, B202**

Background: **R128, G185, B255**

The colors impart a "feel" to the image. The technique seems to work best when you pick a dark and light color. It doesn't matter which is foreground and which is background.

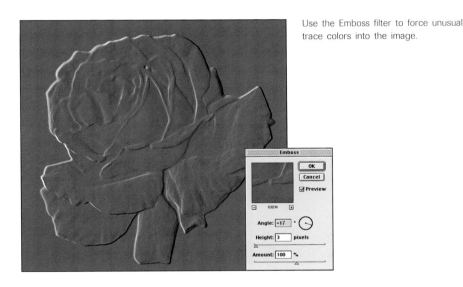

Use the Emboss filter to force unusual trace colors into the image.

4 Choose Filter/Render/Difference Clouds.

The Difference Clouds filter uses the new foreground and background colors that you selected. As it applies the clouds to your image, it changes the original colors as if you were using Difference mode.

Choose the Difference Clouds filter to add new color to your image.

5 Choose Filter/Pixelate/Crystallize. Set Cell Size to 20.

The crystals become the brushstrokes for the water-color. The Cell Size determines the scale of the texture in the image.

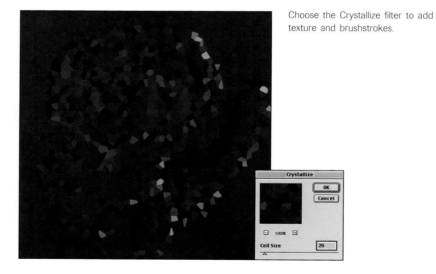

Choose the Crystallize filter to add texture and brushstrokes.

6 Change the Background copy layer to Difference mode.

Difference mode restores some of the original image color. This is one potential stopping point for the technique.

Change the Blend mode for the Background copy layer to Difference.

7 Choose Image/Adjust/Invert.

Inverting the layer makes the colors completely different. Subsequent layers will modify this color shift.

Invert the layer to dramatically change the colors.

8 Drag the Background copy layer to the New Layer icon to duplicate it. Name the new layer Copy 2.

The layer remains in Difference mode, so this puts back an intense version of your starting colors. This is another potential stopping point (especially if you make a layer mask from the black surrounding the Background layer).

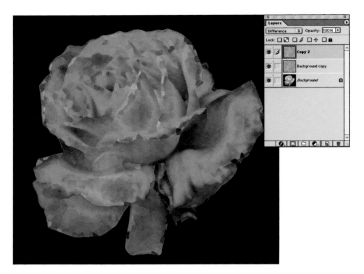

Duplicate the Background copy layer.

9 Choose Image/Adjust/Invert with the Copy 2 layer active. Drag the Copy 2 layer to the New Layer icon to duplicate it. Name the new layer Copy 3. Invert the Copy 3 layer. Choose Filter/Pixelate/Crystallize and set Cell Size to 10.

All these inverted copies in Difference mode change the way the image looks and the colors it contains. You can continue this process as long as you like. The smaller setting on the Crystallize filter adds additional texture.

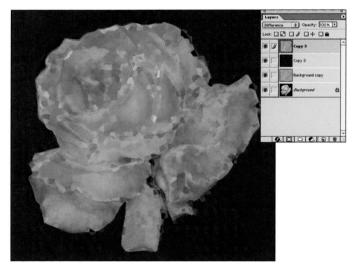

Invert the top layer, duplicate it, and invert the duplicate.

10 Activate the Background copy layer. Choose
Filter/Blur/Motion Blur. Enter these settings:

Angle: **−28°**

Distance: **70 pixels**

The Motion Blur filter adds a feeling of motion and
brush stroke to the image.

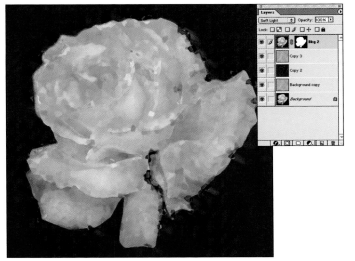

Apply the Motion Blur filter to
the Background copy layer.

11 Drag the Background layer to the New Layer icon.
Name the new layer Bkg 2. Drag the Bkg 2 layer to
the top of the layer stack. Change the Blend mode
to Soft Light. Use the Magic Wand tool with the
following settings:

Tolerance: **50**

Contiguous: **Checked**

Anti-alias: **Checked**

Click in the black area of the layer. Choose Select/
Inverse and change the selection into a layer mask.

This step puts back the original color, but the result
is much softer than the other steps that restored
some of the original color. This, too, is a potential
stopping point.

Duplicate the original image, drag it to
the top of the layer stack in Soft Light
mode, and mask out the background.

12 Drag the Bkg 2 layer to the New Layer icon at the bottom of the Layers palette. Change the Blend mode to Hue. Choose Image/Apply Image, and place the Background copy layer into the new layer.

Of all the many ways to get a new image into the top layer while reusing the layer mask on the Bkg 2 layer, this one is the easiest. It also allows you to preview and decide whether you prefer Background copy, Copy 2, or Copy 3. Each choice gives you a different image.

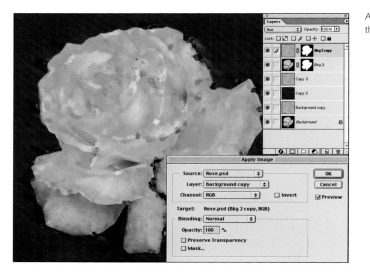

Apply the Background copy layer to the already masked top layer.

ALGORITHMIC PAINTING: FINISHING UP

The only task left is to add back the detail into your image using the Detail Mask you created at the start of this project.

1 Create a new, blank layer at the top of the layer stack.

2 Load the Detail Mask (in the Channels palette) as a selection.

3 Press **D** to set the colors back to the default of black and white.

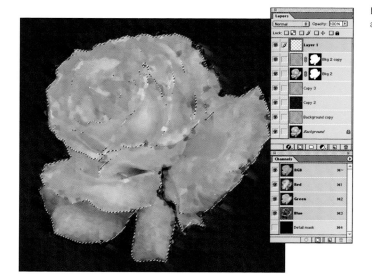

Load the Detail Mask as a selection.

4 Hide the marching ants. Fill the selection on the
   empty layer. You might want to do this two or three
   times. Deselect.

   Because the Detail Mask contains many gray values,
   the selection doesn't permit the full intensity of the
   foreground color to be used. You can, therefore,
   darken the results by filing the selection multiple
   times.

Fill the edge detail selection
with black several times to
add line detail to the image.

ALGORITHMIC PAINTING: HOW IT WORKS

This is really a sneaky trick.

The Median filter sets the stage by blurring the colors, and the Levels command
enables you to alter them and get as much color change as you want.

The Emboss filter makes the color turn neutral, but it also brings out other
areas of contrast in the image. It gives the other filters something to work on.
You also get to pick two colors for your image from the result.

The Difference Clouds filter prepares the image for the Crystallize filter. If you
get flat color from this filter, pick different colors.

The Crystallize filter creates your brushstrokes. The size of the cell is really
important. Larger is usually better, but small cells show more image detail.

Repeating and mixing layers and Blend modes expands your options.

MODIFICATIONS: ALGORITHMIC PAINTING

This project has a huge set of possibilities. Almost any point along the way can be a stopping point. The only requirement is that you like it. Change Blend modes. Try them all. Keep duplicating layers. Add more filters to the layers. Remove some layers.

Here are some of the different results possible from just this image:

The opening image, **ROSESOFT.psd**, uses Color Burn mode for the repeat of the starting image. It has no mask on the top layer, and it uses slightly different starting colors.

ROSEPASTEL.psd skips the section "Changing the Image Colors" and uses the original opening image. It has fewer layers as well.

ROSE14MEDIAN.psd uses a setting of 14 on the Median filter. It is much smoother than the other images. It also eliminates the final Hue Blend mode.

Try using Color Burn mode, as shown in ROSESOFT.psd, instead of Soft Light.

Use the original unaltered image for the Emboss filter, as shown in ROSEPASTEL.psd.

ROSE14MEDIAN.psd uses a larger Median filter setting for a smoother image.

You can create a sketched look by merging the three Difference Mode layers. You might also create a sketch by tossing away some of the layers.

All these variations are in layered files on the accompanying CD-ROM, so you can examine the various permutations of the technique.

You can enhance the technique by using some of the new layer styles in Photoshop 6. Try adding gradient, texture, or color overlays to the images as well.

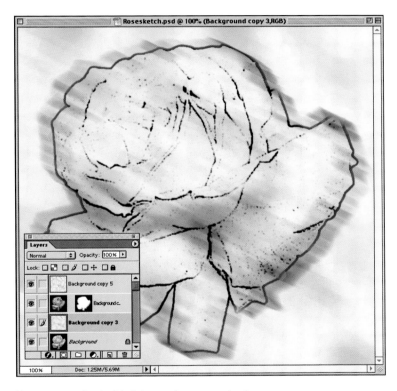

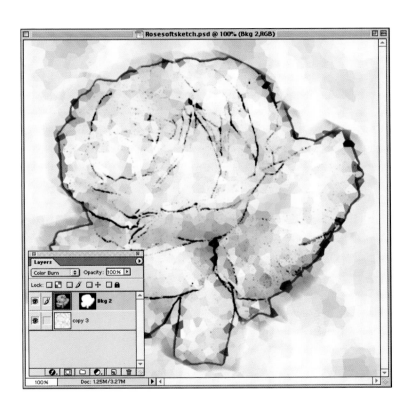

You can get a sketched look by merging or removing layers.

PHOTO PATTERNS

"Repetition does not transform

a lie into a truth."

—FRANKLIN D. ROOSEVELT

TESSELLATIONS AND TONES

You've all seen images comprised of thousands of other tiny images. Those mosaic images require special software (or a huge amount of patience) to construct. You, however, don't need anything more than imagination and a little bit of time to create an image that uses a single pattern and yet accurately reproduces the values in the original image. In the process, you'll also learn one of the "Escher-pattern" tessellation techniques.

Project 6
Photo Patterns

by Sherry London
With creative input
from David Xenakis

GETTING STARTED

To reproduce the values in a photograph through a pattern, you need to create the basic pattern and then create versions of that pattern tile at different degrees of light and dark. Finally, you need to replace the original values in the photograph with the appropriate pattern. In this project, you'll learn how to create a tessellation as the pattern tile. A tessellation is a non-rectangular, interlocking, repeating unit. The most famous artist to use tesellations was M.C. Escher, the Dutch artist who drew the interlocking lizards and the mutating geese.

The basic process is as follows:

- Create, fill, and tile the tessellation.
- Create a rectangular pattern tile.
- Set the midtone tile.
- Create pattern gradations.
- Posterize the photo.
- Add the pattern layers.
- Adjust the pattern scale.
- Colorize the image.

Note: You'll learn how to create a basic tessellation by reading the instructions in this book. However, the rest of the creation process for the tessellation is located in the **06_extra.pdf file in the Projects/06** directory on the CD-ROM. You'll be able to work the rest of the project in the book, if you don't want to try the entire technique, by loading the main image and the already-created patterns from files on the CD-ROM.

CREATING THE TESSELLATION

You can create an interlocking pattern from a rectangle as long as you start by creating a line that touches only three corners of the rectangle. When you duplicate this line, each duplicate becomes one of the four sides to the new shape. Because all four lines are identical, the object automatically is an interlocking pattern tile that can be infinitely repeated. In this section, you'll create the tessellation using a photo as the guide.

1   Open the file **ianphoto.psd** from the accompanying CD-ROM.

     Ian is Alexandra's older brother. He is going to become the pattern that you use to produce Alexandra's picture, shown in the opening image.

2   Use the Rectangular Marquee tool to select an area that is smaller than the ianphoto.psd image and covers Ian's face and elbows.

     Your tessellation shape, which you haven't created yet, is going to be very irregular. You want the finished tessellation tile to fit inside of the ianphoto.psd image. If the tessellation is too big, you won't have enough of Ian's picture to fit inside of it. Therefore, you begin by creating a selection on the actual photo, so you don't make the tessellation tile too big.

Note: The image of Ian was originally the same size as the image of Alexandra. It has already been reduced in size 25%. (It has also been manipulated a bit on the layer that is hidden.) You'll make it even smaller before it becomes the pattern, but this is a workable size without being too small to handle.

Select around Ian's head with the Rectangular Marquee tool.

3 Set your colors to the default of black and white.
Create a new empty layer. Choose Edit/Stroke.
A 1-point stroke is sufficient. Deselect.

The stroked selection allows you to see what used to
be the marquee, and to draw outside of it. Because
the tessellation technique requires you to draw outside
of the selected area, you can't leave the selection active.

Note: An alternative to the stroked selection in a
layer would be to save the selection as a new alpha
channel, and then turn on its Eye icon to preview the
area occupied by the selection. The choice is yours. I
find it easier not to have to cope with the shaded red
area of the alpha channel.

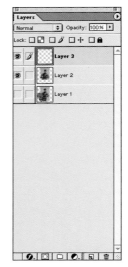

Stroke the selection
on a new layer.

4 Select the Pencil tool and a small brush. Create a new
layer at the top of the layer stack. Draw a line similar
to the one in the screen capture. It needs to touch
three of the four corners in the rectangle. Make sure
that the Pencil touches the corners *inside* of the
stroked rectangle.

Any "half" of a four-sided figure may be defined by
drawing two lines between three points (two end
points with a corner point between them). The line
that you just drew becomes two sides of the shape.
Don't hug the outline of Ian too tightly. If you need
to make the outline smaller before you use it, you
might cut off part of Ian's head. It's better to leave a
bit of extra room rather than too little.

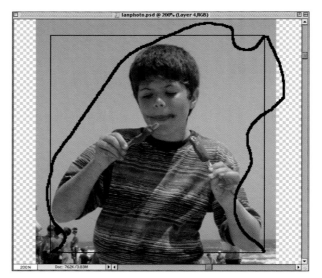

In a new layer, draw a Pencil line that touches
three of the four sides of the rectangle.

5 Create a new 800×800-pixel file. Drag the Pencil outline layer from Ian's photo (the "working" image) into the new file. Turn off the Eye icon on the Background layer.

This is a "scratch file," which is what it will be called when you use it. You'll use this file first to build the tessellation outline, and then to fill it in. The only requirement for the file is that it must be much larger than you need, so that you don't run out of room. Making it three to four times the working file height and width should be sufficient.

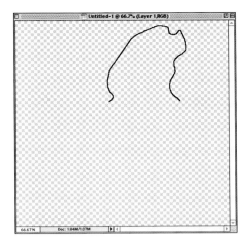

Create a new file, and drag it into the outline you created above.

6 Activate Layer 3 of your working image (Ian). Set the Magic Wand to the following:

Tolerance: **0%**

Anti-alias: **Unchecked**

Contiguous: **Checked**

Click inside of the stroked rectangle. Read the dimensions from the Info palette.

To move the line exactly the distance needed to create the tessellation, you need to know the dimensions of your stroked rectangle. This is the easiest way to figure it out. You might want to write the dimensions on a piece of notepaper.

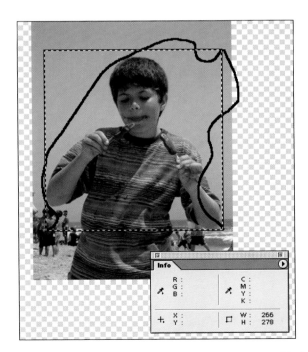

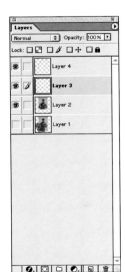

Click inside the stroked rectangle on Layer 3 with the Magic Wand tool, and read the dimensions from the Info palette.

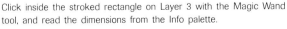

7 In the scratch file, duplicate Layer 1 by dragging it to the New Layer icon in the Layers palette. Choose Filter/Other/Offset. Enter 0 for the Horizontal field and enter the selection height from Step 6 in the Vertical field.

You need three to four copies of the line (depending on its shape) to create a closed object. Use the Offset filter to move the copied line down until it just touches the bottom of the original line.

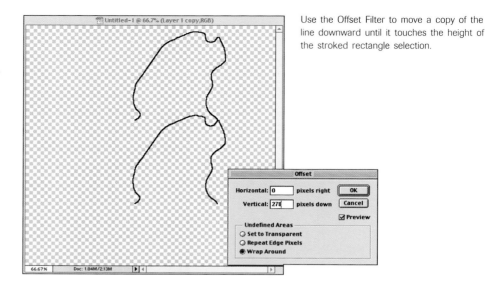

Use the Offset Filter to move a copy of the line downward until it touches the height of the stroked rectangle selection.

8 Duplicate Layer 1 copy, and use the Offset filter to move the shape horizontally to the left of the width of the stroked rectangle. Then duplicate Layer 1 again, and repeat the Offset filter with the previous setting.

You have four copies of the lines. The lines should touch at the three "corner" points that you took such care to create in Step 4. You should have a closed shape somewhere on your image. The closed shape shown here only needed three of the lines. If you had used the first three corners of the stroked rectangle instead of the bottom-left, upper-right, and lower-right, you would have needed all four lines. Skipping one corner, as I did, creates an interesting, although complex, shape.

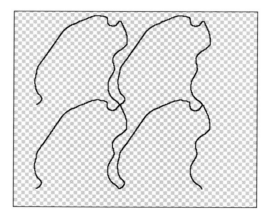

Offset a copy of both line layers horizontally to the right the same distance as the width of the stroked rectangle.

Note: If you discover that your closed shape has over-lapping lines, start over again. The shape won't tile without some major work and experimentation. Simplify your line on your next try. You can get very creative with the shapes, but get a feel for the technique first.

9 Create a new empty layer at the top of the layer stack. Type Shift+Crtl+Alt+E (Shift+Cmd+Opt+E) to merge all of the visible layers into the new layer (Layer 2). Turn off the Eye icons on all of the lower layers.

You need to erase the extra line segments in the next step. It's much easier to do that if the entire shape is in one place. If you forgot to turn off the Eye icon on the Background layer, do it *before* you Alt (Opt)+ Merge Down. You need the top layer to contain transparency.

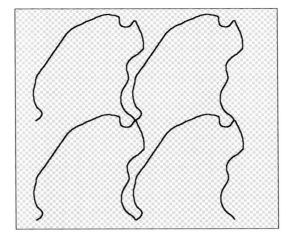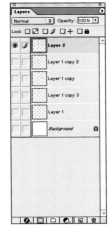

Merge all of the visible layers into a new layer.

Note: Merging visible layers to a new layer is a very useful trick. It allows you to treat your image as a single entity, but keep the original layers available should you want to use them again. You can also select this command by holding the Alt (Opt) key as you select Merge Visible from the Layers menu. I prefer to use the shortcut keys because Photoshop "obeys" them better than the menu command. The result of this operation is stored in the active layer. You'll be using this command a lot, so I will typically refer to it as "do an Option-Merge Visible."

10 Select the Block Eraser tool. Remove all of the line segments on Layer 2 that don't form part of the closed shape.

You need to be very careful when you erase the line segments. Every pixel is critical, and they need to fit together like puzzle pieces in order to tessellate. Only erase up to the places where the lines connect. Don't disturb any of the joints. You use the Block Eraser for the same reason that you used the Pencil tool— the shapes won't interlock exactly if the edges are anti-aliased.

To see how to fill the tessellation with a photo and how to use that tessellation to create a pattern set of 20 different values, work the instructions in the PDF file **06_extra.pdf** from the Projects/06 directory on the CD-ROM.

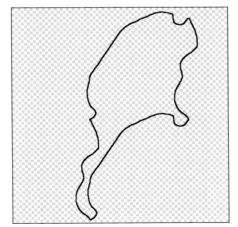

Erase the lines that are not part of the closed shape.

Posterizing the Photo

If you worked the instructions on the CD-ROM, you created 20 small patterns. Each pattern tile is designed to replace a specific value in the main image. (If you didn't create these patterns, you can load them from the CD-ROM). You need to convert Alexandra's image to grayscale, and then posterize it into 20 values. You'll find an action to do this automatically for you in the **GRADATIONS.atn** action folder that you will load into your Actions palette. The Action will work properly on any file that is 1200×1600 pixels.

1   Open the file **ALEXRGB.psd** from the accompanying CD-ROM. Load the **GRADATIONS.atn** file from the CD-ROM into your Actions palette.

ALEXRGB.psd is the file you will pattern. The actions in the Action file make your life much easier. Choose Load Action from the side drop-down menu of the Actions palette to bring the Actions file from the CD-ROM into your Actions palette.

Open the image you want to pattern.

80

2   Select the Make Posterized Grayscale action in
the in the GRADATIONS.atn action folder in the
Actions palette and then click the Play button at
the bottom of the Actions palette. Be sure to check
the box beside each action you want to execute.

Here are the steps that the action performs (so you
can do this without the action):

■   Converts the image to grayscale.

■   Lengthens the image by 50 pixels to allow room
for the selection gradient that you need.

■   Adds a horizontal black-to-white gradient at the
bottom of the image in the new white area of
the canvas.

■   Posterizes the image into 20 steps.

■   Converts the image to RGB mode by converting
it first to Indexed Color and then to RGB. (This
conversion is the result of a bug or anomaly in
Photoshop 6. If you convert directly from
grayscale to RGB, the solid blocks of color in
your posterized gradient are no longer solid—
they dither and the entire replacement technique
for the image falls apart. Taking the grayscale to
Indexed Color and then to RGB, keeps these
blocks of color solid.)

3   Save the file as **ALEXPOSTERIZED**.

4   Choose Edit/Preset Manager. Change the Preset
Type to Patterns and click Load. Select the
IanPatternGrads.pat from the CD-ROM.
Click Done.

This is the pattern file that contains the 20 values of
the tessellation tile. Feel free to use your own tiles.

Play the Make Posterized
Grayscale action.

Note: If you want to use this action with a different size image, you
need to re-record the step that adds 50 pixels to the bottom of the
image and the step that selects that bottom area for the gradient.

Adding the Pattern Layers

Finally, you've come to the step that allows you to create the patterned file. In the previous section, you added a gradient at the bottom of the image that you posterized along with the rest of the image. The gradient makes it easier to select the 20 different colors in the image. The process that you will follow is to select the range of pixels, add a Pattern layer, select the appropriate pattern for that value, and activate the Background layer before selecting the next color. You need to repeat this process 20 times, until each color has been filled with a pattern layer. You may start with the image **ALEXPOSTERIZED.psd** from the CD-ROM if you wish. Your first task is to create a series of selection channels.

1   Activate (or open) **ALEXPOSTERIZED.psd** from the CD-ROM. Choose the Magic Wand tool and set the following:

Tolerance: **0%**

Anti-alias: **Unchecked**

Contiguous: **Unchecked**

You need to turn off the Contiguous flag because you will click on the square at the bottom of your file to select all of the pixels of that color anywhere in the image.

Note: You will also see an action for setting patterns from Magic Wand clicks. This action should be much easier, but it doesn't work. A bug in Photoshop 6 prevents the Magic Wand clicks from making anything other than Contiguous selections. However, it's included in the hope that someday the bug will be fixed.

2   Click on the darkest black square at the bottom of the image. Save the selection to a channel. Accept the default channel name of Alpha 1.

In the next few steps, you will save a channel for each of the 20 values, and you must do it in order from dark to light. Later, to save the channels, you'll use the Set Patterns from Alphas action to automate filling the image with pattern, but it only works if the alpha channels are created from darkest to lightest and left at their default names.

Click to load the darkest blacks in the image as a selection.

3   Double-click the Make Alpha action that is the last action in the GRADATIONS.atn folder that you placed in the Actions palette. The shortcut key should already be set to F1. If you want to select a different shortcut key, do it now, and then close the dialog box.

This is just a time-saving way to help create the alpha channels. You still need to click on the bottom pos-terized gradient to select the values, but if you pick a convenient function key, you only need to click with your "working" hand and press the function key with your other hand.

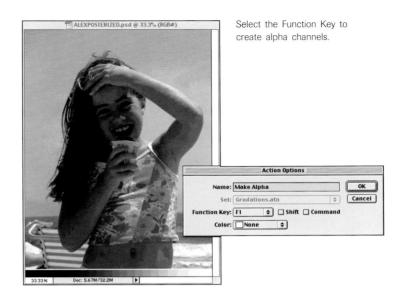

Select the Function Key to create alpha channels.

4   Click the next darkest black at the bottom of the image to load it as a selection. Press the function key that you've chosen to save the selection as a channel. Repeat this process for the remaining colors in the gradient bar.

Selecting the second color is tricky because the first black block is much larger than the other blocks. You might need to click twice before you find the correct block.

Save an alpha channel for each of the 20 colors in the image.

5 Play the Set Patterns From Alphas action. For each layer, the action will pause and ask you to select a pattern. You need to keep track of which pattern is next. Each time you see the Pattern dialog box pop-up, click on the pattern that is shown and choose the next pattern from the Preset menu.

This step saves you an enormous amount of tedium, and should work with any file that is posterized into 20 values with a set of alpha channels to match and patterns numbered as these are. For each value in the image, the action loads the alpha channel, creates a pattern layer, and fills it with the specified pattern value. Don't worry that the patterns are too large for the image, you'll fix that next.

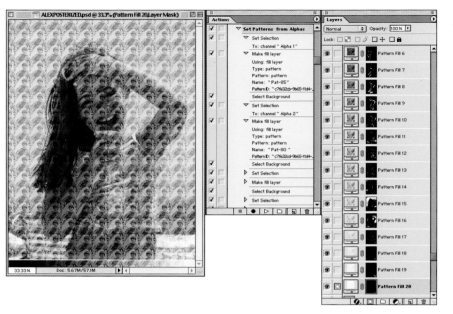

Play the Set Pattern from Alphas action.

Note: You'll find it easier to remember which pattern comes next if you change your view of the pattern presets to one that includes the pattern name. To change the way that you view the presets, click on the small arrowhead to the left of the Done button and choose Text Only, Small List, or Large List from the drop-down menu.

Note: Should you decide to create this entire effect without the use of the actions, you can click on the posterized gradient bar at the bottom of the image to select the specific values in the image, then immediately create a pattern layer. You don't need to save an alpha channel first.

ADJUSTING THE PATTERN SCALE

In this section, you'll set the scale of the patterns in the image to better bring out the values in the original.

1 With the Crop tool, select the entire image except for the 50-pixel gradient at the bottom of the image. Click the Hide button in the Options bar, and then execute the command.

You should find it easier to evaluate the image if you don't have to look at the gradient bar. However, by selecting Hide, you can get it back if you decide that you need it.

2 Set the Move tool option to Auto Select layers.

Auto Select is usually a very bad idea, but it will save you a lot of time trying to figure out which layer you should be adjusting.

Use the Hide option to crop the image and remove the gradient bar.

3 Click on Alexandra's face. Open the Pattern Fill dialog box for the selected layer and set the Scale to 50%.

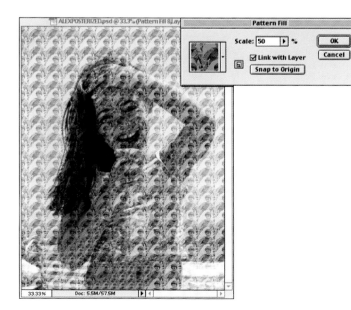

Set the Scale of the selected layer to 50%.

4   Repeat this process for as many of the layers as you
    feel need to be adjusted.

    You might want to let the background sky areas
    remain at 100%. You might also want to seek some
    areas at 50%. Try to scale the layers in divisible units
    (50 is half of 100 and 25 is half of 50).

Scale all of the layers in Alexandra's face to 25%.

HOW IT WORKS

You've learned two major new skills in this technique. One skill is how to create a
tessellation; the other is how to replace grayscale values with patterns.

The tessellation makes use of the geometric principle that a continuous (though wiggly)
line that touches exactly three corners of an imaginary rectangle will create an interlocking
shape if the line is used as a repeat pattern. If you want to learn more about tessellations,
an excellent book is *Introduction to Tessellations* by Dale Seymour and Jill Britton.

The portion of the project that deals with replacing gray values with patterns is the
product of David Xenakis' vivid imagination brought to life by Sherry London. The
premise is, if you posterize a grayscale image and then create patterns that average out to
the values in the posterized image, you can replace values with patterns on a pixel-by-
pixel basis. The final result still retains a single unifying pattern because all of the
replacements use the same pattern image—only the value changes.

The modifications possible for this technique are almost infinite. You can modify the
shape of the tessellation or pattern element, you can modify the pattern content, or you
can modify the colorization method used.

MODIFICATIONS

You might want to change the colors in the image. You can do this in a number of ways. You could simply make the entire image into a grayscale image and create it in gray values. This is an elegant solution because the lack of color allows the pattern to gain importance.

You could simply place a copy of the original color image as the top layer, change its Blend mode to Color, and reduce the opacity of the layer if necessary.

You might want to play color tricks with the image. If you create a grayscale version of your patterned image, you can use the new Gradient Map feature in Photoshop 6 to give a true sepia gradient.

Place the original image on top of the patterns and change the Blend mode to Color.

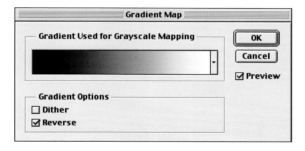

A true sepia gradient goes from white to black with a sepia color in the midtones and can be applied to a grayscale image using a Gradient Map layer.

The Gradient Map layer changes the values in the grayscale to the values in the gradient.

You could also use a multi-colored gradient as the gradient map for a much more abstract effect.

Finally, you could create a Diffusion Dither Halftone image and reconstruct the original colors in your photograph. You can use a flattened version of the image you created in this project, or you can use the image **ALEXGRAY.psd** from the accompanying CD-ROM.

1   Open the image **ALEXGRAY.psd** from the accompanying CD-ROM.

2   Open the image **ALEXCMYK.psd** from the accompanying CD-ROM.

    If you are creating an image to break apart into channels and recombine for print, you should start with a CMYK file because the image will seriously change colors if you create it in RGB and then convert it to CMYK at the end.

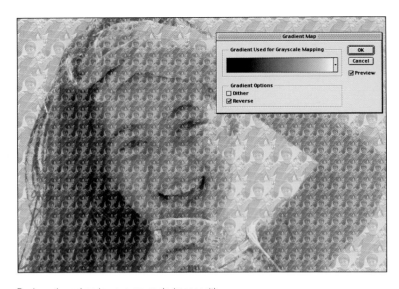

Replace the colors in your grayscale image with a colored gradient for a more wild effect.

3   Choose Split Channels from the drop-down menu in the Channels palette.

Split the image into four channels.

4 Choose Image/Mode/Bitmap and set the Input and Output resolutions to the same number. Choose the Diffusion Dither method.

Your image must be in Grayscale or Multi-Channel mode before you can change it to a bitmap. If you are going to print at a high resolution, you might want to set your Output resolution to at least 300ppi. That makes the image much larger, however, and isn't necessary now.

Convert the channel into a bitmapped image using a Diffusion Dither.

5 Convert the image back into Grayscale mode. Use a 1:1 Size Ratio.

You can't merge channels together if the images are in bitmap mode.

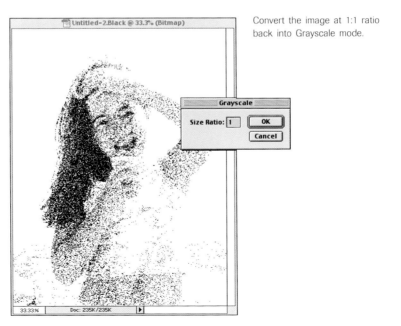

Convert the image at 1:1 ratio back into Grayscale mode.

6 Choose Image/Apply Image. Enter the following settings:

Source: **ALEXGRAY.psd**

Layer: **Background**

Channel: **Gray**

Blending: **Screen**

Opacity: **100%**

Mask: **Unchecked**

By applying the patterned image in Screen mode, the grayscale pixels from the patterned only "cling" to the black pixels in the channel. When you rebuild the channels, the patterns will appear again, but this time in color.

7 Repeat Steps 4–6 for each the remaining three channels.

8 Choose Merge Channels from the Channels palette menu. Select CMYK and 4 channels as the mode. Accept the default names in the dialog box.

You can change the order of the channels used in the merge operation, but your colors won't be accurate if you do. As long as there is a choice of the four printing colors available, Photoshop finds the correct replacements.

Apply the ALEXGRAY.psd image to the channel in Screen mode.

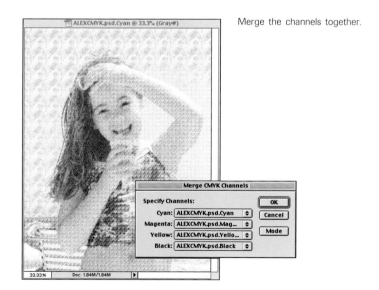

Merge the channels together.

90

9 The image is ready to be printed, and is in CMYK mode, using your CMYK default workspace.

Note: You will find several more modifications in the **06_extra.pdf** file on the CD-ROM.

The finished image is ready for print.

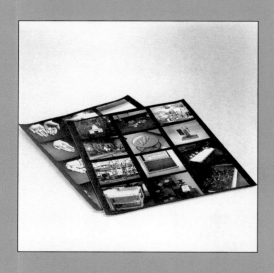

RETOUCHING EFFECTS

"My passport photo is one of the most remarkable

photographs I have ever seen—no retouching,

no shadows, no flattery—just stark me."

—ANNE MORROW LINDBERGH

PORTRAIT RETOUCHING TECHNIQUES

In this project, you'll learn several basic

retouching techniques that when used in

combination can produce some pretty striking

results. You can apply these techniques to a

number of projects, including photography repair

and restoration, cleaning dirty or damaged

scans, and basic color manipulation. In this

example, you'll use the effects to slightly modify

the photograph and give it that "fashion maga-

zine" cover look.

Project 7

Retouching Effects

by Felix Nelson

GETTING STARTED

This effect covers the basic retouching of a typical head or face shot. Use blurring, quick masking, and History Brush techniques for overall corrections, as well as utilizing layer modes to effect changes in the highlights and shadow areas. The example is an image that doesn't need a lot of color correction, but could use just a little help in the retouch department. You'll start by removing some of the dirty areas (white speckles) around the model's shoulders and neck.

1   Open the file **Retouch1.jpg** from the accompanying CD-ROM.

2 Choose Filter/Blur/Gaussian Blur and enter a setting of 3 pixels.

The 3-pixel setting works great for low-resolution images, but for higher resolution images, you should enter a higher value. These settings vary from image to image. What you're trying to accomplish is making the speckles (or dust) blend into the rest of the image.

3 Press **Y** to select the History Brush. Go to the History Options bar and change the Mode to Darken. Choose Window/Show History.

4 In the History palette, click once on the word Open (the first entry in the History list) to highlight it, then click the History Brush source slot to the left of the words "Gaussian Blur."

This sets the source. The History Brush icon source should now appear next to it.

5 Use the History Brush to cover the white speckles from the model's shoulder and neck.

Note: Remember to use a soft-edged brush. If you're not sure whether or not you have a soft-edged brush, simply look at the brush on the left side of the History Options bar. It should look blurry (or soft) on the edges.

Note: If there are any dark areas in the image that you'd like to correct, just change the Mode in the Options bar to Lighten, and then simply paint over the dark areas.

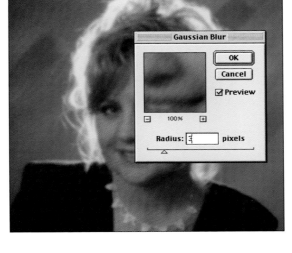

Use a Gaussian Blur to hide speckles and dust on the model's face, neck, and chest.

Use the History palette to set your source.

Change the Mode in the History Options bar to lighten and paint over any dark areas.

6 Switch to Quick Mask mode by double-clicking the toolbar's Quick Mask icon on the bottom right. In the Quick Mask Option window, check Selected Areas and set Opacity to 50%.

7 Use a soft-edged brush to select the areas you want to modify (wrinkles, freckles, and so on).

Be sure not to make your selection too close to the hard edges around the eyes and chin; this might make these edges too soft and unrecognizable.

8 Press **Q** to go back to Normal mode view.

The areas you painted in Step 6 become an active selection in Normal mode, so you can copy them into their own layer.

9 Press Ctrl(Cmd)+J to put the active selection on its own layer.

While in Quick Mask mode, use the Paintbrush to paint over the areas you want to modify.

10 Apply the Gaussian Blur filter with the Radius set to 3.

You can see how this softens the selected areas and removes the undesired wrinkles and freckles from the model's face, neck, and chest.

You'll notice that even after we removed the wrinkles, there are still some dark areas just below the eyes and under the lower lip.

Add a 3-pixel Gaussian Blur to a new layer to remove most of the wrinkles and freckles.

11 Open the Layers palette and choose Flatten Image from the pull-down menu. Select the Rubber Stamp tool and, in its Options bar, set the Mode to Lighten, the Opacity to 20%, and select Use All Layers. Press Alt(Opt)+click on the image just below the dark areas, and use the Rubber Stamp tool to clone these parts away.

Use the Rubber Stamp tool to remove the dark areas under the eyes and chin.

ADDING DETAILS TO THE EYES

We've made some major modifications to the overall image, but now we'll concentrate on adding brightness and details to the eyes. You can use this to draw attention to a specific area of a photograph or image by adding some detail.

Note: You'll continue to use the same image provided on the accompanying CD, but this might be a good time to save your document if you're satisfied with the results up to this point.

1 Switch to the Lasso tool by pressing **L**, and make a fairly tight selection around the eyes.

2 Choose Select/Feather, and enter 3 pixels.

This softens the edges of your selection. The feather amount needs to change based on the size and resolution of your image.

Use the Lasso tool to select around the eyes.

Note: You can also set the feather by choosing Alt+Ctrl+D (Opt+Cmd+D).

3 Put this selection on its own layer by pressing Ctrl(Cmd)+J. Duplicate this layer (Layer 1) by dragging it to the New layer icon at the bottom of the Layers palette (Layer 1 copy).

We'll be using both layers in this part of the project, so pay special attention to which layer we're working on.

Create a feathered selection around the eyes, put this selection on its own layer, and then duplicate the layer.

4 In the Layers palette, click on Layer 1 and change the Blend mode to Multiply and the Opacity to 50%.

Changing the Blend mode gives the eyes some depth. Click back on Layer 1 copy to activate.

5 Choose Image/Adjust/Hue/Saturation or press Ctrl(Cmd)+U and set the following:

Colorize: **On**

Hue: **214**

Saturation: **18**

These settings work well for this project because we're trying to give the model's natural eye color a little punch. You can completely change the eye color in this dialog box. Don't be afraid to experiment a little.

Change the Blend mode of Layer 1 to Multiply and the Opacity to 50%.

Note: Be careful not to make the eye color too vibrant as this gives you an unrealistic effect. You can always lower the Opacity in this layer if the eye color is too bright or vivid.

6   Switch to the Eraser tool. Choose a small soft-edged brush, and erase away the color from the pupil area (the center of the eyes) and the dark areas on the edge of the irises (the outside edges of the eyes) on Layer 1 copy.

Use the Eraser tool to remove the center and the edges of the pupil area on Layer 1 copy.

7   Drag Layer 1 copy to the New Layer icon to create a copy. Set the new layer's Blend mode (Layer 1 copy 2) to Screen, and lower the Opacity to 25%.

8   Choose Filter/Sharpen/Unsharp Mask, and enter:

Amount: **477**

Radius: **20 pixels**

Threshold: **0**

As you can see, the irises are now very crisp, bright, and vivid.

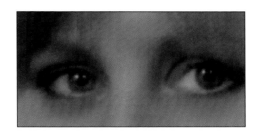

Create a new layer and set it to Blend mode.

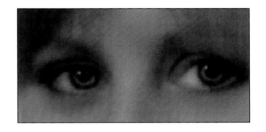

Use the Unsharp Mask to brighten the iris.

9   In the Layers palette, choose Flatten Image from the Layers palette pull-down menu.

After you've completed retouching the eyes, flatten the image.

CREATING COLORFUL LIPS

As with the eyes, we'd like to draw some attention to the area around the mouth and lips. Adding a deep, rich color to the lips creates a cover-girl look.

1   Choose the Lasso tool by pressing **L** and make a selection around the lips.

2   Choose Select/Feather, or Alt+Ctrl+D (Opt+Cmd+D), and enter 2 pixels.

3   Press Ctrl(Cmd)+J to put this selection on its own layer. Change the Blend mode of this new layer to Screen, and lower the Opacity to 15%.

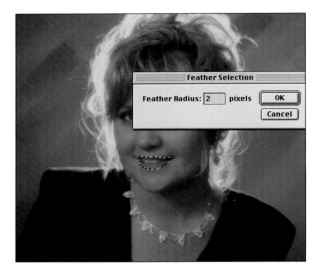

Make a feathered selection around the lips and give them a 2-pixel Gaussian Blur.

4   Choose Filter/Sharpen/Unsharp Mask, and enter:

Amount: **500**

Radius: **4 pixels**

Threshold: **0**

Putting the lips selection on its own layer and adding an Unsharp Mask gives the lips more depth and detail.

RESIZING THE NOSE

Our retouch project has made huge strides, but now we'll have to perform a little plastic surgery. In this part of the project, we'll resize our model's nose. The Transform function is one of the most powerful tools when trying to resize and reshape—especially when proper proportions are a must. The Rubber Stamp tool comes into play again as we try to seamlessly replace the old nose with the new.

1 Activate the Background layer in the Layers palette. Now switch to the Lasso tool, and make a selection around the nose. Make the selection fairly loose, but try not to include any parts of the eyes or lips. Choose Select/Feather, enter 2 pixels, and click OK. Then press Ctrl(Cmd)+J to put this selection on its own layer.

2 Choose Filter/Blur/Gaussian Blur, and enter a setting of 0.5 pixels for Radius.

Make a feathered selection around the nose and put it on its own layer.

3 Press Ctrl(Cmd)+T to bring up the Free Transform tool. Choose Edit/Transform/Perspective, and drag the bottom-right adjustment point toward the left to make the lower part of the nose thinner. Press Enter (Return) to make the transformation final.

This command makes the lower part of the nose thinner. This gives you a more narrow nose at the bottom without affecting the top portion of the nose.

4 Use the Eraser tool to remove the excess image around the nose on Layer 2.

You'll start to see portions of the old nose behind the new one, but you'll remove that with the Rubber Stamp tool.

Use the Free Transform function to alter the shape of the nose.

5　Switch to the Rubber Stamp tool. Set the Mode to Normal and the Opacity to 50% in the Options palette. Use the Rubber Stamp tool (on the Background layer) to clone away the old nose.

6　In the Layers palette, choose Flatten Image from the pull-down menu.

Use the Eraser tool and Rubber Stamp tool to blend in the new, reshaped nose.

LEVELS ADJUSTMENT

As I mentioned in the beginning of this project, you are using an image that doesn't really need a lot of color correction, but a slight Levels Adjustment helps lighten the overall image.

1　Choose Image/Adjust/Levels or press Ctrl(Cmd)+L. Move the white point adjustment slider until it reads 224. Next, move the black point adjustment slider until it reads 10, and click OK.

A slight Levels Adjustment gives a little pop to the final look of the project.

MODIFICATIONS

You can give the jewelry a little sparkle by simply selecting the jewelry, putting it on a separate layer, and then changing the Layer Blend mode to Soft Light.

You can also use some of the techniques learned in the eyes retouching portion of this project to change the color of the model's dress or the color of the background.

RESTORATION TECHNIQUES

"Human beings are the only creatures that

allow their children to come back home."

—BILL COSBY

CLEANING UP A DAMAGED PHOTOGRAPH

Just about everyone has a photo that needs

restoring. The damage to a photo can be as

minor as a slight shift in colors to pieces of the

photo having been broken off or missing. The

range of damages is as wide as the various

techniques used to repair those damages. Each

photo restoration project requires a unique

approach; there is no one quick fix for all

damaged photos.

Project 8

Restoration Techniques

by Gary Kubicek

GETTING STARTED

This project involves restoring a damaged black-and-white photograph. The photo was larger than the scanner and required two separate scans—the top half and the bottom half, with some overlap… You must assemble the two images first, and restore the damaged areas next. The emulsion of the photo (the layer of a photograph that contains the image) has been damaged, creating many large white areas that you'll need to remove using the Clone Stamp tool. Also, there are hundreds of white specks and scratches throughout the photo that you can remove in just a few steps. To add a finishing touch, apply a sepia tone to give the photo that warm, old-time look.

COMBINING TWO IMAGES

As previously mentioned, the photo for this project was larger than the scanner. You might encounter this situation in your own imaging, so it's worthwhile to learn this technique of combining the two halves of one photo.

1   Open the images **Daniel-TopHalf.psd** and **Daniel-BottomHalf.psd** from the accompanying CD.

2   For each image, zoom out enough so the height of each image, and its window, is slightly less than half of Photoshop's workspace.

Open both of the Daniel images.

3   Position the Daniel-BottomHalf image in the bottom half of the workspace; you will be adding canvas to the top of the image and will need to see the entire image. On the Layers palette, double-click the Background layer, and click OK in the New Layer dialog box.

When you add canvas to an image that does not contain a Background layer, the added area is made of transparent pixels, and this is what you want when combining two images.

Place the Daniel-BottomHalf image at the lower half of the workspace and convert the Background layer to a regular layer.

4 Right-click (Ctrl+click) the image title bar in the layers palette and then choose Image/Canvas Size from the menu. Type 10 inches in the Height field, and then click the bottom center anchor.

5 Make the Daniel-TopHalf image active. On the Layers palette, drag the Background layer into the Daniel-BottomHalf image. Close the Daniel-TopHalf image.

6 Zoom in so the width of the image and its window are approximately the width of your screen. Reduce the layer's Opacity to 60%, and choose the Move tool. Move the layer so the hands on each layer overlap as closely as possible. Use the arrow keys for one-pixel nudging.

Note: You'll notice that although the hands align nicely, the sweater is about one or two pixels off. This is due to the top half of the photo being slightly rotated when placed on the scanner. Because areas of the body (in this case, the hands) must be rendered as perfectly as possible, you can let other areas fall out of alignment and correct them later using the Clone Stamp tool.

7 Press **0** to return the layer's Opacity to 100%. At the bottom of the Layers palette, click the Add Layer Mask icon to add a mask to Layer 1.

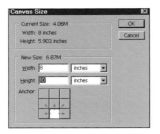

Add more canvas to the top of the image.

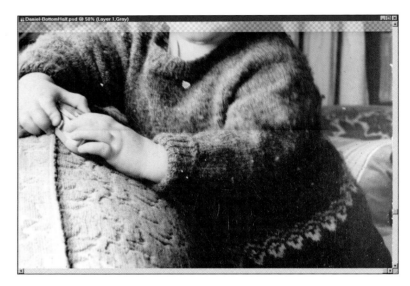

Align the hands on both layers.

8 Choose the Linear Gradient tool and the Foreground to Background gradient fill. Hold down the Shift key and, with the cursor positioned just below the line of the bottom edge of the Layer 1 contents at the hand area, click and drag upward about one-half of a screen inch.

The Gradient tool provides a smooth transition between two layers. You might need to Undo and apply the gradient again if the hands do not blend well. The sweater alignment looks bad, but the hands do align very well with the correct gradient fill on the layer mask.

9 From the main menu, choose Layer/Merge Down.

Apply the linear gradient to create a smooth transition.

10 Choose the Clone Stamp tool and the Soft Round 65-pixel brush from the Brush drop-down menu. Hold down the Shift key and press the] key once to harden the brush by 25%. Clone in the sweater area to remove the misalignment of the two layers. Alt (Opt)+click to establish the source pixel for cloning, and enable Aligned in the Options strip. Leave the image open.

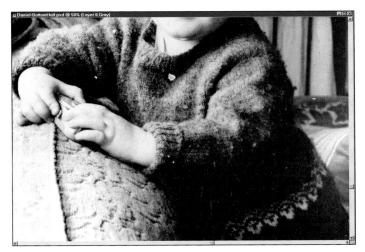

Clone over the areas of the sweater that do not align.

RESTORING THE DAMAGED AREAS

In this section, you will eliminate the large white specks and minimize the hundreds, if not thousands, of scratches in this image. But, before tackling those defects, you'll crop the image to the essential elements.

You can continue with the image from the preceding section or open image **Daniel_1.psd** from the accompanying CD.

1   Press Ctrl(Cmd)+0 to fit the image on your screen. Choose the Crop tool and drag a marquee so the top and sides are just inside the photo's borders and the bottom side of the marquee is just below the white design on the sweater.

   By cropping the image, you will have a better composition, and in the process reduce the amount of areas that require restoration. Cropping any image that you are repairing should always be considered.

Crop out the extraneous areas of the photo.

2   Choose the Lasso tool and drag a selection outlining Daniel's face and neck, but do not include the shadow on the right side of his face or his hair. Hold down the Shift key and drag a marquee along the outline of his hands.

3   Choose Select/Inverse, and then choose Select/Feather and type 12.

   The Dust and Scratches filter, used in the next step, would blur the face and hands—something you do not want to do! Creating a selection that includes all image areas except the face and hands restricts the filter from affecting these important areas. Feathering the selection softens the transition between the filtered and non-filtered areas.

Drag a marquee outlining the face and hands.

4 Choose Filter/Noise/Dust and Scratches, and type 3 for the Radius and 0 for the Threshold.

Apply the Dust and Scratches filter to remove hundreds of white specks and scratches.

5 Press Ctrl(Cmd)+D to deselect. Choose the Clone Stamp tool and remove the remaining white specks that are scattered throughout the image. Zoom in to see the smaller specks that need removing.

Remove the remaining white specks.

Note: In this situation, it is generally a good idea to use a brush tip size that is slightly larger than the speck. And because the specks vary in size, use the bracket keys to easily increase (]) or decrease ([) the size of the brush tip.

APPLYING A SEPIA TONE

Sepia tone, the brownish-red color often seen in old (as in 100 years or more) photographs can be created in Photoshop. If you ask five different Photoshop users how to add sepia tone to an image, you'll probably get five different techniques. In this section, the technique described uses an adjustment layer to create the sepia effect. The advantage of this technique is that you can easily change the settings later without altering the original image.

You can continue with the image from the preceding section, or open image **Daniel_2.psd** from the accompanying CD.

1 From the main menu, choose Image/Mode/RGB Color.

Note: The image needs to be converted from grayscale to a color mode, so that you can add the sepia tone. This process, however, has increased the image size to 18MB. If your computer has difficulty with files this large, you can choose Image/Image Size, and reduce the Width setting to decrease the image size. For example, a width setting of 1000 pixels reduces the image to 3.24MB.

2   Click the Create New Adjustment Layer icon at the bottom of the Layers palette and choose Hue/ Saturation from the flyout menu.

3   Select the Colorize option. Set the Hue to 33 and the Saturation to 25%.

This setting creates an accurate sepia tone. But you can move any of the three sliders from their current settings to customize the sepia to your liking.

4   Click the Create New Adjustment Layer icon at the bottom of the Layer's palette, and choose Curves from the flyout menu.

5   Alt(Opt)+click the graph to toggle to 10 divisions in each direction.

The 4×4 grid division is Photoshop's default setting.

6   Move the double arrow in the center of the gradient so that black is at the left and white is at the right.

The white-to-black gradient is Photoshop's default setting.

7   Drag the white control point straight down by one-half of a grid. Drag the black control point directly right by one-half of a grid. Now, click on the curve halfway between the white and black points, and drag diagonally upward and to the left about one-half of a grid.

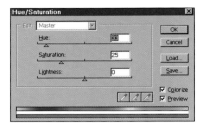

Adjust the Hue to 33 and the Saturation to 25%.

Note: After completing Step 6, the highlight control point is now located in the upper-right corner of the graph, and the black control point is in the lower-left corner.

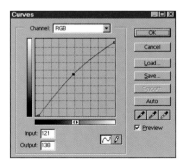

Move the curve to the points shown here.

Note: Moving the white point decreases the amount of washed-out highlights; moving the black point increases the black tonal range; and moving the midtone control point lightens the midtones. These Curves settings are purely an artistic call. You might choose a different curve setting, or even find that not using the curves produces a more pleasing effect.

8   Choose Layer/Flatten Image.

Flatten the layers.

MODIFICATIONS

There are as many techniques to repair a damaged photo as there are types of damages—
and that's a lot! You can pick and choose a technique from this project to help you
complete a restoration. You can also use the method described previously for sepia
toning and apply that technique to any photograph.

You could also take the restoration a little further by adding a border to the photograph.
Borders on photographs were extremely popular until only a couple of decades ago. So, in
keeping with the look of an aged photograph, you can create a border for the restoration.

If you like, continue with the image from the preceding section or open image **Daniel.psd**
from the accompanying CD.

1   On the Layers palette, double-click the Background
    layer, and then click OK in the New Layer dialog box.

    This converts the Background layer to a regular layer.

2 Choose Image/Canvas Size. Type 8.3 for Width and 9.3 for Height.

3 Click the New Layer icon at the bottom of the Layers palette and drag the new layer, Layer 1, under Layer 0 in the layer stack.

Add canvas to all sides of the image.

4 Use the Eyedropper tool to sample the color on the lightest area of Daniel's cheek. Press Alt+Backspace (Opt+Delete) to fill Layer 1 with the sampled color.

You want the color of the border to be similar to a very light area of the photo—after all, in a black-and-white photo that has a border, the border is white.

5 Choose Filter/Noise/Add Noise. Type 7.82 for the Amount and select Gaussian and Monochromatic.

The image of Daniel is grainy, and these settings for the Add Noise filter create a similar grain pattern (different photographs will show different size and intensity of grain).

6 Choose Filter/Blur/Gaussian Blur and set Radius to 1.

The grain pattern, like everything else in the photo, is not in sharp focus. Gaussian Blur softens the focus of the grain.

Fill the new layer with the color sampled from Daniel's cheek.

7 Click on Layer 0 in the Layers palette, and then choose Select/Load Selection. Click OK to load the contents of the layer as a selection. Choose Select/Modify/Contract and type 3.

The edge of the Daniel image (Layer 0) is too sharp and needs to be softened.

8 Choose Select/Feather and type 3 to soften the selection's edge.

Contract the selection created from Layer 0's contents.

9 Click on the Layer Mask icon at the bottom of the Layers palette.

The feathered selection area maintained visibility when the layer mask was created and created a soft 3-pixel wide border around the edges of the photo of Daniel.

Using the technique discussed in these steps, the edges of the photo are uniformly softened.

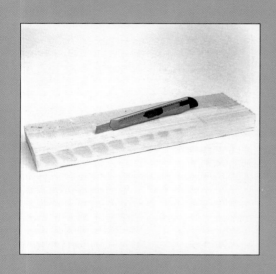

ALTERING ATMOSPHERE

"I've looked at clouds from both sides now

From up and down and still somehow,

Its cloud illusions I recall

I really don't know clouds at all."

—JONI MITCHELL, ***BOTH SIDES NOW*** **(1969)**

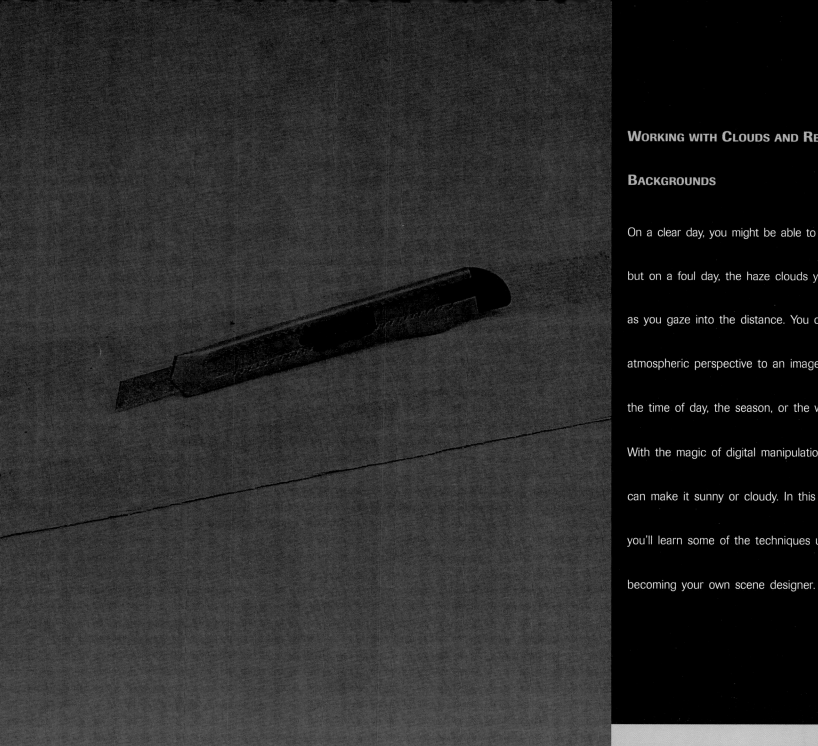

WORKING WITH CLOUDS AND REFLECTED

BACKGROUNDS

On a clear day, you might be able to see forever, but on a foul day, the haze clouds your vision as you gaze into the distance. You can add atmospheric perspective to an image to change the time of day, the season, or the weather. With the magic of digital manipulation, you can make it sunny or cloudy. In this project, you'll learn some of the techniques used for becoming your own scene designer.

Project 9
Altering Atmosphere

by Sherry London

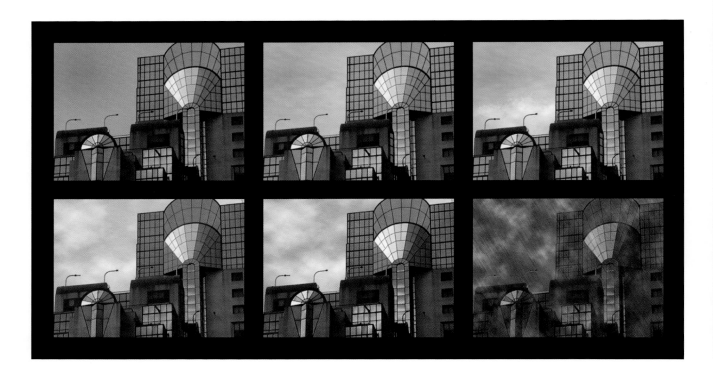

GETTING STARTED

On a recent trip to San Francisco, the city remained stubbornly cloudy the entire length
of our stay. In this project, you'll use an image of a mirrored building taken with a
digital camera, and change the sky to reflect different atmospheric conditions. You'll
learn how to create your own clouds and how to change the lighting reflected in the
building's mirrors. This technique uses layers, layer masks, channels, gradients, filters,
image distortions, and imagination to alter the atmosphere surrounding the original
building. You'll build a composite that resembles a story board of six different weather
conditions throughout the day.

ON A CLEAR DAY...

You might not be able to see forever, but you can change the original image to reflect a cloudless sky.

1 Open the image **Building.psd** from the accompanying CD-ROM.

You can use this as your starting image, or any image with a sky that is in need of adjustment (or re-creation).

Choose an image with a less-than-spectacular sky.

2 Create an alpha channel to isolate the sky.

To save time, the alpha channel is already in your image, and is called Sky. This channel was easy to build with the Magic Wand tool set to a Tolerance of 55, Contiguous On, and Anti-alias checked. Project 18, "Blending Images," and Project B, "Compositing," (on the CD-ROM) show you more ways to create alpha channels for compositing.

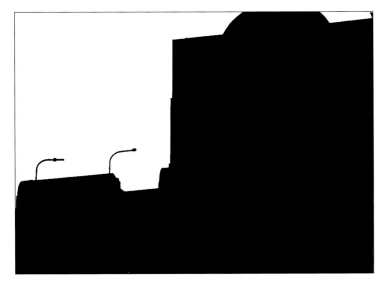

Create an alpha channel that selects only the sky.

3 Create a new Gradient layer from the New Fill or Adjustment Layer pop-up on the Layers palette or select Layer/New Fill Layer/Gradient from the top menu bar. Click on the Gradient bar swatch to show the Gradient Editor and select Load. Load the **SKY.grd** gradient set from the accompanying CD-ROM. Then click to select the Sky gradient swatch. Click OK to close the Editor, but don't close the Gradient Fill dialog box yet.

> **Note:** You can build your own gradient for the sky colors. One easy way to select accurate sky colors is to sample colors from a sky scene photo.

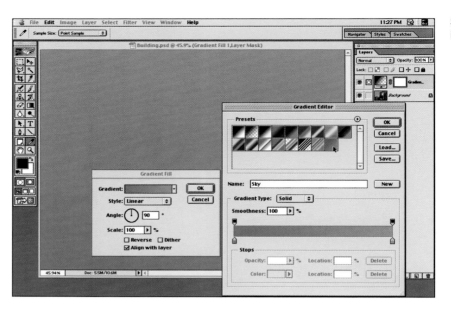

Select the Sky gradient in the Gradient Editor.

4 Change the Gradient Style to Radial. Clear the Align with Layer check box. Set the Scale to 70%. Move the deeper blue center of the gradient into the upper-left quarter of the image. Don't allow it to touch the image edges, however. Check the Dither box.

The Dither flag should prevent the banding that might otherwise occur in colors this close in value and hue.

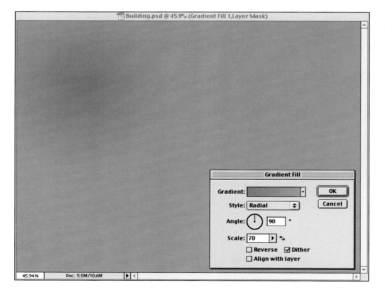

Drag the radial gradient into the upper-left quarter of the image.

5 Choose Image/Apply Image and enter the following settings:

Source: **Building.psd**

Layer: **Merged**

Channel: **Sky**

Blending: **Normal**

Opacity: **100%**

Mask: **Unchecked**

Apply Image is the fastest and most efficient way to transfer the contents of the Sky alpha channel into the layer mask for the gradient. Because you are selecting an alpha channel in the command, the layer that you choose is actually irrelevant.

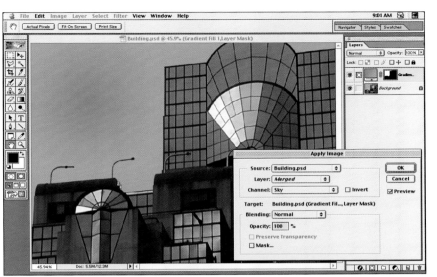

Use the Apply Image command to transfer the Sky alpha channel into the layer mask of the Gradient layer.

6 Turn off the Link icon between the gradient and the layer mask in the Gradient Fill 1 layer. Double-click the Gradient swatch to open the Gradient Fill dialog box. Change the Scale to 82%, and move the center of the gradient closer to the upper-left corner of the image.

It's easier to adjust the Gradient Fill once the layer mask is in place. Make any adjustments that you want. If you want to move the Gradient Fill, you need to do it in the Gradient Fill dialog box, or you will either move the mask or the building—neither of which were the intended actions.

7 Duplicate the Gradient Fill 1 layer by dragging it to the new Layer icon at the bottom of the Layers palette.

8 Set Image/Apply Image to the Windows Only alpha channel.

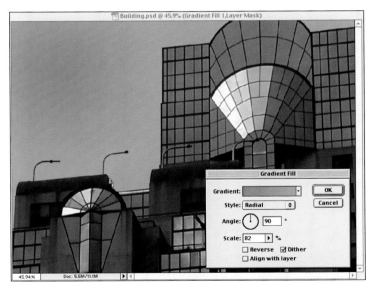

Adjust the location and size of the gradient.

The change in sky color makes the sky look sunny, but you also need to adjust the color of the windows (and of the entire building) to reflect the change in atmosphere. You'll fix the way the color interacts with the windows in the next step, but you first need to get the correct mask in place.

9   Change the Blend mode for Gradient Fill 1 copy to Soft Light.

Color and Lighten modes also work, but I prefer the luminosity of Soft Light mode, which gives just a hint of sky color to the windows.

10 Add a Hue/Saturation layer (Layer/New Adjustment Layer/Hue/Saturation) at the top of the layer stack. Click OK to close the dialog box, but don't change the settings yet.

It's easier to adjust the settings after the mask is in place.

11 Set Image/Apply Image to the Building Not Windows alpha channel.

Once this channel is placed in the mask for the Hue/Saturation 1 layer, the changes only affect the concrete of the building.

12 Open the dialog box for the Hue/Saturation 1 layer and enter the following settings:

Colorize: **Checked**

Hue: **50**

Saturation: **67**

Lightness: **+1**

Turn the Opacity down to about 22%, or the color change is much too strong. The sunlight adds a yellow cast to the building and makes it look much warmer than the original photo.

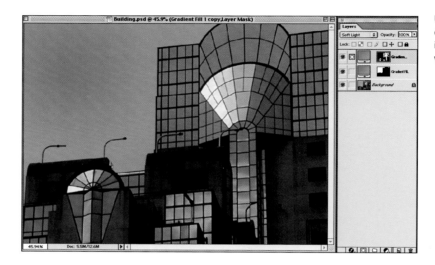

Use the Windows Only alpha channel to apply the Sky gradient in Soft Light mode only to the windows of the building.

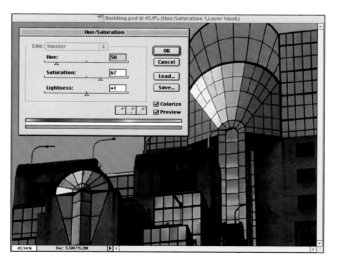

Adjust the Hue/Saturation settings to colorize the building with a warm yellow tone.

STARTING THE STORY BOARD

The end-point of this project is a small time-lapse story board. You'll save a small version
of the building image, at this point, to add as the first frame of the story board.

1   Choose Image/Duplicate/OK.

    Create a copy of the **Building.psd** image. You won't
    flatten it, however, because you might want to adjust
    some of the settings when you put the entire image
    together.

2   Set Image/Image Size to resample the image at
    300ppi to 2 inches wide.

3   Save the resized image as **Building1s.psd**. Close
    the image.

4   Save the large version of the image as **Building1.psd**,
    and leave it open as the starting point for the next
    section.

Resample the Building copy
image to 2 inches wide.

SOME FLUFFY CLOUDS

As the day progresses, some fluffy little "fair weather" clouds begin to dot
the sky. The Clouds filter is not the appropriate way to create these clouds
(although you will use it later in this project). Instead, you'll use a technique
for creating clouds that is based on a technique developed in the late 1980s by
John Derry. Although I've modified it over the years, John's cloud technique
is based on using the Free Transform command to stretch a tiny section of an
airbrushed image so it breaks up into areas of elongated pixel formations.

Note: John Derry has been part of the Painter design team for many
years, but when I first met him, he had just written the user's manual
for a graphics program called Lumena. This very-high-end graphics
program was the first PC program to use a 24-bit color card that
was even remotely within the price range of an individual user (it cost
$5000 for the Hercules graphics card and Lumena software). I liked
John's cloud technique so well that I've used it ever since (with his
permission, of course).

1 Create new image that is the same size and color space as **Building1.psd**.

The new image is where you will create the first set of clouds.

Note: You can quickly match image sizes when you create a new image by first selecting File/New. With the New Image dialog box open, pull down the Window menu and click on **Building.psd**. The image dimensions and other characteristics are transferred to the New Image dialog box. You need only click OK at that point.

2 Add a new Gradient layer and select the same Sky gradient that you used before. You may leave this as a linear gradient, but check the Reverse box so that the darker blue is on top.

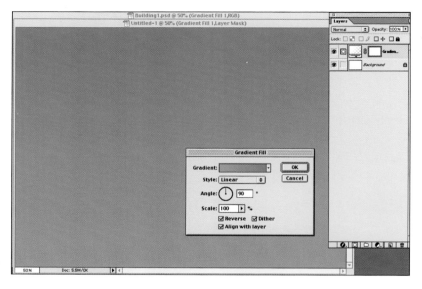

Add a Gradient layer using the Sky gradient.

3 Choose Layer/Rasterize/Fill Content.

This makes the Gradient layer editable, so that you can create your clouds inside of it. You could also use the Rasterize/Layer Content command in this instance. Because you have nothing in the layer mask, it makes no difference what commands you select.

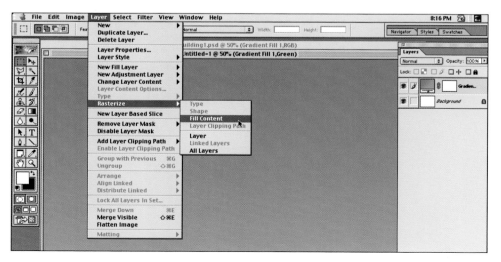

Rasterize the Gradient layer.

4 Create a new 28×28-pixel file. Make black your foreground color. Choose the Paintbrush tool and the 28-pixel Spatter brush. Stamp the brush in to the new image.

Stamp the 28-pixel Spatter brush into a new file.

The brush shape is perfect for helping to create clouds, but it is much too small. Clicking on the brush on the Brush drop-down shows that it is 28 pixels, therefore, you created a 28-pixel square file to hold it. Your next step will be to enlarge the image and define it as a new brush.

5 Choose Image/Image Size and resample the image at 400%. Choose Edit/Define Brush. Name the brush Spatter 112.

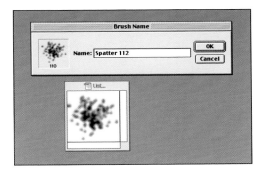

Define the enlarged brush.

6 Choose the Airbrush tool. Open the Brush palette in the Brush area of the toolbar and select the Spatter 112 brush that you just created. Set the Spacing to 120%. Close the 28-pixel square image without saving it.

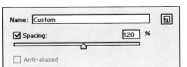

Change the brush Spacing to 120%.

You need to click the Brush drop-down arrow to open the Brush palette, but you need to click the Brush icon with Brush palette closed in order to open the Brush Options dialog box. Changing the spacing of the brush temporarily creates a new custom brush, which remains until you select a different brush. A setting of 120% means the brush cannot paint a continuous line. You'll stamp with this brush rather than paint with it anyway.

7 Set the Airbrush tool Pressure to 20%. Make white your foreground color. Scatter the brush strokes near the upper-left quadrant of the image. Double back over some areas to make them more white.

You'll need to stretch a portion of the image to cover most of the image (in Step 11), so you're only doing extra work if you paint over your entire image. This small area will be sufficient. However, if you want to try out a variety of brush strokes, you may use the entire image and then, in Step 9, select the area you like the best.

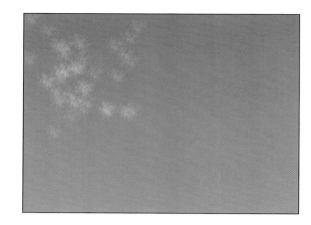

Scatter areas of the Spatter 112 brush in the upper-left quadrantof the image.

8 Select the 300-pixel airbrush with a pressure of 10%. Lightly spray a few small areas with this brush. Select the 65-pixel airbrush, and spray a few lines with the brush.

Use whatever brushes you want to build some texture in the upper-left quadrant of the image. Leave a lot of blue sky, however. You aren't painting clouds. Rather, you're spraying shapes to stretch into clouds.

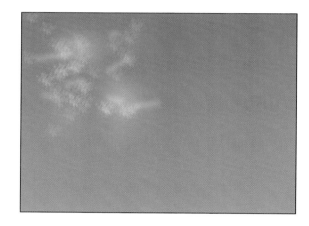

Spray additional strokes in several different brushes onto the image.

9 Use the Rectangular Marquee tool to isolate an interesting area of the image. Change the selection into a new layer (Layer/New/Layer Via Copy or Ctrl[Cmd]+J).

You need to define "interesting" for yourself. Pick the area you think works best. You can always change your mind. After a few tries, you'll begin to get a feel for the forms that stretch into good clouds. Keep the selection somewhat on the small size. The larger the selection gets, the less it's able to stretch.

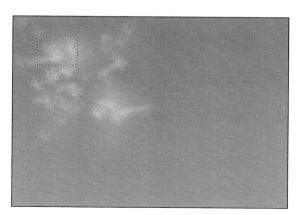

Select an area of interest and copy it into its own layer.

10 With Layer 1 active, choose Edit/Free Transform, and move the boxed area to the upper-left corner.

You need to start the scaling in the upper-left of the image because that is where the clouds will appear in the Building.psd image.

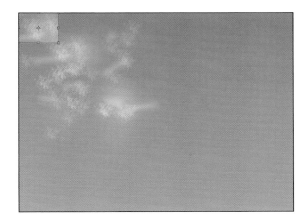

Move the bounded area to the upper-left corner.

11 Stretch the box to the right side of the image, and about ⁴/₅ down the length of the image. Press Enter (Return) to execute the transformation.

The Free Transform command enables you to stretch a tiny image, to scale it asymmetrically. It's this uneven scaling that creates the clouds.

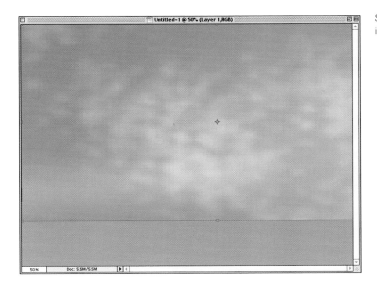

Stretch the bounded area until it covers most of the image.

ADDING CLOUDS

You don't need to settle for your first cloud formations. You can layer clouds on top of clouds, and re-stretch areas of clouds to build your sky. This section shows you how to enhance the clouds that you just created.

1 Make a rectangular selection in the stretched layer (Layer 1). Create a new layer via copy.

If you create a selection that is taller than it is wide, you'll be able to stretch the image more sideways without distorting the height of the cloud formation.

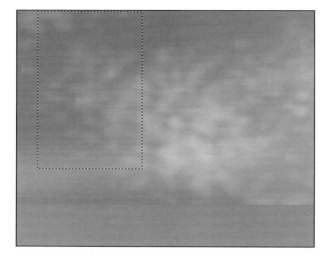

Create a selection taller than it is wide, and copy it to a new layer.

2 Use the Free Transform command to stretch the content of Layer 2 over the same areas of the image that you did before. Lower the Opacity of the layer if you have lost too much of the clouds.

By building the clouds in layers, you can mix various approaches to cloud design.

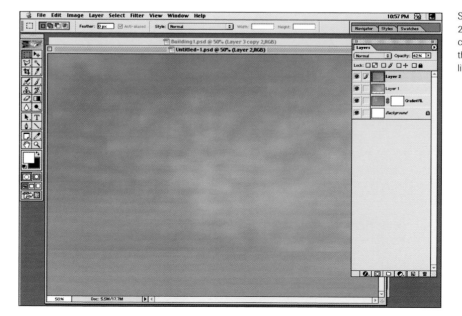

Stretch the contents of Layer 2 using the Free Transform command, and then lower the layer Opacity until you like the result.

3 Activate Gradient Fill Layer 1 and select a tall, narrow strip of the airbrushed area (hide Layers 1 and 2 so you can select the area). Copy it to a new layer at the top of the layer stack and stretch it. Reduce the Opacity to mix it with the other layers.

You can continue this process until you like the sky. Toss away layers if you don't want them. Select areas of already stretched layers and re-stretch them. If an area becomes over-stretched and acquires a hard edge, you can either use the Blur tool or apply a Gaussian Blur to a highly-feathered selection.

4 Create an empty new layer at the top of the layer stack. Merge your layers into this empty layer (Shift+Ctrl+Alt[Shift+Cmd+Opt]+E).

It's easier to place one layer into the Building image than it is to place multiple layers. However, you might want to revisit the layers in the clouds image. Choosing Merge Visible with the Alt (Opt) key pressed down takes a snapshot of the composite image and places it into the active layer.

5 Save your image as **CLOUDS.psd**. Don't close it yet.

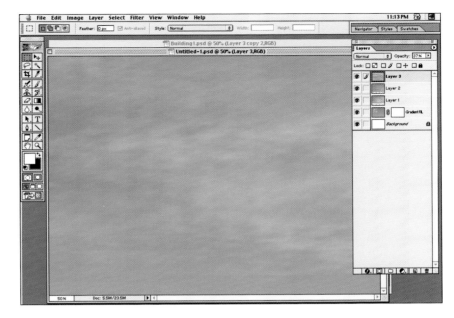

Continue to build and stretch more layers of clouds until you like the results.

MAKING A SUNNY DAY

Now that you've built the clouds, you need to get them back into the **Building1.psd** image to fill the sky. You may continue in the **Building1.psd** image that you previously saved or start with **Building1.psd** on the accompanying CD.

1 Create a new layer and move it to the top of the layer stack.

Because you are going to add several layers of clouds to the sky, a clipping group (of which this new layer will form the base) makes more sense than a layer mask that only masks a single layer. You'll convert the Gradient Fill 1 layer into the top layer of the group in the next step.

2 Move the Gradient Fill 1 layer to the top of the layer stack and discard the layer mask (Layer/Remove Layer Mask/Discard). Choose Layer/Group with Previous (Ctrl[Cmd]+G).

Your entire gradient seems to disappear (because the clipping group base layer is empty). You'll fix that next.

Note: If you've not used them before, clipping groups are a wonderful feature. The base layer acts like glue on a piece of paper. The image in any layer that is grouped with it "sticks" only to the portions of the base layer that aren't transparent (as if you were dropping glitter onto the glue and then brushing off the residue).

3 Activate Layer 1. Choose Image/Apply Image and enter the following settings:

Source: **Building1.psd**

Layer: **Merged**

Channel: **Sky**

Invert: **Unchecked**

Blending: **Normal**

Opacity: **100%**

Preserve Transparency: **Unchecked**

Mask: **Checked —Building1.psd**

Layer: **Merged**

Channel: **Sky**

The Sky alpha channel was designed to select the sky. Therefore, you can save several steps by using the Apply Image command through the sky mask. You only want the sky itself in the clipping group base layer because a clipping group needs a base layer with transparency in it (if the base layer has no areas of transparency, then no clipping occurs). As soon as the sky is transferred to Layer 1, your gradient reappears.

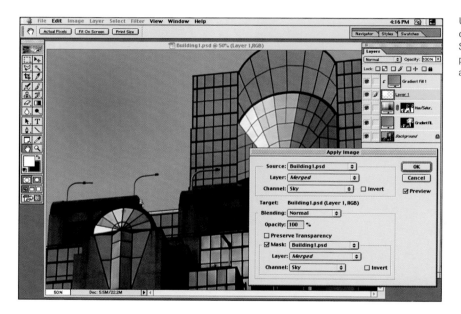

Use the Apply Image command through the Sky alpha channel to place only the sky area into Layer 1.

4 Drag the Layer 4 thumbnail from the CLOUDS.psd Layers palette (with the Shift key pressed) and drop it into the Building1.psd image as the top layer. Choose Layer/Group with Previous.

It's easier with images this size to drag and drop them from the Layers palette. The Shift key keeps the images in register. You could also have used the Apply Image command into a new layer and saved yourself some mousing around. The clouds layer occupies only the sky area as soon as you group it with the previous layers.

Place the clouds layer into the Building image and add it to the clipping group.

5 Set the Layer Blend mode to Hard Light.

Hard Light mode makes the white clouds stand out more, and changes the time of day to closer to noon. It makes the image look more sunny.

6 Activate the Gradient Fill 1 copy layer. Change the Blend mode to Hard Light (instead of Soft Light). Lower the Opacity of the layer to 85% if you want.

Changing the reflection on the windows to Hard Light looks more realistic for the sunny day. If you find the effect too harsh, adjust the Opacity.

Change the Blend mode to Hard Light.

7 Open the Hue/Saturation dialog box for the Hue/Saturation layer and set the Lightness to +14.

This makes the building's walls also reflect the warmth of the sun.

8 Save the building image as **Building2.psd**. Choose Image/Duplicate, and then resize the duplicate to 2 inches wide at 300ppi. Save the smaller copy as **Building2s.psd**.

The sunny day gives you a taste of this technique. You can use **09_extras.pdf** on the accompanying CD to learn how to make the day progressively more cloudy and to create rain and fog. All of the instructions needed to create the story board are in this PDF file.

Change the Lightness setting on the Hue/Saturation layer to +14.

HOW IT WORKS

When you alter atmosphere, you need to change not only the sky, but also any of the lighting conditions affected by the sky. You need to create selections and alpha channels to make these changes easy to create. Once you have selections created, you can create your sky conditions. Clouds can be formed by stretching airbrushed images, modifying the result of the Clouds filter (either by stretching it or removing opacity, or both), or by layering clouds on top of one another. You can make the day lighter using Overlay or Screen mode, or darker with Multiply.

MODIFICATIONS

You can create an infinite variety of clouds. If you study the sky, you'll notice that you can see clouds that look as if they were done in Photoshop, layered in Multiply mode, or flattened over the "wrong" color background and then cut and pasted. Look at the weird clouds that appear in an almost cloudless sky. Sometimes, they are hard edged and sharp as they reflect the sun (think Blend modes backed with white) and sometimes they are Gaussian Blurred into one another. You should have the basic tools to create all of these clouds now.

You can also create the effect of sunlight after the storm with a rainbow peeking through. You can add Gradient layers to poke colors into the clouds. This image, which is on the accompanying CD-ROM so you can examine its layers, uses a Rainbow gradient scaled to 10% in Overlay, Screen, or Soft Light mode and merged into the image using a layer mask.

You can also create a rainbow.

DROP SHADOWS
AND REFLECTIONS

"I never saw an ugly thing in my life:

for let the form of an object be what it

may—light, shade, and perspective

will always make it beautiful."

—JOHN CONSTABLE

ADDING DEPTH TO FLAT IMAGES

Need a glossy product shot today? With no

time to set up a photo shoot? Never fear. If you

have a product image, you can recreate a full-

studio environment—complete with shadows

and reflections. This project shows you how.

Project 10

Drop Shadows and Reflections

by Scott Kelby

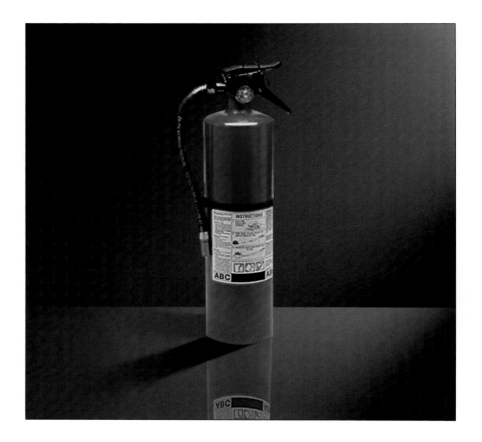

GETTING STARTED

In this project, you are going to set up and create a product shot entirely from scratch using Photoshop's tools to create shadows, reflections, and lighting. Use Layer Styles, Layer Sets, image transformations, and the Lighting Effects filter to make it work. First, you need to create a background for your image, place the product, simulate lighting, create reflections, and cast shadows. Finally, tune your image to perfection.

In the Background

Start by creating your own custom background, because behind every great project is a background (get it, a background? Ah, forget it).

1 Create a new Photoshop document that is 468×468 pixels, 72 ppi, and in RGB mode.

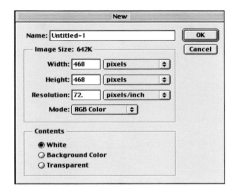

Create a new file that is 6.5 inches square and filled white.

2 Choose the Gradient tool. Open the Gradient Editor by clicking once on the Gradient thumbnail in the Options bar.

With the Gradient tool active, open the Gradient Editor.

You're going to create a custom gradient for this project in the next step. Opening the Gradient Editor in Photoshop 6 is tricky, but once you know to just click the preview Gradient thumbnail, the editor works mostly as it did in earlier versions.

3 Choose the Black-White gradient as your model. Double-click the bottom-left color stop to bring up the Color Picker. Select a 60% gray (R122, G122, B122). Open the bottom-right color stop and select a 20% gray (R209, G211, B212). Make sure that the top transparency stops are both set to 100%. Click New, and name the new preset 60-20% gray.

The small markers below the current gradient are called color stops. The markers on top of the gradient are the transparency stops.

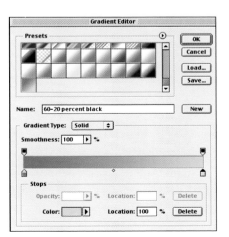

Create a new gradient that goes from 60% black on the left to 20% black on the right.

4 Add a Gradient layer from the Create New Fill or Adjustment Layer pop-up menu. Set the Angle to −90°, and choose the 60-20% gray gradient that you created.

This gradient forms the base for your background. By using a Gradient layer, you give yourself the flexibility to change the gradient or its angle at any point in the image development cycle.

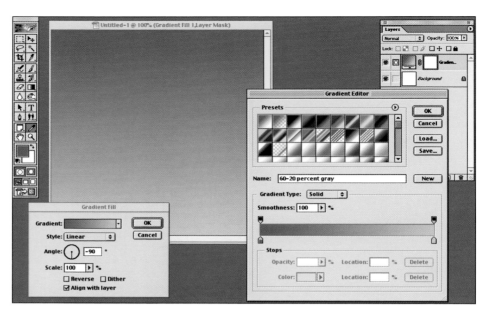

Fill a Gradient layer with the 60-20% gray gradient.

5 Add a Hue/Saturation layer (Layer/New Adjustment Layer/Hue/Saturation) on top of the Gradient layer. Click the Colorize box, and change the Hue slider to 263.

This colors the gradient purple. I liked the colors better using Colorize in the Hue/Saturation layer than I did by applying the same color to the image as a Color Overlay effect in Color mode. Of course, in your own work, you could use the Color Overlay effect if you prefer it.

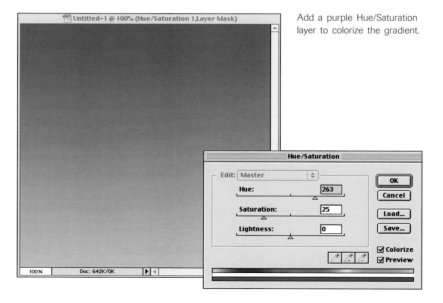

Add a purple Hue/Saturation layer to colorize the gradient.

INTRODUCING THE OBJECT

You need to select an image that you want to use in your studio shot. It can, of course, be any type of image, but if you are going to create shadows and reflections, you should choose an object that can look like it is sitting on a reflective table surface (which means that cows and other large animals are probably not appropriate). In this project, you are going to use a fire extinguisher. I've prepared the image for you so that it has no background. If you start with an image that does have a background, you need to extract it first. Project B, "Compositing," on the accompanying CD-ROM shows you more about extracting images from backgrounds.

1   Open the image **FIREXT.psd** from the accompanying CD-ROM.

Open the image FIREXT.psd.

2   Keep the Shift key pressed down as you drag and drop the fire extinguisher into the untitled image. Close FIREXT.psd.

The Shift key makes the dragged object appear in the center of its new file.

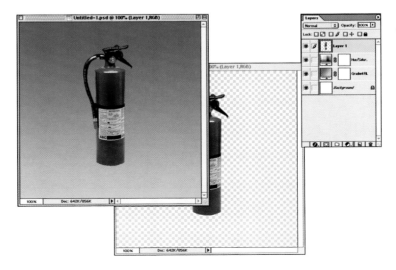

Drag the fire extinguisher into the center of the gradient image.

ADDING REFLECTIONS

Now it's time to create a reflection of the fire extinguisher, and make it look as if it is a natural reflection rather than a computer-generated one. You duplicate and flip the layer, change the layer opacity, and apply a Motion Blur filter.

1 Duplicate Layer 1 by dragging it to the New Layers icon at the bottom of the Layers palette. Right(Ctrl)+ click the layer name, select Layer Properties, and rename the layer Reflection.

This duplicate fire extinguisher becomes the reflection.

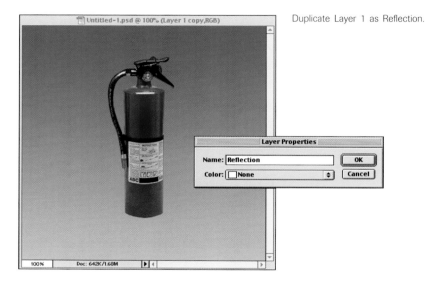

Duplicate Layer 1 as Reflection.

2 Choose Edit/Transform/Flip Vertical.

Even though you are selecting one specific type of Transform command, you have a "Free Transform" box that you can use to access almost all of the menu features on the toolbar at the top of the Photoshop 6 interface. Although there is no "Flip" command, you could also flip your image vertically by setting its height on the Options toolbar to −100%.

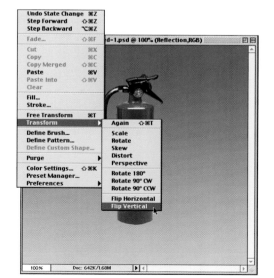

Flip the Reflection layer vertically.

3 Holding down the Shift key and using the Move tool, drag the flipped copy of your object downward until the bottom of the fire extinguisher in the Reflection layer almost reaches the bottom of the original object in Layer 1. In the Layers palette, drag the Reflection layer below Layer 1.

It is easier to position the object first, before you change the order of the Reflection layer. You need to drag from the top portion of the fire extinguisher (which is actually its bottom) or Photoshop thinks you are trying to drag the object out of the image. Most of the flipped object is not visible after it has been moved.

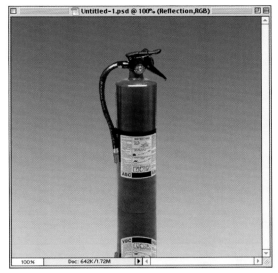
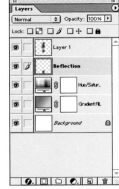

Move the fire extinguisher until its bottom touches the bottom of the original, and then move the Reflection layer below Layer 1.

4 Lower the Opacity of the Reflection layer to 40%.

Lowering Opacity helps to create the effect of a reflection. You can experiment with this setting; it might need to go as low as 20% to give the appearance of a reflection.

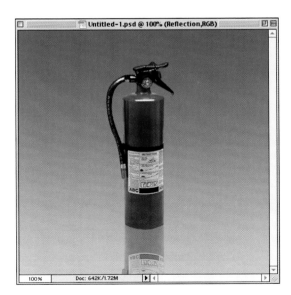
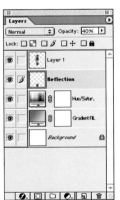

Change the layer Opacity of the Reflection layer to 40%.

5 Choose Filter/Blur/Motion Blur. Set Angle to –90°
and Distance to 12 pixels.

This reflection was very mirror-like and crisp, and
sometimes can look a bit too crisp and artificial. I like
to add a filter to take the attention off the reflection.
The settings that you used add enough blur to the
reflection to make it look more realistic.

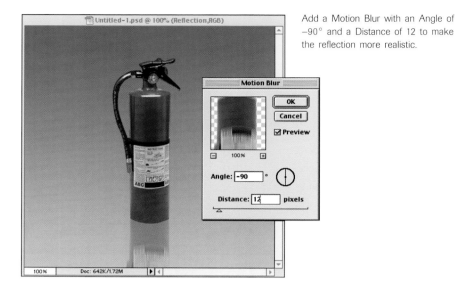

Add a Motion Blur with an Angle of
–90° and a Distance of 12 to make
the reflection more realistic.

CREATING A LIGHT SOURCE

If you are to have realistic shadows and reflections, you need a light source to help you
create shadows that add to the illusion. Create a light source by using the Lighting Effects
filter to simulate the light and enhance the "shot in the studio" effect. Use a Hard Light
layer filled with a neutral color as the layer for your light source. This enables you to keep
the Gradient and Hue/Saturation layers as live layers.

1 Hold the Alt(Opt) key and click the New Layer icon
at the bottom of the Layers palette to enter the Layer
Options dialog box. Choose a Hard Light layer
(name it Light Source), and click on the check box to
fill the layer with a neutral color.

Hard Light mode's neutral color is 50% gray, and it
looks as if it is transparent. When you apply the
Lighting Effect filter in the next step, all you can see
on this layer is the light itself.

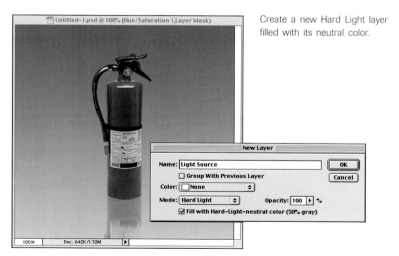

Create a new Hard Light layer
filled with its neutral color.

142

2 Choose Filter/Render/Lighting Effects. Click the end point of the oval light in the preview window and rotate the beam of light around so the light is coming from the upper-right corner. Enter the following settings:

Style: **Default**

Light Type: **Spotlight**

Light: **On**

Intensity: **35**

Focus: **69**

Gloss: **0**

Material: **69**

Exposure: **0**

Ambience: **8**

Texture Channel: **None**

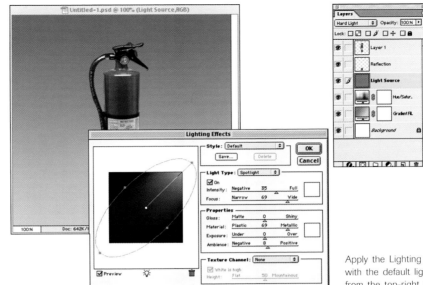

Apply the Lighting Effects filter with the default light coming from the top-right corner.

Note: These are the default settings if you've never used the Lighting Effects filter (or you've just trashed your Preferences). If your Filter dialog box already has these settings, all you need to do is set the angle and stretch the lighting to match the dialog box shown here. The result is a beam of light coming from the upper-right corner of the image.

BUILDING A CAST SHADOW

In this part of the project, you're going to build a cast shadow. There are a number of ways to do this, but I'm going to show you how we did it back when I was kid, when we had to walk seven miles in the snow, up hill both ways, just to use Photoshop. Use the Transform command to make it work.

1 Duplicate Layer 1 and name it Cast Shadow 1.

Turn this duplicate into a cast shadow.

2 Choose Edit/Transform/Distort. Grab the top-left corner of the Transform bounding box and drag it down and to the left until it's almost aligned with the base of the extinguisher. Don't set the transform yet.

If you actually align the copy with the base of the extinguisher, you cannot see a preview because the distortion is too great. Make sure you can still see the distorted image.

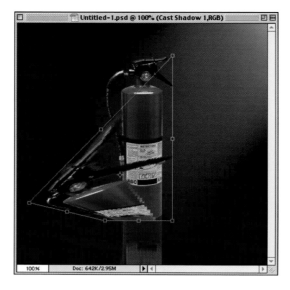

Distort the copied layer by dragging its upper-left corner down and to the left.

3 Grab the upper-right Transform handle and drag it down and to the left, but not as far down as the first point. Grab the top center point and pull away from the image to stretch it. Don't set the transform yet.

You're trying to create a version of your extinguisher that's nearly lying on the ground, facing away from your light source. You can adjust the left and right corners as you see fit to make this transformed copy look like it's being cast by the light source.

Note: Another way of achieving the same result is to Choose Edit/Free Transform, scale the image from the top-center until it is level with the bottom of the label on Layer 1, and then hold the Shift+Alt (Shift+Cmd) keys. These modifiers change the Free Transform Scale command into the Skew command. Drag the top-center handle to the left until the left-most point is off the image.

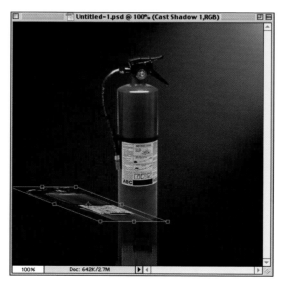

Skew the right side of the cast shadow and stretch the shape.

4 Choose Edit/Transform/Flip Vertical. Click inside the bounding box, and drag your flipped layer to meet the base of the extinguisher. Press Enter (Return) when you are satisfied.

Flip/Vertical flips your image in the direction of the light source.

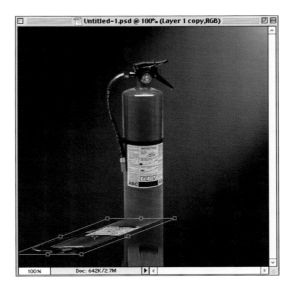

Flip the cast shadow vertically and reposition it so that its bottom touches the bottom of the extinguisher.

Note: If you wanted to accomplish all of the changes by only using the Options toolbar, you can enter the following settings:

X: **142.0 pixels**	Angle: **0°**
Y: **408.5 pixels**	Horizontal Skew: **−68.5°**
W: **100%**	Vertical Skew: **0°**
H: **−21.4%**	

5 Drag the Cast Shadow 1 layer below Layer 1 in the Layers palette.

You might need to reposition the layer slightly once you have changed its layer order.

6 Load the transparency of the Cast Shadow 1 layer (Select/Load Selection/Cast Shadow/Transparency). Leave the object selected, but drag the layer itself to the Layers palette trashcan. Then create a new layer.

Loading the Layer transparency still leaves some partially transparent pixels along the edges of the object. These pixels would detract from the final image because they would not get filled properly in the next step. The easiest way to cope with them is to trash the layer and create a new one.

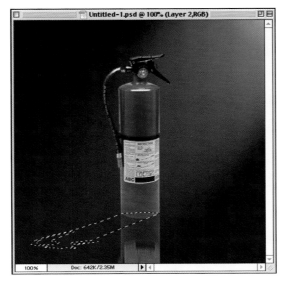

Select the cast shadow, trash the layer that it is on, but leave the selection in place as you create a new layer.

7 Set your colors to the default (press the **D** key). Select the Gradient tool and open the Gradient Editor. Choose the Foreground to Transparent gradient, which is the second preset on the top row.

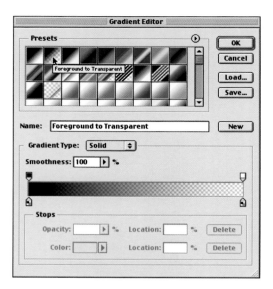

Choose the Foreground to Transparent gradient preset.

8 Place the Gradient tool on the base of selection (the top-right side), and drag diagonally down to the left side of your selection. Deselect.

This gives the illusion that your shadow starts at the base of the object, and then fades away naturally as it moves farther away from the object. You're not done quite yet, however.

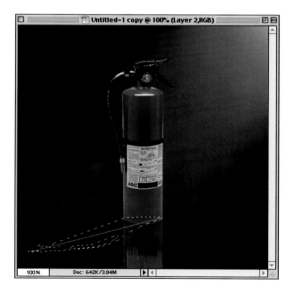

Fill the selection with the gradient, so the area near the base of the extinguisher is almost opaque.

9 Choose Filter/Blur/Gaussian Blur. Set the Radius to 1.

A 1-pixel blur just gives the shadow a hint of softness. To make this as realistic as possible, you are going to make the shadow less blurry nearest the extinguisher, and progressively blurrier as it moves away from the extinguisher (just like in real life—or at least in real life as portrayed on TV).

Apply a Gaussian Blur of 1 to the cast shadow in Layer 2.

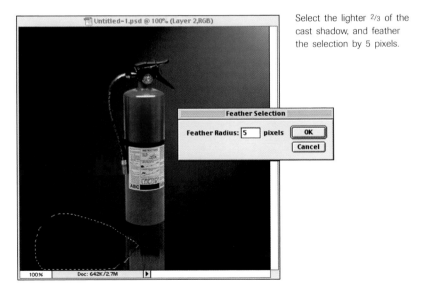

10 With the Lasso tool, very loosely select the lighter $^2/_3$ of your gradient shadow (leaving the area just below and to the left of the extinguisher unselected). Choose Select/Feather and set a Feather of 5 pixels.

This smoothes the transition between the 1-pixel blur you added earlier and the heavier blur applied in the next step.

Select the lighter $^2/_3$ of the cast shadow, and feather the selection by 5 pixels.

11 Choose Filter/Blur/Gaussian Blur. Enter a Radius of 3. Click OK to apply the filter but don't deselect.

The top of portion of the shadow is now much softer than the area closest to the extinguisher. You're going to use the current selection in the next step.

12 Using the Lasso tool, drag the selection away from the object (out of the image) until only the lightest third is selected. Apply a Gaussian Blur of 3 or 4 to this new selection. Deselect.

The blur makes the almost transparent portion of the cast shadow very soft.

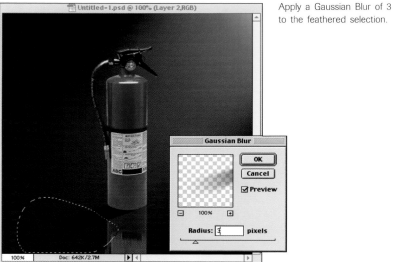

Apply a Gaussian Blur of 3 to the feathered selection.

13 Lower the Opacity of this shadow layer (Layer 2) to about 70%.

Lowering Opacity for the layer helps to place less emphasis on the shadow.

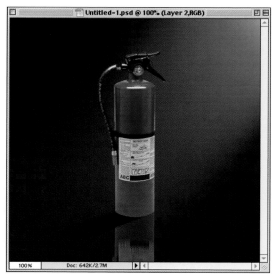

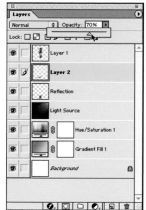

Set the layer's Opacity to 70%.

CREATING MULTIPLE LIGHT SOURCES

As hard to believe as this might sound, there are photographers that own not just one, but two lights (shocking!) The good news is: From multiple light sources, you can have multiple shadows (and I always say "the more shadows the merrier"). Besides, we've come too far not to toss in another gratuitous shadow, so I say let's go for broke and add another, as if there was a second light source. To do this, simply copy our existing cast shadow layer, change its angle, shrink it a little, and lower its opacity.

1   Rename Layer 2 to Cast Shadow 1 by Right(Ctrl)+ clicking on the layer name to open the Layer Properties dialog box.

2   Duplicate the Cast Shadow 1 layer and name it Cast Shadow 2.

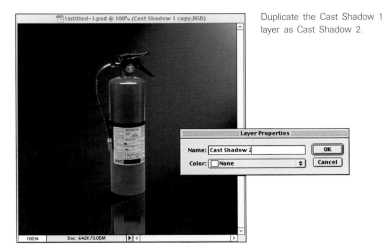

Duplicate the Cast Shadow 1 layer as Cast Shadow 2.

3   Choose the Free Transform command, hold the Ctrl(Cmd) key, and drag the center-left control point upward until the Vertical Skew amount on the Option toolbar reads approximately 21°. Release the Modifier key and drag the same center-left control point toward the right until the Width on the Options toolbar reads approximately 82%. Press Enter (Return) to lock in the transformation.

These settings skew the second cast shadow, so it moves up and gets smaller, as if a second light were shining on it from a different direction.

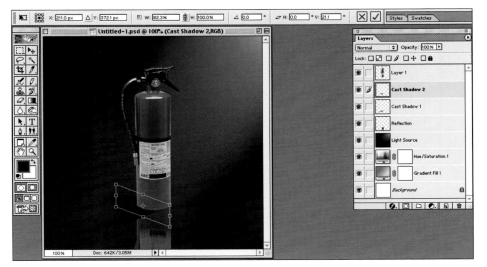

Skew the second cast shadow.

4   In the Layers palette, set Opacity for the Cast Shadow 2
layer to 35%.

This completes the second light source shadow.

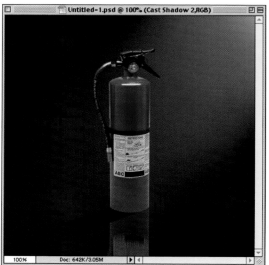

Change the opacity of
the second cast shadow
to 35%.

CREATING A TABLETOP

To further enhance this studio shot, you can make it look as if the extinguisher were
resting on a very reflective tabletop. Create and duplicate a Layer Set (a new Photoshop 6
feature), so you can keep your special layers "live," and then apply a layer mask to the
duplicate Layer Set and position it to act as a tabletop. Before you work through this
section, be sure to read the sidebar that addresses the issue of banding.

LIVE EFFECTS AND BANDING

If you look closely at the Light Source layer, notice that there seems to be
a lot of banding—color breaks where it seems you can see circular, sharp
changes of color. This is happening because of the interaction between
the Gradient layers, Hue/Saturation layers, and the Hard Light mode of
the Light Source layer. I wanted you to have the opportunity to use live
layers in this project. This is, however, really the point that you should
decide if you like the colors or not and change them until you're happy.

The banding would not occur as badly if you were to rasterize and merge
the Gradient Fill 1 layer and Hue/Saturation layers and apply the Lighting
Effects filter directly to the merged layer. At this point in the project, it is
still easy to do this. Simply trash the Light Source layer. Then, click
the Gradient Fill 1 layer and choose Layer/Rasterize/Layer. Activate
the Hue/Saturation layer and choose Layer/Rasterize/Layer and
Layer/Merge Down. You can discard the layer masks. Finally,
choose Filter/Render/Lighting Effects. Your changed light should
still be there.

This is how you would work if you were completing your own project.
For the purpose of seeing how to use live layers and how to work
with Layer Sets, please follow the main set of instructions in the
project. Know, however, that I am aware of the banding issue, and
you can correct it at this point in the project.

Should you choose to keep live layers throughout your own projects
(with your own images), you can still cover the banding at the end.
You need to apply a small but different amount of noise (using the
Add Noise filter in monochromatic, Gaussian mode) to at least two
of the three channels in the image (or three of the four channels if
you convert the image to CMYK before printing). Apply the noise
only to the Light Source layer in the Tabletop Layer Set. The tabletop gets a bit less reflective, but you'll notice much less banding.

1 Activate the Light Source layer. Click the Link icon next to the Gradient Fill 1 layer and the Hue/Saturation 1 layer. Choose New Set From Linked in the Layers palette side drop-down menu. Name the new set Backdrop.

A new feature in Photoshop 6 allows you to create hierarchical Layer Sets where a set can hold many layers. The set can share many of the same properties as a regular layer—you can mask and move a set as if it were a single entity. You need to keep this layer set just above the Background layer.

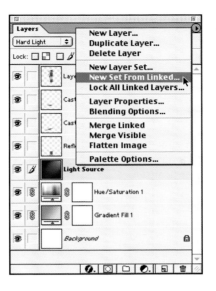

Link the Hue/Saturation and Gradient Fill layers to the Light Source layer and create a new Layer Set from the linked layers.

2 Choose Duplicate Layer Set from the side drop-down menu on the Layers palette.

You can't duplicate a Layer Set by dragging it to the New Layer icon on the Layers palette as you would a plain layer. You could, however, have used the Duplicate Layer Set command on the Layers menu instead. Make sure the TableTop Layer Set stays just above the collapsed Backdrop Layer Set. If it gets higher in the list, you can lose the reflections.

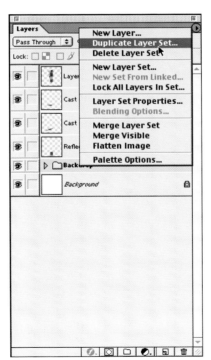

Duplicate the Backdrop Layer Set.

3 Name the copied Layer Set Tabletop.

Notice in the dialog box that you can copy a Layer Set to a totally new or different file. You do not want to right now, but you could if you wanted to.

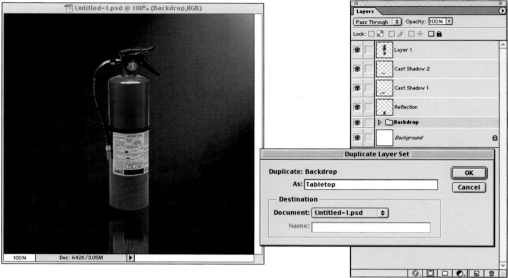

Name the duplicated Layer Set Tabletop.

4 Activate the Tabletop Layer Set and draw a Rectangular Marquee selection around the bottom half of the image.

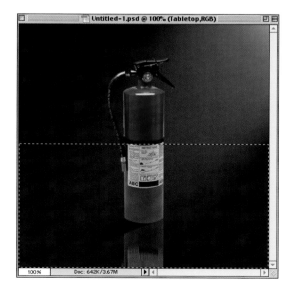

Select the bottom half of the image.

152

5 Click the Add a Mask icon at the bottom of the Layers palette. With the Move tool, hold down the Shift key and drag the layer straight down until the edge of this layer appears just above the bottom of the extinguisher image.

This makes the object appear as though it is sitting on a table, further enhancing your "shot in a studio" effect. The Shift key constrains the movement of the masked Layer Set to keep it aligned.

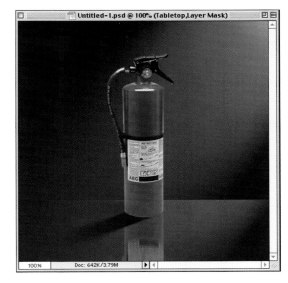
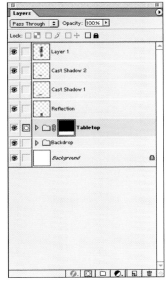

Add a layer mask to the Layer Set and drag the set down until it is just higher than the bottom of the extinguisher.

6 Twirl down the twisty on the Tabletop Layer Set to reveal all of the layers in the set. Activate the Light Source layer. By clicking the Create New Fill or Adjustment Layer icon, add a new Levels layer on top of the Light Source layer. In the Levels dialog box, drag the White Input slider to 180.

You can enhance the "extinguisher is on a table" effect by brightening the table a bit. You cannot use the Levels command on an entire Layer Set—it only affects the layer mask, which isn't what you want. A Levels Adjustment layer on top of the Light Source layer, however, does the trick. Notice the effect of the Levels change is localized to the Layer Set. You can set the Levels highlight to any degree of brightness that you prefer.

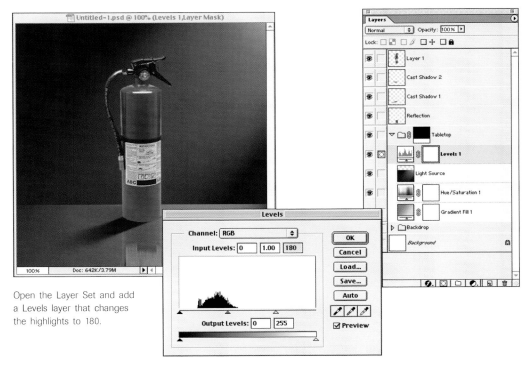

Open the Layer Set and add a Levels layer that changes the highlights to 180.

153

FINAL TOUCHES

OK, one last tweak (this one's picky, but you've come this far, why not go all the way?).
It makes the reflection a bit more realistic by adding a perspective effect.

1 Activate the Reflection layer. Choose Edit/Transform/
Perspective. Choose View/Zoom Out twice to shrink
your image area. Then grab the lower-right corner of
your image window and drag it to the right and down
until you can see the entire bounding box around the
reflection. Grab the bottom-right control point and
drag it slightly toward the left.

This adds a slight perspective effect and helps make
the reflection just a tad more realistic. Press Enter
(Return) to set the transformation.

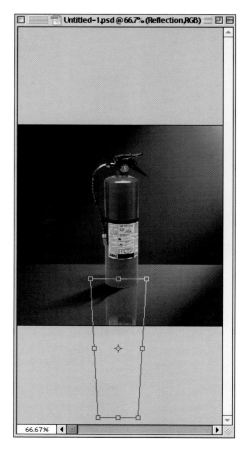

Add a Perspective effect to make
the reflection look as if it is getting
smaller at the bottom.

MODIFICATIONS

That's it—you've done it! From a blank white image to a photographic studio shot in about 34 quick steps. It's pretty amazing how the use of some simple shadows, lighting, and reflections adds so much depth and visual interest to what otherwise could be flat, dull images.

How could you change the effect? You can easily change the angle of your lighting. If the object that you are using shows any evidence of light direction, then you need to be sure to match the angle that is already blended into the object.

For more complex scenes, you could composite together multiple objects and use many more shadows and light sources. Just remember that the lighting needs to be internally consistent or your viewer has the nagging sense of discomfort that something simply "doesn't look right"—even if the actual cause of the discomfort eludes them.

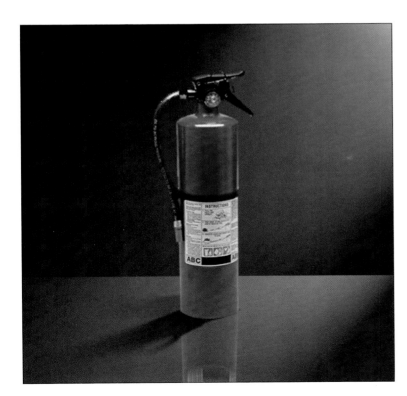

As perfect a studio shot as you can find.

VIGNETTES AND EDGES

"Think of all the beauty still

left around you and be happy."

—ANNE FRANK, *DIARY OF A YOUNG GIRL*, 1952

A Decorative Treatment

A traditional vignette is an oval area cut from

an image and given a softened edge. You

can be extremely creative with a vignette by

changing the shape of the featured area,

or by adding decorative edges and textures.

Photoshop 6's new Shape tool makes it even

easier to create interesting vignette outlines.

Project 11

Vignettes and Edges

by Sherry London

GETTING STARTED

This project shows you how to create a heart-shaped vignette and add texture to it by embedding it inside of a larger composition. You'll eventually transform the composite image into a new vignette. You'll use the Shape tool to create the original vignette heart. You'll learn how to build soft selections in a channel, and add texture to specific areas in a channel. This project makes heavy use of the Apply Image and Calculations commands, and shows you how to combine channels. By learning how to manipulate the channels, you can create any type of edge treatment you want.

Note: So that you can concentrate on the unique techniques of pattern and texture-filtering the edges of the vignette, the first and last portions of this project have been included in the **11_extras.pdf** file on the CD for you to work with. You can work through this project in its entirety by using the 11_extras.pdf file, or you can work through the more-focused portion of the project included here in the book by using pre-built files instead.

CREATING EDGE MASKS

In this section, you'll learn how to create edge effects that allow some portions of the image to be visible, but cause other area along the edges of the image to disappear. You'll use a combination of layer masks and clipping groups to achieve this result. Open **brideheart3.psd** from the accompanying CD.

Note: If you want, the **11_extras.pdf** file included on the accompanying CD will show you how to build the composite image we're starting with here.

1 Create a new layer above the Background layer. Use the Lasso tool to create the outline of a jagged shape that runs near the edges of the window, but doesn't ever touch it. Fill this shape with white.

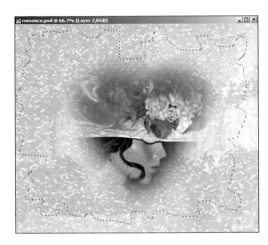

Create a jagged shape to become another vignette frame.

2 Click the Save Selection as Channel icon in the Channels palette to create Alpha 1. Deselect. Double-click the thumbnail and change the name of the channel to Hard Edge Original Panel.

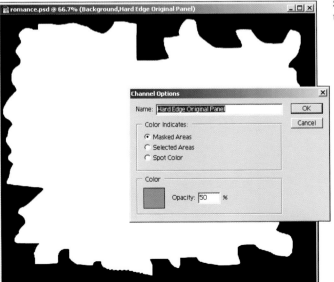

Save the jagged selection to a new channel.

159

3 Activate the Background layer. Use the Eyedropper tool to select a light green from the image, and then create a new solid layer from the Create New Fill or Adjustment Layer drop-down on the Layers palette. Set the Opacity of the new layer to 54%.

Note: Select the color for the solid layer with the Eyedropper tool before you add the Solid layer. You need to do this first, because as soon as you add the solid layer, the Eyedropper tool adds the foreground color to the soild layer, and you can no longer pick a different color from the image itself. However, you could select a color from a different image with the New Solid dialog box open.

Note: When you increase the canvas size, a solid layer (new to Photoshop 6) "grows" with the increased size of the image. A colored background layer (the Photoshop 5 way of doing things) would show a white border around it unless the background color swatch was set to match the background layer color before increasing the canvas size.

4 Activate Layer 0. Choose Layer/Group with Previous to clip Layer 0 to the white shape.

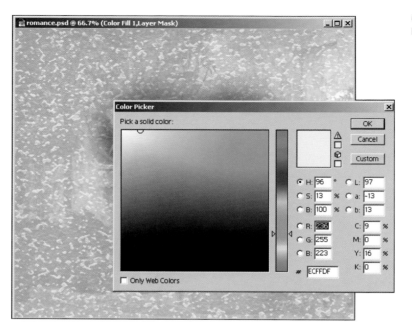

Create a solid layer using a light green in the image.

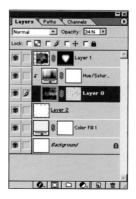

Group Layer 0 to Layer 2.

5 Activate Layer 2 and choose Filter/Blur/Gaussian Blur. Set the amount to 34 pixels.

Grouping the layers before you blur the clipped-to layer allows you to preview the final effect as you apply the Gaussian Blur.

6 In the Channels palette, press the Ctrl (Cmd) key and click the Hard Edge Original Panel channel to load the alpha channel as a selection. Choose Select/Modify/Border to set a 50-pixel border. Set 5 pixels of feathering (Select/Feather). Save the selection to a new channel. Name the channel Decorative Edge. *Don't* deselect.

7 From Filter/Noise/Add Noise set:

Amount: **130%**

Distribution: **Gaussian**

Monochromatic: **Checked**

8 In Filter/Pixelate/Crystallize, set the Cell Size to 20. Deselect.

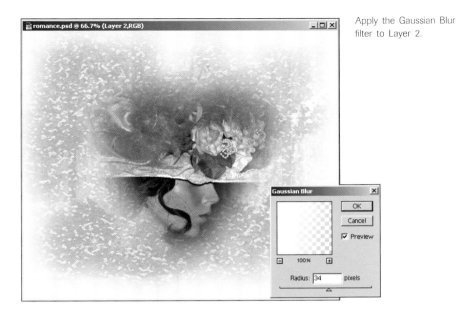

Apply the Gaussian Blur filter to Layer 2.

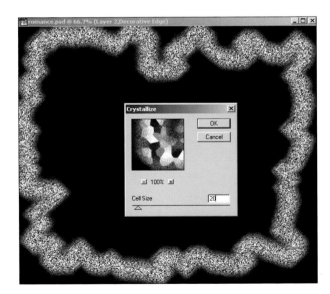

Crystallize the noise in the channel selection.

9 Select Image/Adjust/Invert to invert the values in the channel. Set the Threshold to 60.

You want to leave some black in the channel, but not an enormous amount.

10 Activate Layer 2. Add a layer mask. Leave the layer mask active and choose Image/Apply Image. Place the Decorative Edge channel into the layer mask.

Note: The Apply Image command allows you to "project" the contents of a channel or image into a new location. In the process, you can combine the projected image and the original image in a variety of ways. Apply Image is one of the oldest commands in Photoshop, but it is still an incredibly useful one. It doesn't use clipboard memory and is one of the only ways to paste images into a channel. The only "gotcha" is that you can only use the Apply Image command when both images contain exactly the same number of pixels. You can't make a mistake with this, because Photoshop only shows you the "legal" images in the dialog box. However, if you want to use an image in the Apply Image dialog box and you don't see it as an option, check your image size to find the difference.

11 With Layer 2's layer mask still active, choose Filter/Blur/Gaussian Blur and enter 1.5 to soften the hard edges a tiny bit.

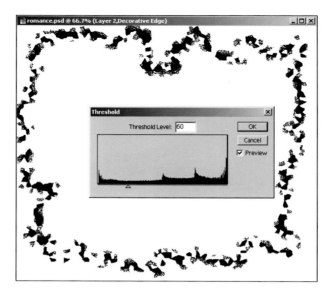

Use Threshold to remove the gray values in the channel.

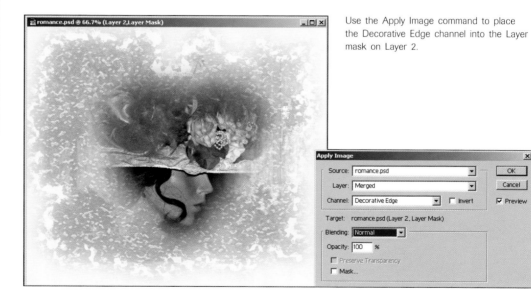

Use the Apply Image command to place the Decorative Edge channel into the Layer mask on Layer 2.

CREATE ADDITIONAL FRAMES

Additional frames can enhance a vignette. While adding some to the example, you'll learn how to import an Adobe Illustrator image and paint freely on a layer, and then use the Calculations command to make another layer mask. You can continue to work in the current image, or you might use **brideheart4.psd** as your starting point.

1   Drag Layer 0 to the New Layer icon to copy it. Right-click (Ctrl+click) the image thumbnail in the Layers palette and choose Layer Properties from the menu. Rename the copied layer as Layer 3. Drag Layer 3 into position above the Color Fill 1 layer. Discard Layer 3's layer mask (don't apply it). Change the layer's Opacity to 100%.

Using Apply Image should have been faster than duplicating Layer 0 and removing its mask, but the Apply Image command would have applied both the image *and* the layer mask to the new layer.

2   Create a new, empty layer (Layer 4) above the Color Fill 1 layer. Open **freepaint.psd** from the CD and then make Layer 4 of your working image active again. Choose Image/Apply Image and set:

Source: **freepaint.psd**

Layer: **Layer 1**

Channel: **RGB**

Click OK. Activate Layer 3 and select Group with Previous to preview the way the dark lines look. Alter Layer 4 until you like the effect.

Alternatively, you can paint your own frame in the empty Layer 4.

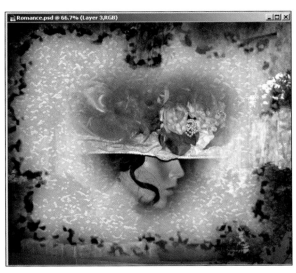

Create Layer 3 from an unmasked duplicate of Layer 0.

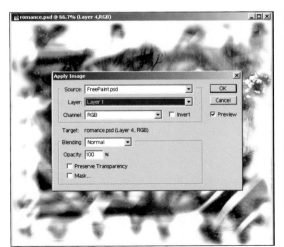

Apply the freely painted lines in freepaint.psd to a new layer in your working image, and then preview the results by grouping Layer 3 with the new Layer 4.

3 Press the Ctrl (Cmd) key and click the thumbnail of Layer 4 to load the transparency of the layer as a selection. Click the Save Selection as Channel icon in the Channels palette. Name the channel FREEPAINT and deselect. Delete Layer 4.

Tip: If you want to create your own dark frame (because this is what you are working toward), you can group Layer 3 to Layer 4 and then paint freely on Layer 4 to add areas where the dark image in Layer 3 is visible. Use white when you paint just in case you want to lower the opacity of Layer 3 at any time. You can soften your painting in Layer 4 by choosing Filter/Blur/Motion Blur. The settings used in freepaint.psd are Angle at 53 and Distance at 44, but you can choose your own if you want.

4 Activate the Color Fill 1 layer. Choose File/Place and open frame.ai. Accept the default size and press the Enter (Return) key. Load the transparency of the frame.ai layer and save the selection to a channel. Name the channel frame.ai and deselect. Delete the frame.ai layer.

Note: How could you create your own frame.ai? Frame.ai began as a simple rectangle in Illustrator 9. The Object/Path/Add Points command used multiple times added new points to the object. Applying the Sketchy style added three randomly spaced strokes onto the single object. If you open frame.ai in Illustrator 9, you can look in the Appearance palette to see the modifications made to the Sketchy style so that each stroke has a different weight.

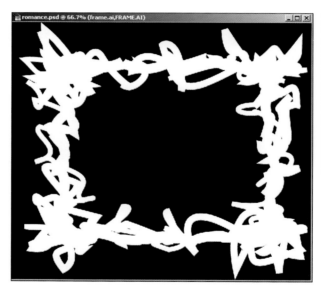

Place frame.ai into a layer above Color Fill 1, and save the transparency of the layer as a channel.

5 Activate the frame.ai channel. Apply a Gaussian Blur filter with a pixel radius between 5 and 9 pixels. Choose Filter/Distort/Wave, and set:

Number of Generators: **5**

Wavelength (Min): **35**

Wavelength (Max): **135**

Amplitude (Min): **35**

Amplitude (Max): **35**

Scale (H and V): **100%**

Type: **Sine**

Undefined Areas: **Repeat Edge Pixels**

Choose Edit/Fade Wave and fade the filter to 100% Lighten. Apply another Gaussian Blur filter with a pixel radius between 5 and 9 pixels.

6 Choose Image/Calculations. Both sources are in the current document and the layer selection does not matter. Enter the following settings:

Source 1 Channel: **freepaint**

Source 2 Channel: **frame.ai**

Blending: **Subtract**

Opacity: **100%**

Offset: **0**

Scale: **1**

Don't select a mask. Place the result in a new channel and click OK. Name the new channel Layer Frame.

7 Load the Layer Frame channel as a selection. Activate Layer 3, click the Add a Mask icon in the Layers palette.

8 Choose Image/Canvas Size and increase both Width and Height by 100 pixels. Leave the anchor in the center.

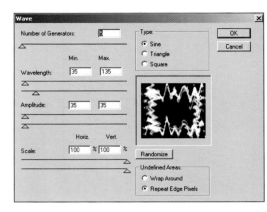
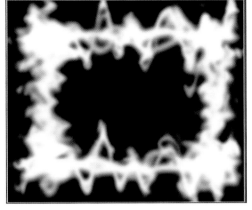

Apply the Wave filter faded to 100% Lighten mode and then apply a Gaussian Blur filter of 5 pixels.

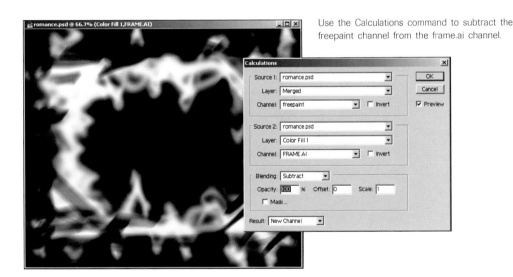

Use the Calculations command to subtract the freepaint channel from the frame.ai channel.

Note: The Calculations command combines two channels and places the result into a new channel, new document, or new selection. It only works with grayscale data. If you need color, use the Apply Image command.

9 Activate Layer 1 and create a new layer (Layer 4). Type Shift+Crtl+Alt+E (Shift+Cmd+Opt+E) to merge all the visible layers into the new layer. Turn off the Eye icons on all of the lower layers.

> **Note:** Merging all visible layers to a new layer is a very useful trick. It allows you to treat your image as a single entity but keep the original layers available if you want to use them again. You can select this command by holding the Alt (Opt) key as you select Merge Visible from the Layers menu. The result is stored in the active layer.

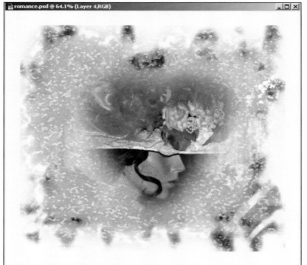

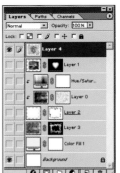

Merge all the visible layers into a new layer.

10 Activate Layer 4. Choose the Elliptical Marquee tool. Drag an elliptical selection around the original image borders (from the upper-left corner to the bottom-right of the area that is not part of the solid light green border). Click the Add a Mask icon in the Layers palette to create a layer mask.

You need to remember to set the Fixed Size marquee back to the Normal style.

11 Load the layer mask as a selection by Ctrl(Cmd)+ clicking on the layer mask thumbnail in the Layers palette. Choose Select/ Inverse. Activate the Layer 4 image (not the layer mask). Choose Select/Feather and set Feather to 15 pixels. Apply a Gaussian Blur of 15 pixels to the selection. Deselect.

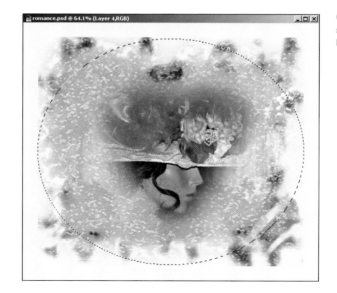

Create an Elliptical Marquee selection to use as a new layer mask.

12 Activate the Layer 4 layer mask. Apply a Gaussian Blur filter of 15–30 pixels to the layer mask. Blur any visible hard edges in the Layer 4 image with the Blur tool.

You've created a composite vignette that could stand on its own if you wanted to stop now. You can, however, take this technique even further.

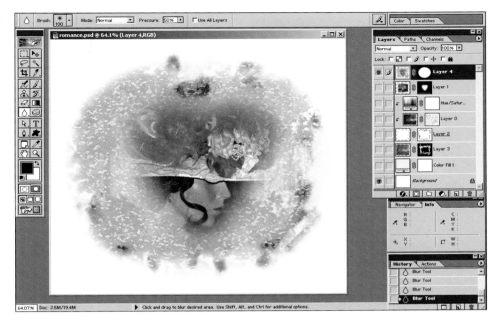

Blur the layer mask by 15 pixels and then touch up any hard edges in the image with the Blur tool.

CREATE THE VIGNETTE EDGES

The vignette isn't quite finished. You can use patterns in the edges of the vignette to produce amazing texture variations. You don't need to settle for just a blurred edge to the vignette. You can continue with your working image or use **brideheart5.psd** from the accompanying CD as your starting point.

1 Activate Layer 4 and then activate the Channels palette. Drag Layer Mask 4 to the Create New Channel icon to copy it. Name the copied channel Blurred Oval. Drag-duplicate the Blurred Oval channel and name it Flower Channel.

The blurred edge of the oval gives your flower channel the gray values it needs.

2 Choose Edit/Preset Manager and select Patterns from the Preset Type menu. Then click on Load. Select the file **VigPats.pat** from the accompanying CD.

These are the patterns you'll use in the vignette edges.

Load some new patterns into your pattern preset library.

3 Ctrl(Cmd)+click the Flower Channel to load it as a selection. Choose Edit/Fill/Pattern and fill it with the flower pattern (flowerbrick). Don't deselect.

The soft edges in the loaded channel make the pattern fill fade from the center of the oval toward its edges.

4 Make sure your background color is set to white. Choose Select/Modify/Contract and contract the selection by 60 pixels. Press the Backspace (Delete) key to remove the pattern from the selection. Deselect.

By contracting the selection by 60 pixels, you're removing the edges of the oval from the selection. When you delete, therefore, you're removing the pattern from the part of the oval that wants to remain plain and not from the edges of the oval.

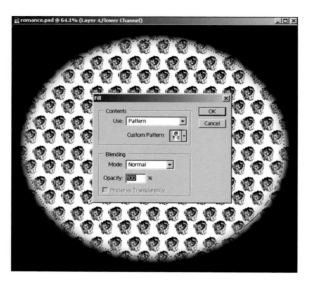

Fill the selection in the channel with the flower pattern.

5 Choose Image/Adjust/Levels and move the Input black point slider to 128. Click OK. Choose Image/Adjust/Threshold and move the slider to 45-50. Do not deselect.

6 Create a new channel and name it Stripe Channel. Fill it with the stripe pattern you loaded into your preset patterns from VigPats.pat.

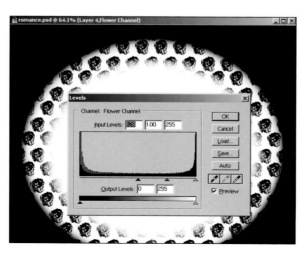

Use the Levels command to change the black Input point to 128.

7 Ctrl(Cmd)+click the Blurred Oval channel to load it as a selection. Press the Shift+Ctrl+Alt (Shift+Cmd+Opt) keys and click the Stripe channel to intersect the blurred oval with the stripes. Save the result to a new channel and name it Striped Oval.

8 Your background color must still be white. Ctrl (Cmd)+click the Blurred Oval channel to load it as a selection. Choose Select/Modify/Contract and contract the selection by 60 pixels. Activate the Striped Oval channel. Press the Backspace (Delete) key. With the selection still active, choose Image/Adjust/Levels and move the Input black point slider to 86. Deselect.

You don't need to feather the selection because the Blurred Oval channel is already blurred on the edges. This blurred selection also helps the Levels command to create different degrees of darkness, but the setting of 86 guarantees that the finished object does not have a true black in it. As you are creating a layer mask, the lack of black in the stripes means that some part of the masked image is visible.

9 Activate the Flower Channel. Choose Image/Apply Image and multiply the Blurred Oval channel onto the flowers.

The flowers are solid black and remain so. They "cut out" the layer when used in a mask. The Blurred Oval channel restores some of the shading lost in the Threshold command.

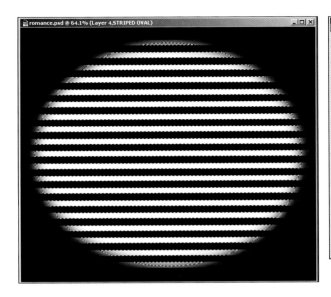

Save a new channel that is the intersection of the Blurred Oval and the Stripes channels.

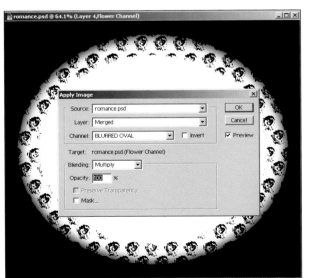

Multiply the Blurred Oval channel onto the Flower Channel.

10 With the Flower Channel still active, choose Image/ Apply Image and apply the Striped Oval channel to the Flower Channel set in Darken mode. Repeat this command a second time.

The second Apply Image command adds more darkness to the channel, but controls it based on the underlying values.

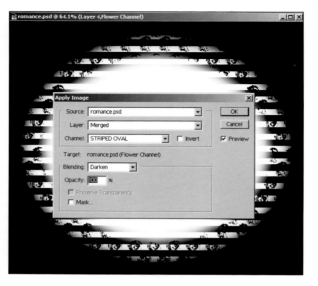

Darken the Flower Channel with the Striped Oval channel.

11 Activate the RGB channel and make the layer mask on Layer 4 active. Choose Image/Apply Image. Apply the Flowers Channel to the layer mask in Darken mode.

If you want to create a vignetted border around this image using some additional but similar methods, you can work the "Create the Border" instructions that are in the **11_extras.pdf** file on the accompanying CD-ROM.

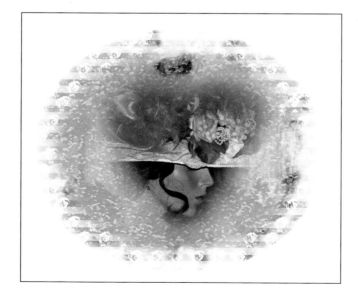

Apply the Flower Channel to the Layer 4 layer mask in Darken mode to create an interesting edge for the vignette.

How It Works

By creating a variety of channels with different patterns, textures, or value ranges in them, you can create an endless variety of vignette and edge effects. The technique makes heavy use of the various blend modes available in the Apply Image command. The basic premise is that you can create a blurred-edge channel in whatever shape you want your vignette to be and then place patterns or textures into the outer edges of the mask. You can use Levels or Threshold to further refine the values in the channel to make them lighter to reveal more of a layer or darken them to create cut out areas.

Modifications

You have many ways you can modify the project. Anywhere you were directed to change an opacity setting or to apply a specific blend mode or filter setting, you can opt for a different setting. The settings for the Wave filter, shown here, differ from the ones you used. These settings make a noticeable change in the final result.

You can choose to add or not include the border, or to stop at any point along the way. You can choose to substitute a different image for the one used here, but use the same set of instructions.

You can apply a vignette to any image that you prefer. Although the time-honored preference is for "people shots," non-human subjects also make good vignette candidates. You've seen several examples of different shapes that are used as layer masks, but any shape works.

As well, the techniques you've learned in this project can be used to manufacture your own edge effects. Both AutoFX and Extensis have sets of "image edges" that help to keep every image from having a sharp, rectangular profile. You can make your own with the techniques that you've learned. Instead of blending the original image softly with the masks, you can use masks to cut out hard edges. At a smaller scale, you can use these same techniques on text to create decorative edges. You can also apply the texture-in-a-mask techniques to the inside edges of borders to make frames for images like you did in this project. However, you can vary the shape of the border and the textures you poke into the edges.

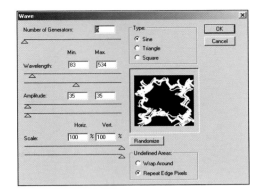

A change in the filter settings makes a definitive change in the final image.

Inverting the Final Edge channel that you created makes an excellent edge treatment for this skater image (skater.psd on the accompanying CD). Because of the skater's position, you wouldn't be able to vignette her easily. However, using the border mask as an edge works very well.

CARICATURE

"If we would build on a sure foundation

in friendship, we must love friends for

their sake rather than for our own."

—CHARLOTTE BRONTE

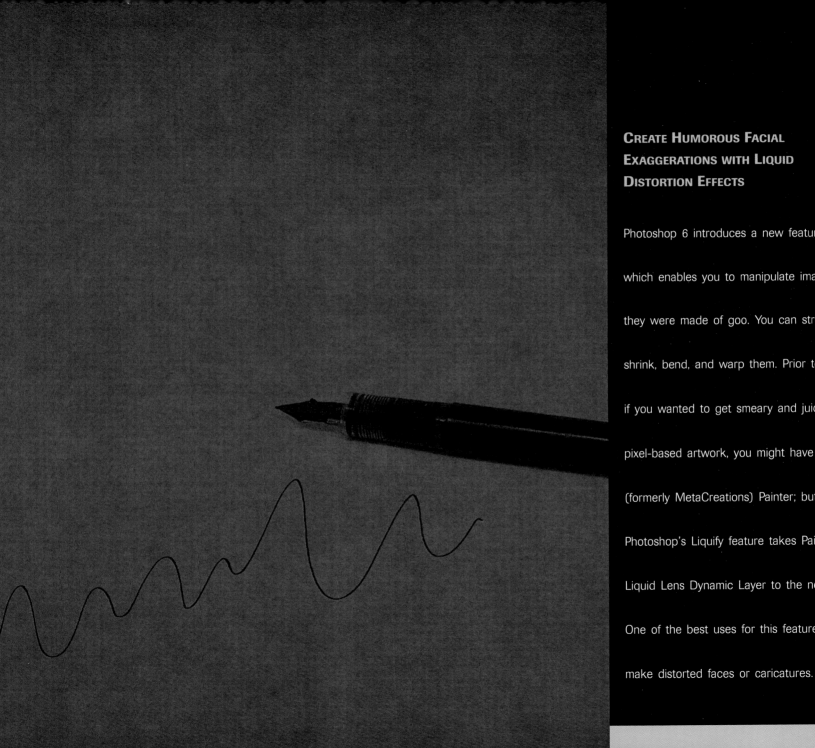

CREATE HUMOROUS FACIAL EXAGGERATIONS WITH LIQUID DISTORTION EFFECTS

Photoshop 6 introduces a new feature, Liquify,

which enables you to manipulate images as if

they were made of goo. You can stretch,

shrink, bend, and warp them. Prior to version 6,

if you wanted to get smeary and juicy with

pixel-based artwork, you might have used Corel

(formerly MetaCreations) Painter; but

Photoshop's Liquify feature takes Painter's

Liquid Lens Dynamic Layer to the next level.

One of the best uses for this feature is to

make distorted faces or caricatures.

Project 12

Caricature

by Rhoda Grossman

THE ART OF CARICATURE

As a professional caricature artist for many years, I pride myself on knowing both the proper spelling and pronunciation of the word! Beyond that, here are some practical guidelines for approaching a caricature assignment. What is required is a distortion of some or all of the components of a face, without losing the essential likeness or personality of the subject. So, if the subject has a larger than average nose, make it even bigger. If he has smaller than average eyes, reduce them to little beady spots.

The angles and volumes of the face are as important as the size and position of eyes, mouth, nose, and (occasionally) ears. Exaggerate any important aspect of your subject and simplify the rest. Careful observation and experience will sharpen your ability to determine what to focus on and what to ignore.

Caricature can be used for political commentary or humor. It can be created with any technique, from traditional pen-and-ink to new media collage.

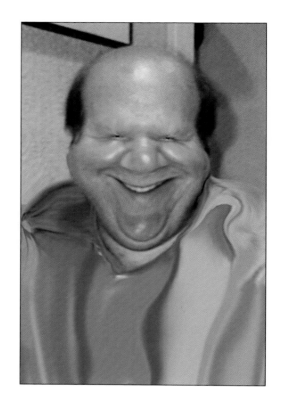

Note: When you choose the Liquify command at the bottom of the Image menu, your image appears in the center of a dialog box providing tools to warp, twirl, shift, pucker, and bloat pixels. Other options are included for selective reverting or freezing pixels to ensure they remain unchanged.

Pucker and Bloat are similar to Pinch and Spherize in the Distort filter group. The Liquify tools, however, offer considerably more power and control over distortions than the filters in the Distort family. Applying brush strokes directly to the pixels you want to alter is more natural than making selections and previewing settings.

GETTING STARTED

You will begin with a photograph of a person and use the Liquify tools in Photoshop 6 to distort the face in a fluid, painterly style. You'll practice recommended hand movements for best results, and you will learn how to protect or reconstruct parts of your image.

MANIPULATE FACIAL FEATURES

My friend Anthony has agreed to let you distort a photograph of him to practice caricature technique. You will begin by making some of his features larger and some smaller, using Bloat and Pucker. Then alter the shape of his head and face with the Warp tool.

1   Open the image **ANTHONY.tif** from the accompanying CD and choose Image/Liquify.

    You remain in the Liquify environment for all these steps. Do not click OK until after you have completely finished with the distortions.

2   Select the Pucker tool and draw in a circular motion around each of Anthony's eyes. Use a Brush Size of about 60 pixels and Brush Pressure around 50%.

    The Pucker tool makes an area smaller. For better control, use small circular movements with your stylus (or mouse). This will help you reduce the eyes without distorting them in other ways. Change the Brush Size or Brush Pressure in the Liquify dialog box as needed. Tablet users can enable the Stylus Pressure check box.

Begin with the snapshot of Anthony.

Reduce the size of Anthony's eyes with the Pucker tool.

Note: Liquify is not just a command, but an entire desktop environment with its own special toolbar and options. The Brush Size and Brush Pressure settings in the Tool Options section of the Liquify dialog box are completely independent of the size and pressure controls in the Photoshop options strip. You can use the bracket keys to alter brush size one pixel at a time (left bracket reduces brush size, right bracket increases it), but the numeric keys do not enable you to change pressure (opacity). The hot spot for each Liquify tool is at the center of the brush. Therefore, you might want to use Preferences/Display and Cursors to make the brushes "precise" while you are working with Liquify effects.

3 Apply the Bloat tool to Anthony's nose. Begin with tiny circular strokes over the nostrils and slightly larger ones in the center of the nose. Set Brush Size to about 40 pixels.

Enlarging the nostril areas first should keep them from being obliterated when you bloat the center of the nose. If the highlight on the nose becomes too dominant, soften its edges with short strokes from the Bloat tool, using very light pressure. That procedure works much more efficiently than dismissing the Liquify dialog box so that you can use the standard Blur tool.

4 Select the Warp tool and set the Brush Size to around 80 pixels. Drag each corner of Anthony's mouth out and up.

The brush should be large enough to spread pixels around the mouth realistically. Too small of a brush will create a thin line, and too large of a brush will spread the distortion to other parts of the face. We will get to those other parts in the next step.

5 Continue using the Warp tool, but enlarge the Brush Size to about 100 pixels. Pull Anthony's cheeks out and his chin down, creating more curves in the outline of his face.

You can also pull (or is it push?) his temples slightly in toward the eyes. It is not enough to just change each feature by reducing or enlarging it. A good caricature also exaggerates the shape of the face and head, adding considerably to the humorous effect.

Enlarge his nose with the Bloat tool.

Spread that smile with the Warp tool.

Create more curves to reshape Anthony's face.

Note: Photoshop's menu strip is unavailable while you are in the Liquify dialog box, but you can undo your preceding brush stroke with the usual keyboard combination Ctrl(Cmd)+Z.

6 Fine-tune your distortions with the Reconstruct tool. Choose the Mode for Reconstruction and the size and pressure you need for best control. When you are satisfied with the results, click OK to dismiss the Liquify dialog box.

If any parts of Anthony's face are distorted too much, you can reconstruct the original pixels in a specific area by painting with the Reconstruct tool. Smooth mode is ideal for fixing minor problems. As you stroke, pixels slowly return to their original state, giving you lots of control over where to stop. If you want to redo a portion of the face completely, use Revert mode for painting the original pixels back quickly, with no intermediate stages.

Note: the Reconstruct button automatically re-creates the original pixels in the entire image, in accordance with the mode you have selected. So with Smooth mode, pressing the Reconstruct button allows the original to slowly emerge from the distortions. You can stop the process at any moment by pressing the Spacebar. Rigid and Stiff modes reconstruct the image more quickly, but still give you time to stop the process if you like an intermediate stage.

Do not use the Revert button unless you want all changes to disappear instantly. Fortunately, you can undo the Revert command.

Here's an example of some overly enthusiastic distortion and the effect of a few seconds of automatic reconstruction in Smooth mode.

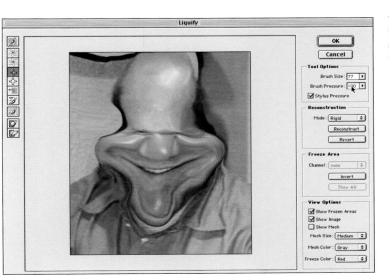

You can reconstruct Anthony's face using the Reconstruct tool or redo parts completely with the Revert mode.

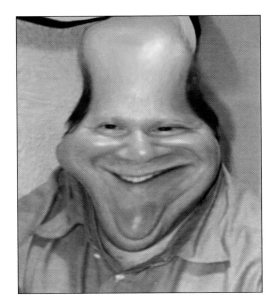

Begin with wild distortion, and then slowly reconstruct in Smooth mode.

DISTORT THE BODY

You will add more space at the bottom of the image and use Liquify tools to give Anthony's shirt a fluid look. You will learn to protect portions of the image you want to remain unchanged.

1 Use Image/Canvas Size to add about a 1/2 inch of white space at the bottom of the image. Set the anchor in the top row to keep Anthony at the top.

2 Fill the white space with a medium blue sampled from Anthony's shirt. Add a few roughly vertical brush strokes with other shades of blue. Liquify effects will be added to this area.

Tip: You can avoid distorting areas of an image you want to remain unchanged by using the Freeze tool in the Liquify dialog box. After you have prepared frozen areas, avoid using the Revert button, because it will undo your work with the Freeze tool as well as other effects. Instead, rely on the Reconstruct tool.

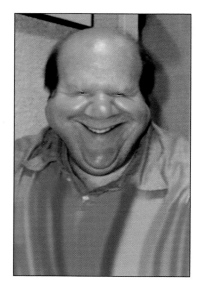

Fill and paint the white area with blue to give the Liquify tools more material to work with.

3 Paint over Anthony's head and the upper part of the background with the Freeze tool. Be sure to cover all skin-tone pixels, including the chest.

It is useful at this stage to keep Anthony's face static while you work freely with other parts of the image. The Freeze tool creates a mask to protect pixels from distortion. Paint over areas you want to protect, and the familiar 50% red (indicating a mask) appears to show which pixels are frozen. You can switch to the Thaw tool to release pixels from the mask. You can toggle the visibility of the mask from a check box in the View options.

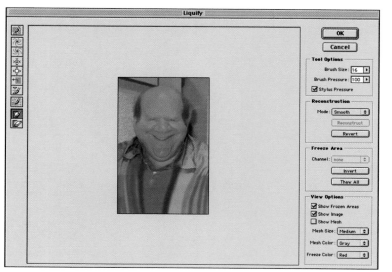

Freeze the pixels you want to protect from further distortion.

4 Use the Bloat and Pucker tools with vertical strokes on the shirt to create smoother curves in the fabric.

A little experimentation with placement of the Bloat tool should reward you with some beautiful shading effects. Recall that you can undo any stroke.

5 Switch to the Twirl Clockwise tool to give Anthony's shirt collar a little more personality.

The Twirl tools both respond well to circular brush strokes, as do the their neighbors, Pucker and Bloat. It does not seem to matter which direction your strokes turn. The Clockwise Twirl always produces a clockwise distortion and the Counterclockwise Twirl is true to its name as well. (Users in the Southern Hemisphere might find the reverse is true.) The finished caricature is shown at the beginning of this project.

Use the Twirl Clockwise tool (center) on Anthony's shirt collar.

MODIFICATIONS

The various tool choices, brush sizes, and your hand movements make many effects possible. Therefore, Liquify must involve some trial-and-error.

The Reconstruct feature invites experimentation. Rather than attempt to distort each feature individually, why not purposely mess a face up beyond all recognition and then gradually reconstruct it?

Use a photo of the author to experiment with Liquify effects.

A photo of me, **RHODA.tif**, is available on *the Photoshop Effects Magic* CD-ROM. Use bold strokes with the Warp tool on the forehead, cheeks, and chin and a few Twirls on the eyeglasses to make extreme distortions.

Use the Reconstruct tool in Smooth mode to reduce the distortion one brush stroke at a time. Smooth mode might not enable you to go back as far as you would like. If you want to continue reconstruction after Smooth mode has reached its limit, use Stiff mode.

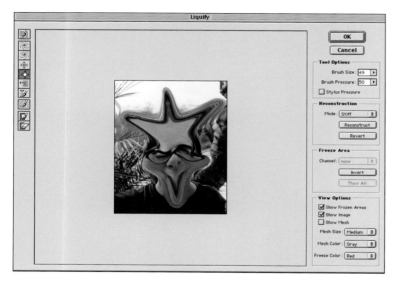

Create serious distortions quickly
with Warp and Twirl tools.

Reconstruct in Smooth mode or Stiff
mode until you like the result.

Liquify can suggest a painterly look, which you can emphasize with one or more filters in the Artistic category. Here is the effect of the Paint Daubs filter with settings of 8 for Brush Size, 7 for Sharpness, and Simple for Brush Type.

For the look of paint on canvas, apply a canvas texture available in the Texture/Texturizer filter. Settings here are 100% Scaling, 7 Relief, and Light Direction from the top.

At this point, you are probably ready to deface a copy of the Mona Lisa, and you have my full support.

Produce a more painterly effect with the Paint Daubs filter.

Add a canvas texture to complete the painterly look.

CREATING WITH FILTERS

"You'd be surprised how much

it costs to look this cheap."

—DOLLY PARTON

PHOTOSHOP'S FILTERS BRING LIFE TO DIGITAL IMAGERY

Working with filters and discovering their magic

in Photoshop is probably the most exciting part

of this medium. In this chapter, you watch a

simple drawing, a "chicken scratch" if you will,

come to life with the aid of filters. The use of

filters and layers with different opacities can

provide the necessary tools to help anyone feel

like an "artiste."

Creating with Filters

by Kelly Loomis

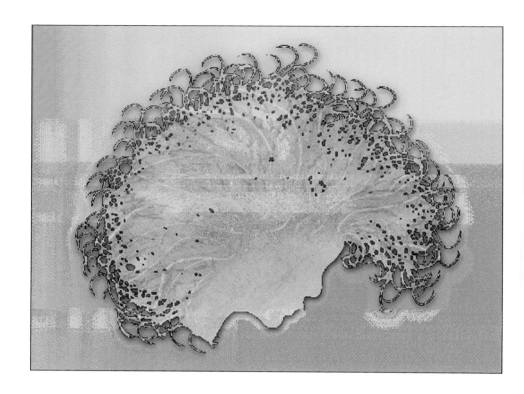

GETTING STARTED

In this project, you'll add "fantasy" hair to a pre-drawn image of a woman's face in a profile. Using filters such as Difference Clouds, Accented Edges, and Ripple, to name a few, you apply the texture, color, and density without the time-consuming task of conventional painting.

CREATING THE NECESSARY LAYERS

The first phase in this project is to make some of the necessary layers. You need five layers to work through this project. One is the Background layer, and the remaining four are for painting the hair, opacity, textures, and highlights. Great imagery relies on density, color, and highlighting. To achieve those same effects in digital design opposed to conventional graphic design, layering techniques are used with different opacities.

1   Open **head1.tif** from the accompanying CD-ROM. The Background layer of the image is empty, but the image contains an alpha channel. Choose Select/Load Selection and load the Alpha 1 channel.

    The Select/Load Selection dialog box defaults to the Alpha 1 channel. You'll use this selection to create four layers.

2   Leave the selection marquee active and choose Layer/ New/Layer Via Copy (Ctrl[Cmd]+J). Turn off the Eye icon on the Background layer. This creates Layer 1.

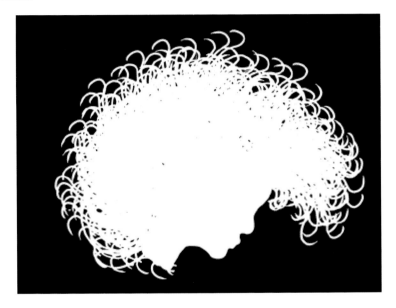

Load this alpha channel as a selection by choosing Select/Load Selection.

3   Press Ctrl(Cmd)+J three more times to create Layers 2, 3, and 4.

Tip: Keep in mind, if you make the layers in a different manner, such as duplicating Layer 1, the layer names will not match up with this tutorial.

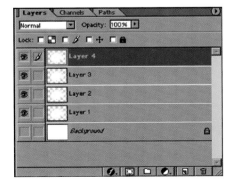

Create Layers 2 through 4 by choosing Layer/New/Layer Via Copy three times.

FILLING THE BACKGROUND

In the next phase, you add color to the background using the Gradient tool.

1   Turn off the Eye icon in Layers 1 through 4. Turn
    on the Eye icon in the Background layer and make
    the layer active.

2   Activate the Gradient tool and choose Linear
    Gradient/Darken mode at 28% Opacity. Click the
    Gradient to open the Gradient Editor. Use three
    color stops positioned at 0%, 50%, and 70%, with
    these corresponding colors: R0, G18, B255; R0,
    G255, B96; R0, G255, B139. Drag the Gradient
    cursor from left to right across the image. Hold the
    Shift key to constrain the gradient to a horizontal
    direction.

    All colors throughout this tutorial are in RGB mode.
    The Opacity is set to 28% so that the layer allows a
    blend of the white background and the colors togeth-
    er. The colors should be somewhat pastel–like and
    not too bright. This is the backdrop for your painting
    and should not take away from the head image.

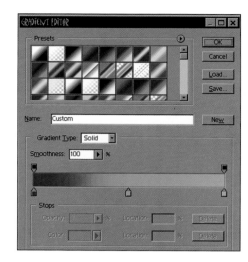

Create a new gradient using the specified color stops
in Step 2 and click on the New button in the dialog
box to change it into a preset for future use.

ADDING TEXTURE

The Difference Clouds filter works by generating a random cloud pattern using the foreground and background colors and then applying this cloud formation to the original layer
in Difference mode. You use this filter to create the beginning texture for the profile.

1   Change the foreground color to R194, G194, B194.
    Change the background color to R0, G0, B0.

2 Activate Layer 1, and choose Filter/Render/
Difference Clouds.

Applying the Difference Clouds filter gives the
image a subtle texture that the Fine Edges filter uses
later. Because the head is white, you are seeing the
same effect as using the Clouds filter and then the
Image/Adjust/Invert command. You don't need
a selection because the Difference Cloud filter
cannot change transparent pixels, so it only works
on the head.

Apply Difference Clouds. Because
the clouds are applied in a
"random" order, your image might
not look exactly like the figure.

3 Choose Filter/Stylize/Find Edges.

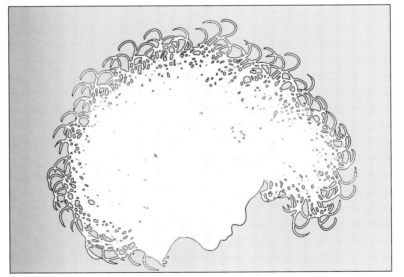

Accentuate the edges of
the head with the Find
Edges effect.

4 Choose Layer/Layer Style/Drop Shadow. Set the following:

Blend Mode: **Multiply**

Color: RGB **0, 0, 0**

Opacity: **50%**

Use Global Light: **Checked**

Angle: **120°**

Distance: **5 px**

Spread: **4%**

Size: **10 px**

Contour: **Linear**

Noise: **0%**

Anti-aliased: **Unchecked**

Layer Knocks Out Drop Shadow: **Checked**

When you add the Drop Shadow filter, the image takes on a more three-dimensional look.

5 Turn off the Eye icon in Layer 1.

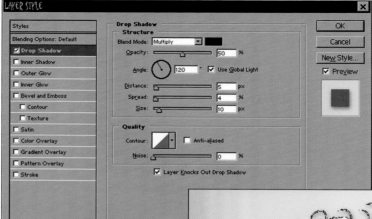

Use the settings in the Drop Shadow Layer Style menu to add dimension and depth to the image.

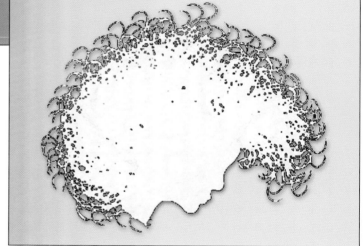

PAINTING AND TEXTURING HAIR

Next you add two layers of hair. The first layer brings complexity to the image by painting in the hair with different brush sizes, whereas the second layer (which you paint in another step later) adds highlights. Adding accentuating and distorting filters to Layer 2, while lessening the opacity, adds an abstract effect to the strands.

1 Activate Layer 2. Change the foreground color to R119, G119, B119. Select the Paintbrush tool. Use a 6-pixel brush with the following settings:

Hardness: **0**

Spacing: **1**

Roundness: **100%**

Change the Brush Options Bar as follows:

Mode: **Normal**

Opacity: **100%**

Wet Edges: **Unchecked**

The result is firm small hair strands with no breaks in each stroke/strand.

2 Paint 1/3 of the desired hair strands. Change to a 4-pixel brush for the next 1/3, and finish the remaining 1/3 with a 2-pixel brush. Intertwine the strands as you go.

Use the image shown here or **head2.tif** on the accompanying CD-ROM as a model. You do not have to count the strands, just try to come as close to the number on the image as possible. By varying the strands, you make a more life-like head of hair and give the image a more complex look and feel.

Tip: A pressure-sensitive tablet is most effective for painting the hair. If you use one, you can just keep the same brush size and vary the pressure.

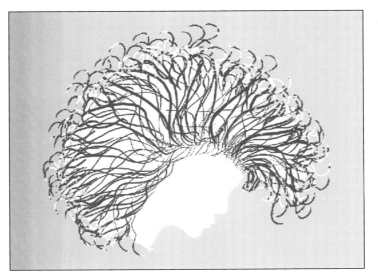

Paint the hair in different sizes while intertwining the strands.

Tip: To make it easier to paint the hair, click on the Lock Transparent Pixels box in the Layers palette.

3   Set the Magic Wand to a Tolerence of 0 and check
Anti-aliased. Do not check Contiguous. Click on the
white background of the head to select the white
pixels. Choose Select/Inverse. Hold the Alt (Opt)
key and click on the transparent area around the head
to remove the transparent area from the selection.
Only the hair that you created is selected.

4   Choose Filter/Brush Strokes/Accented Edges. Set the
following:

Edge Width: **5**

Brightness: **28**

Smoothness: **7**

By applying the Accented Edges filter, you can add
contrast and definition to the hair strands. You might
need to lessen the Edge Width and lower the
Brightness depending on how your strands are
painted. So be sure to play with the settings. The
number of strands applied and the extent of their
variety determine the outcome of this action. Each
action might not result in an exact copy of the
figure shown.

5   Choose Filter/Stylize/Find Edges.

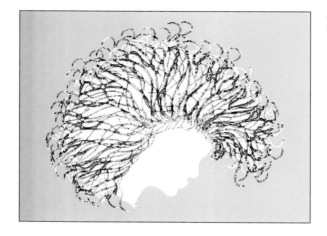

Apply the Accented Edges filter to add hard
lines, soft lines, and curves to the hair.

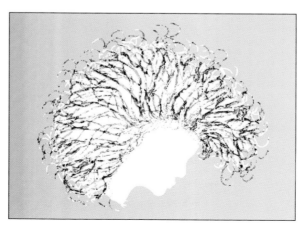

Use the Find Edges filter to distort
and add contrast to the strands.

6 Choose Filter/Distort/Ripple and set Amount to −100% and Size to Large.

7 Change the Opacity in Layer 2 to 20%.

I used a setting of 20% Opacity, but you are free to choose a different percentage.

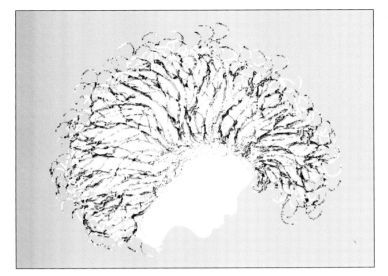

Add a ripple and squiggling effect to the strands with the Ripple filter.

8 Turn on the Eye icon in Layer 1.

With the Eye icon (visibility) activated in Layer 1, you can now see how the layer should look after the filters are applied. You can play with the settings in all three filters to achieve "almost" the same look or a different look. For instance, decreasing Brightness in the Brush Strokes/Accented Edges filter turns the strands much darker. Add texture to each strand by increasing Ripple in the Distort/Ripple filter and by playing with the size in the Size drop-down menu. Again, these are great tools that enable you to achieve (with patience and exploration) many different abstract as well as natural effects.

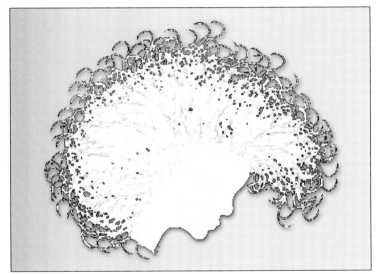

Add filters and change the layer opacity to add a marbleized texture to the face and hair while giving the strands a lacy look with depth and contrast.

ADDING COLOR

To add color depth and density to the profile, use the Gradient tool and change the layer's opacity.

1   Deselect Layer 2, activate Layer 3, and click on the Lock Transparent Pixels box in the Layers palette. Change the layer's Opacity to 40%.

2   Activate the Gradient tool, and choose Linear Gradient/Darken Mode at 28% Opacity.

Set the gradient transparency in the Gradient menu bar.

3   Open the Gradient Editor and change the color stops to 0%, 50%, 100%, with corresponding colors RGB 0, 18, 255, RGB 0, 255, 96, and RGB 0, 18, 255.

This is the same gradient with which you filled the Background layer.

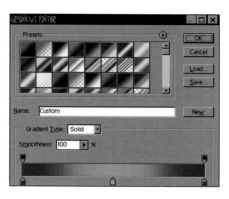

Create a new gradient using the three color stops shown in this figure.

4   Apply the gradient starting with the lower-left hairline and ending at the upper-right hairline. Again, you might not get an exact copy of the image shown.

5   Change the foreground color to RGB 60, 0, 255; and be sure the background color is still RGB 0, 0, 0.

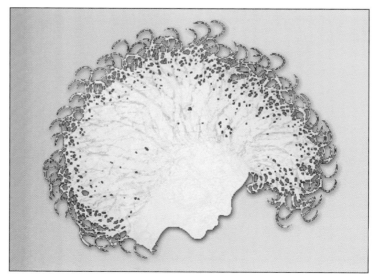

Add color to the face to tie together the background and the head profile.

6 Choose Filter/Render/Difference Clouds.

It might take a bit of time trying to find the right Difference Cloud application. The objective here is to try to apply dark clouds on the upper-right and lower-left areas of the hair while the face remains light. This objective might take many different applications. While searching for the right one, be sure to undo before re-applying. Difference Clouds blends in a cloud pattern by generating random values between the foreground and background color, so be sure to use the background and foreground colors in Step 5.

You can give the Difference Clouds filter more contrast by pressing the Alt (Opt) key as you select the filter from the menu. Apply the filter multiple times to create an ever sharper contrast.

7 Change the foreground color to RGB 168, 0, 255.

8 Change the Brush Options bar settings to Normal mode and 20% Opacity. Choose the 59 Spatter brush at approximately 115% Brush Spacing. Be sure Wet Edges is not checked in the Options bar. Paint sections of the hair as illustrated, keeping the brush on the right and left sides of the hair. Change the foreground color to R32, G32, B124 and continue painting in the edges of the hair.

Do not paint all the curled strands. Paint in a random order, splattering the paint as if you were using a squirt bottle on a houseplant. This adds highlights to the hair while keeping the color values similar with the background.

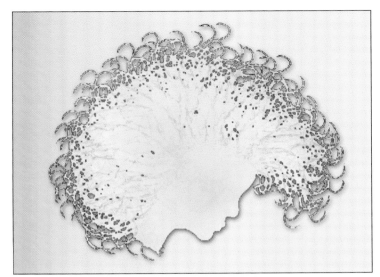

Apply Difference Clouds and be sure to use the foreground and background colors indicated in Step 5.

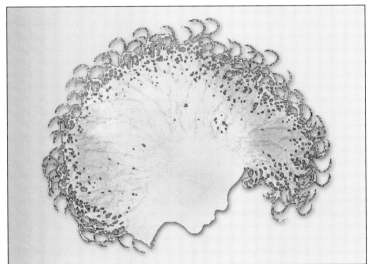

Adjust the color.

9 Choose Layer/Layer Style/Inner Glow. Change the settings as follows:

Blend Mode: **Screen**

Opacity: **25%**

Noise: **0%**

Gradient: Same as Step 2, Filling the Background

Technique: **Softer**

Source: **Edge**

Choke: **0%**

Size: **5 px**

Contour: **Linear**

Anti-aliased: **Unchecked**

Range: **50%**

Jitter: **0%**

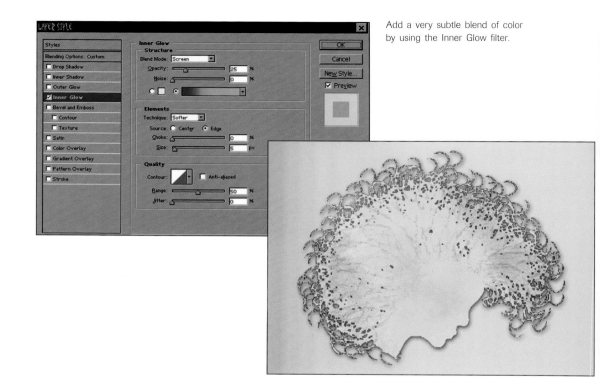

Add a very subtle blend of color by using the Inner Glow filter.

With the chosen settings, the applied filter seems very subtle, almost blending the colors for a more finished look. By playing with the settings, however, you can bring on a whole new personality and a completely different feel to the image. By changing the Structure in Blend mode to Difference and the Opacity to 75%, Technique in Elements to Precise, and the Source to Center, for instance, the image takes on a very 1960s psychedelic look.

Tip: How your Difference Clouds were applied to the profile in Step 6 determine how much paint you need to add to hair sections.

ADDING HIGHLIGHTS

This section finishes off the project. Adding more hair strands and distorting, as well as adding shadows and glow filters, truly demonstrates these amazing tools when applied to a simple drawing.

1   Activate Layer 4, and turn on the Lock Transparent Pixels box in the Layers palette.

2   Change the foreground color to R177, G177, B177; and paint hair strands on the profile using the same brushes as in "Painting and Texturing Hair," Step 1.

Remember that this is the highlight layer and not nearly as many strands are needed. You might need to paint only 1/4 of what was painted in the first layer.

3   Set the Magic Wand to a Tolerance of 0 and check Anti-aliased. Do not check the Contiguous box. Click the white background of the head to select the white pixels. Choose Select/Inverse. Hold down the Alt (Opt) key and click on the transparent area around the head to remove the transparent areas from the selection.

4   Choose Filter/Stylize/Find Edges.

These strands will be the most pronounced strands of hair on the image, and Find Edges brings texture and complexity to them.

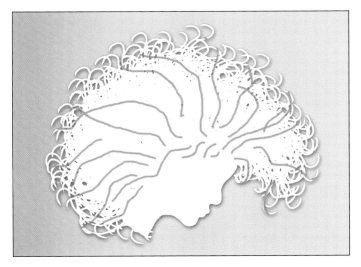

Paint new hair strands to add highlighting effects to the image.

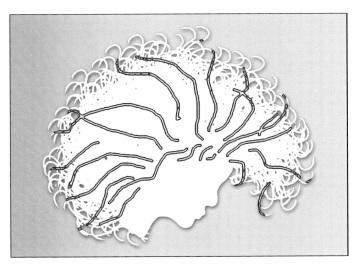

Apply the Find Edges filter.

5 Choose Filter/Distort/Ripple. Set Amount to 100% and Size to Medium.

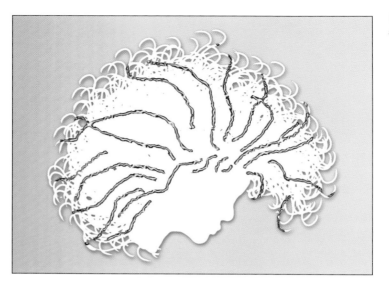

Distort the strands by adding curves and squiggles with the Ripple filter.

6 Copy the selected hair strands and paste them into a new layer called Layer 5. Turn off the Eye icon in Layer 4.

7 Change Opacity in Layer 5 to 20%.

The emphasis in Steps 7 through 9 is to add a highlight by applying a light yellow to the strands, while applying a widespread drop shadow that subtly enhances the strands, thus enhancing the image as a whole. You might have to adjust these two filters, and you might need to adjust the layer's opacity until you get it close enough to the corresponding illustrations.

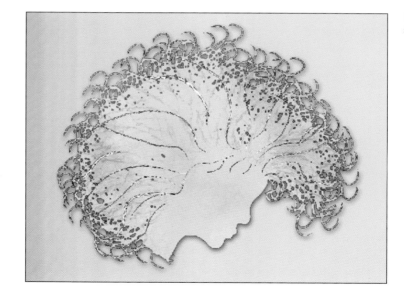

Notice the pronounced strands on the image.

8 Choose Layer/Layer Style/Inner Glow and set the following:

Blend Mode: **Normal**

Opacity: **75%**

Noise: **0%**

Color Picker: RGB **249, 249, 230**

Technique: **Softer**

Source: **Edge**

Choke: **0%**

Size: **5 px**

Contour: **Linear**

Anti-aliased: **Unchecked**

Range: **50%**

Jitter: **0%**

Do not click OK. Go on to the next step.

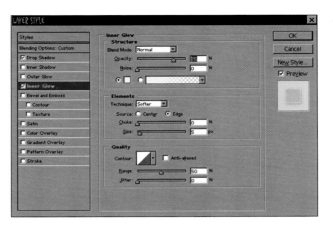

Adjust the settings on the Layer Style/Inner Glow drop-down menu and apply the filter.

Tip: To choose the right color for Inner Glow, you might have to experiment. You might want it lighter or darker and might have to redo Steps 7 and 8 (because they are applied together).

9 Choose Drop Shadow. Set the following:

Blend Mode: **Multiply**

Color: RGB **0, 0, 0**

Opacity: **75%**

Angle: **120°**

Use Global Light: **Checked**

Distance: **5px**

Spread: **12%**

Size: **32px**

Noise: **0%**

Contour: **Linear**

Anti-aliased: **Unchecked**

Layer Knocks Out Drop Shadow: **Checked**

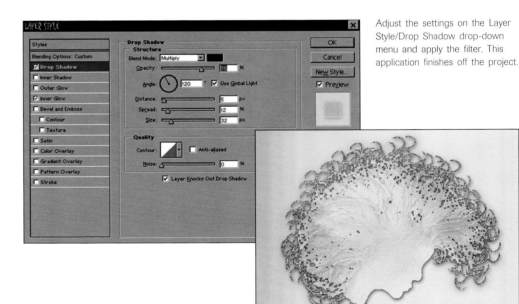

Adjust the settings on the Layer Style/Drop Shadow drop-down menu and apply the filter. This application finishes off the project.

MODIFICATIONS

You have completed the project! At this point, you can either delete Layer 4 or you can use it by creating different layers with highlights or adding filtering effects with different blend modes and colors. The accompanying figures show some finishing touches. See what changing layer opacities, adding different layer styles, using different filters, changing the color hues, and adding subtle gradients can do when using the layers already created in this project. An explanation of all the different techniques used in these figures would take nine more projects, so from this point on you are free to explore, create, and, more importantly, have fun with Photoshop's filters.

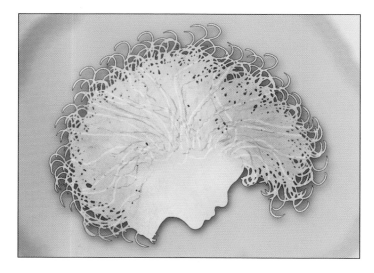

Adjusted layer opacities, deleted layers, applied outer glow, a heavier drop shadow, a gradient, the Neon Glow filter, and highlighted new strands of hair.

Adjusted layer opacities, deleted layers, adjusted hue and saturation, changed color values, an outer glow, and a gradient.

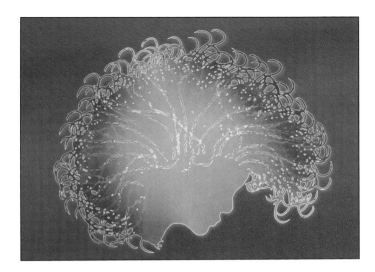

Adjusted layer opacities; deleted layers; adjusted hue and saturation; adjusted contrast and brightness; an added stroke, a gradient, new hair strands, and the Find Edges filter.

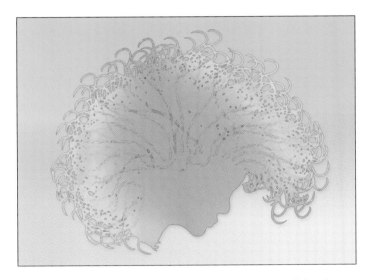

Adjusted layer opacities, deleted layers, a new gradient, more rippled and distorted hair strands, and Accentuated Edges and Find Edges filters applied again.

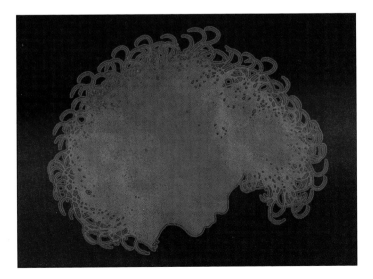

Adjusted layer opacities, deleted layers, changed gradients, adjusted hue and saturation, adjusted color balance, applied Poster Edges, Stroke, and Outer Glow filters.

Adjusted layer opacities, deleted layers, changed gradients, adjusted hue and saturation, adjusted color balance, adjusted brightness, applied Diffuse Glow, and Solarize filters.

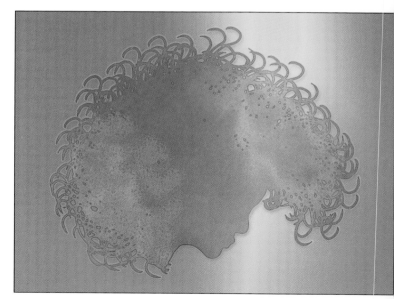

Adjusted layer opacities, deleted layers, adjusted hue and saturation, and an added gradient.

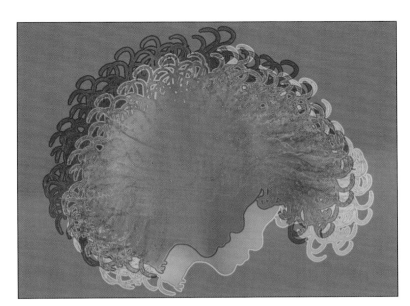

Adjusted layer opacities; deleted layers; changed gradients; adjusted hue and saturation; adjusted color balance, contrast, and brightness; applied Diffuse Glow, Emboss, and Solarize filters.

Adjusted layer opacities, deleted layers, added Solarize, and added Neon Glow filters.

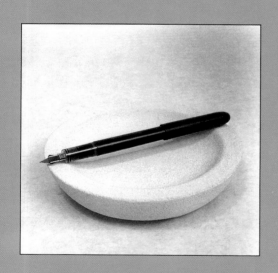

HIDDEN DETAIL REVEALED

"The most beautiful thing we can

experience is the mysterious. It is the

source of all true art and science."

—ALBERT EINSTEIN

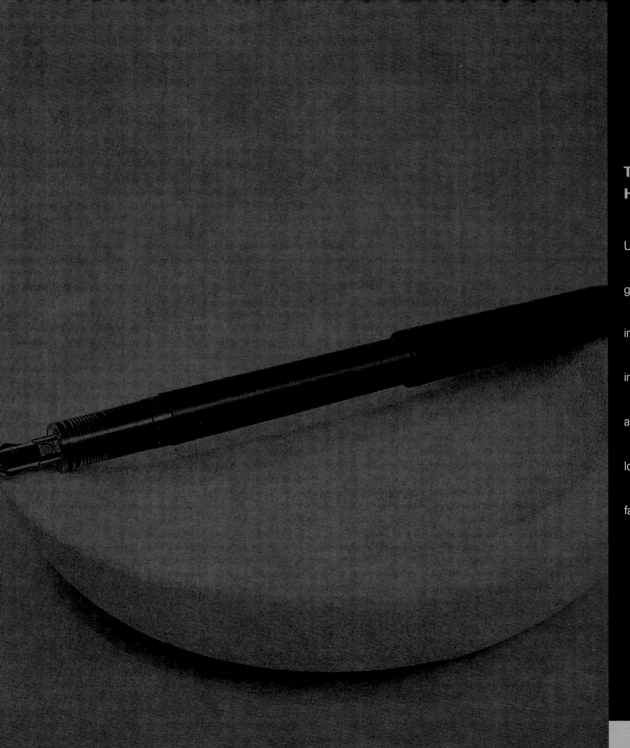

TAKING THE CLOUDS FILTER TO HIGHER LEVELS

Use these recipes to create a unique background, a distinctive texture, or an abstract image. They all begin with the same basic ingredient: Photoshop's Clouds filter. You can add a sequence of other filters to create the look of rock strata, marble, or compelling fantasy effects.

Project 14
Hidden Detail Revealed

by Rhoda Grossman

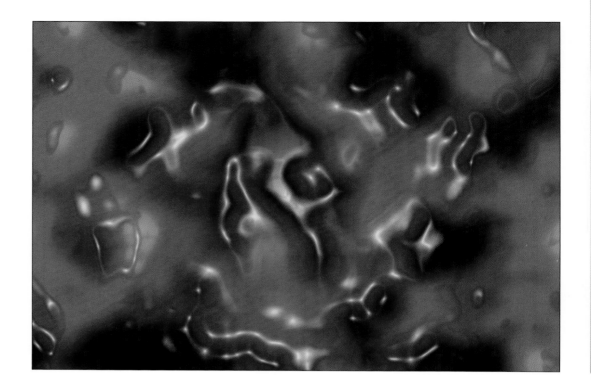

GETTING STARTED

The Clouds filter fills your image, or a selected portion of the image, with fluffy patches. To achieve this effect, all you need to do is choose the foreground and back-ground colors. There are no settings to control what kinds of clouds are produced. Although that may sound limited, you can take those puffy patches into completely new territory by using them as raw material for other filters, such as Find Edges, Smart Blur, Posterize, and Plastic Wrap. The first step is to expand the range of values in your cloud fill, and then apply filters to reveal pixel data that was not visible before.

Note: The fluffy patches are random, so you'll never get exactly the same result twice. To produce the clos-est match of the examples that follow, use the settings and resolution specified.

CONSTRUCTING ROCK STRATA

The key to turning clouds into rock is the Find Edges filter. This aptly named effect takes fluffy clouds and makes a complex array of shapes similar to a topographical map.

1   Make a new white RGB immage. The example is 6x4 inches at 200 ppi. Choose the foreground and background colors.

This example uses white and brown (R121, G89, B87).

2   Apply Filter/Render/Clouds.

3   Use Image/Adjust/Levels to examine and improve the value distribution of the image.

The purpose of adjusting these levels is to maximize the amount of pixel data available for the next steps. Notice that all or most of the pixels are distributed toward the right of the histogram. Only the upper half of the baseline value range is represented.

Apply the Render Clouds filter.

4   Spread the values across the full range of light-to-dark by clicking and dragging the black point to the right until you reach the left edge of the histogram.

You probably won't need to adjust the mid-range values, but you can change the position of the center triangle.

Note: You can use Brightness/Contrast to get nearly the same results. Photoshop pros generally prefer using the Levels adjustment for better control.

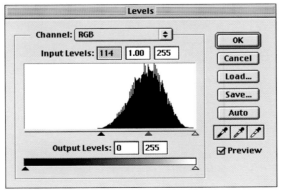

Increase the range of values.

5 Apply the Find Edges filter, found in the Stylize group.

There are no settings or other controls available for the Find Edges filter. The dark areas will be eliminated, and the continuous tonality of the cloud formations will be transformed into a tracery of flat shapes.

The result is mostly white with delicate striations similar to handmade paper. You could stop here if you want a subtle texture, perhaps for something like a Web site background, but there is more detail to be found.

Apply Filter/Stylize/Find Edges.

6 Use Image/Adjust/Levels to increase the range of values as you did in Step 3. Drag the black triangle to the right until the preview shows the degree of depth and detail you want.

I moved the black triangle until it reached the left edge of the histogram. This created the effect of eroded rock strata from an aerial view.

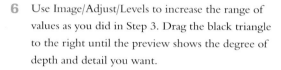

Note: There are some tiny lines in a variety of pastel colors, seen especially well at higher magnification. If you want to emphasize those colors, use the Hue/Saturation adjustment to add saturation. In the same dialog box, you can change the hues to other positions on the color wheel.

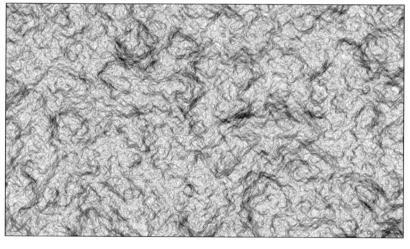

Use Image/Adjust/Levels again to darken the lines and reveal subtle color.

CONVERT CLOUDS TO POLISHED GRANITE

After you've squeezed and teased enough rock strata detail out of the clouds, try reducing detail to see what can happen. Smart Blur softens portions of the image, depending on the settings you use.

1   Continue with the rock strata texture you just created or open the source image **ROCKTEX.tif** from the accompanying CD-ROM.

2   Choose Filter/Blur/Smart Blur and enter the following settings:

Radius: **22**

Threshold: **48**

Quality: **High**

Mode: **Normal**

The subtle variations between crisp areas and soft gradations resemble a watercolor effect.

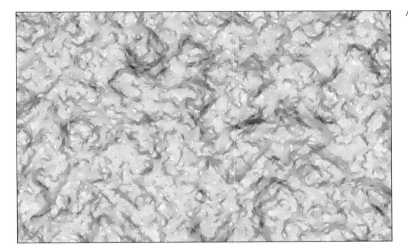

Apply the Smart Blur filter.

3   Apply Smart Blur again with these settings:

Radius: **23**

Threshold: **36**

Quality: **High**

Mode: **Overlay Edge**

Click OK, but don't save the result.

Apply Smart Blur again with different settings.

This time the outcome was similar to polished granite. It's important that you don't save your work at this point or do anything else to the image, because the next step requires you to fade the previous effect.

4   Use the Edit/Fade command to alter the Smart Blur effect by reducing the Opacity slider to around 80%. Change the Blending mode to Hard Light.

The result is an effect like veined marble.

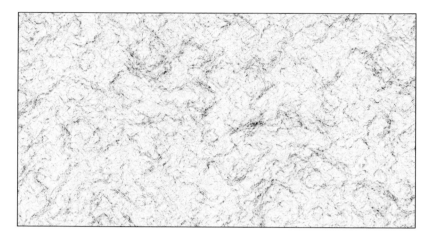

Fade the blur and change the Blending mode.

DESIGNING COSMIC CHROME

This recipe results in an exotic sci-fi kind of atmosphere or terrain. As before, you can find hidden edges in a cloud fill, but this time you'll use the Posterize command. The final addition of Plastic Wrap produces shiny, organic shapes against a dramatic background.

1   Make a new image as for the rock project and fill it with black and red clouds. For the red use R208, G91, B91.

It doesn't matter whether red is the foreground or background color.

2   Adjust the levels by moving the white triangle toward the upper (right) extreme of the histogram.

Because you began with black instead of white plus a color, you need to extend the value range in the higher (lighter) direction.

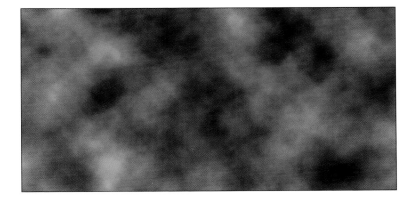

Render some red and black clouds and adjust their levels.

3   Apply Image/Adjust/Posterize, and set Levels to 5.

This reduces the continuous tonality of the clouds to a limited number of flat colors. Using fewer than four levels would simplify the image too much.

Don't confuse Posterize's Levels option with the Levels adjustment, also in the Image menu.

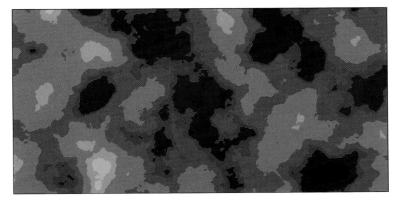

Posterize, using five levels to reduce the tonality to a few flat colors.

4   Use Filter/Blur/Gaussian Blur with a Radius setting of 12 or 13 pixels, which softens the edges created with the Posterize command.

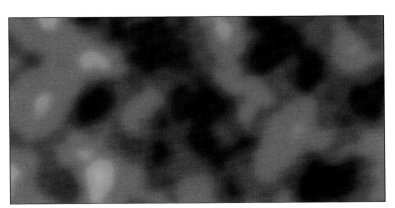

Apply Gaussian Blur to soften the edges.

5 Use Filter/Artistic/Plastic Wrap with these settings:

Highlight Strength: **18**

Detail: **9**

Smoothness: **7**

Suddenly your black-and-red image has mysterious new shapes that glow with a rich luster. They seem to flow in and out of the background. The Detail setting can vary quite a bit without producing a noticeable effect, but Smoothness should not be too low, or unpleasant striations will occur. Use the maximum Highlight Strength and fade if it's too strong.

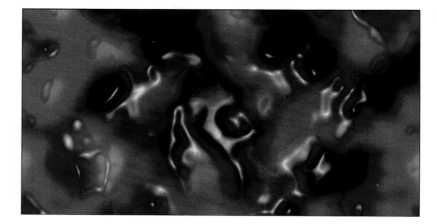

Add the Plastic Wrap effect.

MODIFICATIONS

Significantly different looks will result if you perform steps in a different order or use widely different settings. Consider using the Image/Adjust/Invert command to reverse the hues and values before you proceed to the next step in a recipe. Here is what happens to the cosmic chrome look if you skip the Gaussian Blur.

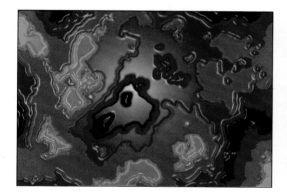

Skip the Gaussian Blur step for a plastic map effect. It is not necessary to adjust Levels correctly, the way you would choose to optimize a photograph. You can push the darker values even more, in anticipation of later benefits, such as more intense color.

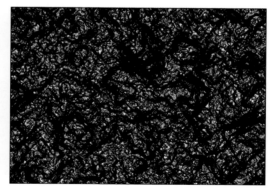

Adjust Levels darker to intensify color later. The Find Edges filter usually produces pastel shades. Use Hue/Saturation adjustments to enrich the colors.

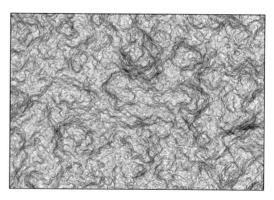

Increase Saturation after completing the Find Edges step.

Here is an image that began with a cloud fill using white and a deep egg-yolk yellow and then had the Paint Daubs filter from the Artistic group applied. Paint Daubs has settings for Brush Size and Sharpness, as well choices for Brush Type. I used the maximum for size and sharpness, and the Wide Sharp Brush Type. Paint Daubs alone can keep you busy all afternoon.

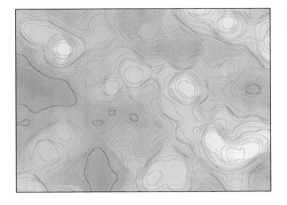

Apply the Paint Daubs filter to a cloud fill.

The icy water effect began with a blue-green and white cloud fill and the usual Levels adjustment. Then the Chrome filter from the Sketch group was applied and faded using Hard Light.

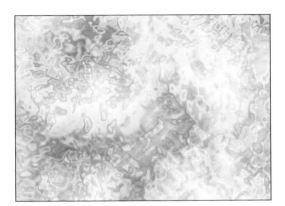

Use the Chrome filter and fade with Hard Light mode. Consider other ways of using a cloud fill as raw material for development. Just pick a color, any color, and render some clouds. Then try one filter after another. Using the History Brush, you can create a richly textured image by painting portions of previous states into the current one.

Beginning with purple and black clouds, the Palette Knife filter was used, followed by the Watercolor filter. The History Brush restored some of the Palette Knife state while in Screen mode. Because Screen mode always lightens pixels, I concentrated on the strokes in the darker regions of the image.

Begin with purple and black clouds, and then add the Palette Knife, Watercolor, and History Brush effects.

PATTERN PLAY

"Keeping your clothes well pressed will

keep you from looking hard pressed."

—COLEMAN COX

CREATING PATTERNS AND TEXTURES

Patterns are ubiquitous. Patterns surround you

in your home or office, and you don't even

notice them because you are so used to seeing

them. They are on your walls, on your floor,

and on the clothes you wear. They shape your

life as you speak of "patterns of thought"

or "patterns of behavior." Patterns don't just

happen. Someone needs to create them.

After you open your eyes to the patterns that

surround you, you'll be amazed at the design

possibilities they contain.

Project 15

Pattern Play

by Sherry London

With head, hat, and jewelry images by
Kelly Loomis, and brushes and two pattern
source images by Joni Ruethling

GETTING STARTED

Photoshop 6 has a new feature that makes *using* patterns easier than ever before. It doesn't, however, make *creating* the patterns any easier. Photoshop can still use a rectangular repeat only and blindly duplicate it again and again. The standard pattern types in wallpaper and fabric design (the brick and the half-drop pattern) are impossible to create automatically in Photoshop. Photoshop still lacks Corel Painter's ability to create seamless repeats with a minimum of fuss. In this project, you'll learn ways to minimize the fuss required. You'll create a quilt of Victorian women and learn how to create, apply, and adjust patterns to fill their clothing. In the process, you'll learn a dozen different pattern-creation techniques (which is still only scratching the surface of what's possible).

Pattern-making has a strong mathematical component, and knowing the size of your tile is a very important part of making pattern seams match up. You'll use the Offset command and precise selection methods to help build the pattern units. After you understand the variety of pattern types that you can create, you can use these skills to create seamless patterns to take into 3-D applications, to use as backgrounds, or to mix into your work.

Almost as important as the pattern-repeat methods is the knowledge of how to prepare images for use as patterns. As you create the patterns, you'll learn a variety of ways to find or create the pattern content. You can work with photographs, paint random images, or develop geometrics. You can also use filters to stylize or make abstracts from photographs that you decide to use for pattern content.

Note: Because all of you might not share my love of patterns, I've included some of the key pattern-making techniques in this chapter and have placed a number of other pattern-creation techniques on the accompanying CD-ROM. You can open the **15_extras.pdf** file from the Projects/15 directory on the CD-ROM and re-create all of the various patterns if you wish, or you can to try a few patterns here and then add the final quilting to a flattened version of the image that contains all of the patterns already applied to the image.

CREATING A PLAIN-MOTIF REPEAT

The easiest form of pattern-making in Photoshop is to simply select a rectangular piece of an image and define it as a pattern. You'll take a photograph, load the pre-created alpha channel, and define the result as a pattern.

Note: If you have not created any patterns before, you can try creating a plain-motif repeat by working this section on the CD-ROM.

CREATING A HALF-DROP REPEAT

The half-drop repeat is the most common pattern type in both fabric and
wallpaper design. In this repeat system, the motifs appear to be in columns
with the motifs in the "even" columns falling halfway between the motifs in
the "odd" columns. To define a half-drop repeat pattern so that it forms the
necessary rectangular pattern unit, you need a file that is twice the width of
your original motif. You'll use the **FlowerBug.psd** tile from the Companion
CD-ROM as your source pattern. The pattern definition technique that you'll
use to prepare this new pattern shows you how you can make any motif-based
rectangular pattern into a half-drop pattern.

1   Create a new 210×112-pixel file at 72ppi with a
transparent background.

These dimensions are twice the width of the original
FlowerBug tile and use the same height. A transparent background saves you the trouble of removing or
hiding the Background layer of the image.

2   Choose Edit/Presets Manager and the select the
Patterns presets. Click on Load and Load
Ladypattern.pat from the CD-ROM. Choose
Edit/Fill and fill with the **FlowerBug.psd** pattern
from the Companion CD.

You'll get two perfectly spaced copies.

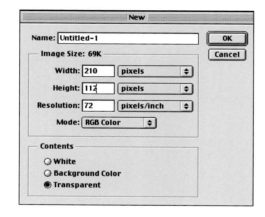

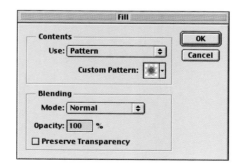

Fill the new image with the FlowerBug pattern.

Create a new document that is
210 pixels wide by 112 pixels high.

Note: If you want to use your own image to make a
half-drop repeat:

1   Make sure the file only contains the image you want
to use as the pattern.

2   Duplicate the layer that contains the image motif so
you have two layers with the same motif.

3   Use the Canvas Size command to double the
width of the tile. Place the anchor for the image
in the center-left anchor spot in the Canvas Size
dialog box.

4   Use the Offset filter (Filter/Other/Offset) to move the
copied layer the same number of pixels to the right
as the *original* width of the image (before you used
the Canvas Size dialog box).

3 Set your foreground and background colors to the default of black and white. Choose Filter/Sketch/Photocopy and set Detail to 10 and Darkness to 12.

This is another way to develop pattern content from photographic images. The Photocopy filter changes the image to a slightly stylized version that uses the foreground and background colors in the Toolbox. You could have chosen any two colors and the results from the Photocopy filter would have used them instead. For this example, however, black and white give you the most control over the Blend mode when you apply the finished pattern.

4 Select the flower on the right with the Rectangular Marquee tool, and cut it to a new layer (Shift+Ctrl [Cmd]+J).

You need to remove the rightmost motif from Layer 1 and place it onto Layer 2 so that you can offset it in the next step.

5 Choose Filter/Other/Offset. Set the Horizontal pixels right to 0, and the Vertical pixels down to 56. Click the Wrap Around radio button.

The Offset filter does the half-drop pattern for you. To make certain that the pattern drops halfway, set your vertical offset to half of the image height.

Note: If you wanted to create a pattern that took four steps before it repeated and in which each motif moved 1/4 of the image width, you would set your file to be four times the original pattern width. You would offset the left-most image not at all, the second copy 25% of the image height, the third copy 50% of the image height, and the fourth copy 75% of the image height.

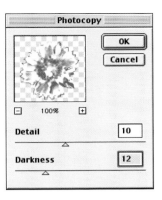

Choose Filter/Sketch/Photocopy to change the image to a black and white version.

Note: If you simply want to make a half-drop pattern, you don't need to include Step 3 in the process. It is merely a way of changing pattern content. You could have used any filter you wanted, and, had you not started with a pattern as the original source, you could have applied the filter to the motif before you duplicated it.

Note: Step 4 is not strictly necessary because Photoshop 6 seems to do a decent job of offsetting images within a selection Marquee. Earlier versions of Photoshop, however, had trouble with the wrap-around feature of the Offset filter, so this is a "safety" precaution to avoid potential problems.

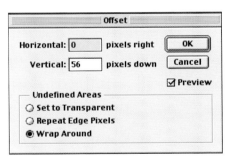

Offset the rightmost copy 56 pixels down.

6 Choose Edit/Define Pattern. Name this HalfDrop Flower.

Define the pattern tile as HalfDrop Flower.

7 Load **LadyQuilt.psd** from the Companion CD, add a Pattern Overlay effect to the Bustle layer of the BustleLady dress. Choose the HalfDrop Flower pattern at 25% Scale in Overlay mode.

Overlay mode enables the black and white in the pattern to take on the color of the original Bustle layer.

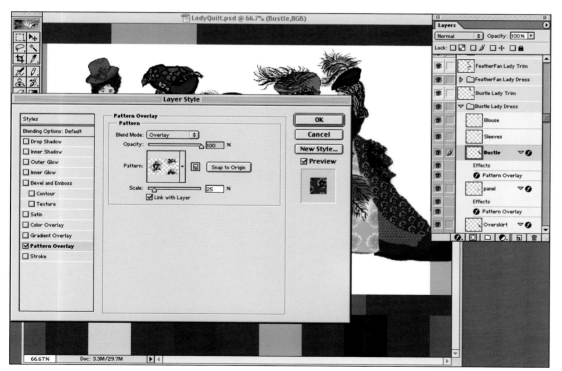

Fill the Pattern Overlay effect with the HalfDrop Flower pattern on the Bustle layer of the BustleLady doll.

CREATING A SEAMLESS REPEAT

Have you ever admired a pattern made up of endless jellybeans, or cookies, or whatever, and wondered how you could create one from your own photos or images? The Brushed Mask seamless method does an almost magical job of making "endless" patterns from photographic or textured sources. You have total control over the results. You can also make a seamless pattern repeat from two different images at the same time. This method uses the Offset filter and a layer mask to position the tile and make it seamless. You'll see how you can use a photo for this technique.

1   Open the image **FLOWERPHOTO.psd** from the accompanying CD-ROM.

Open the FLOWERPHOTO.psd image.

2   Duplicate the Background layer. With Background copy layer active, select Filter/Other/Offset with Wrap Around selected. Set the Horizontal pixels right to 100 and the Vertical pixels down to 75.

The original image is 200×150 pixels. The offset needs to be one-half of the image dimensions. The seam lines are centered and very obvious.

Offset Background copy layer by 100 pixels right and 75 pixels down.

219

3 Create a layer mask. With black as the foreground color, and a fairly large, soft paintbrush, paint over the center seam of the image in both directions until you create an image with no seams.

Try to make as few changes to the edges of the image as possible. Fix as much as you can inside of the image perimeter. The actual image or photo that you use dictates exactly what you brush in or out in the mask. To make this floral image seamless, for example, you might want to reveal an entire flower from the layer beneath even if it means removing more from the top layer than just the center seam line area.

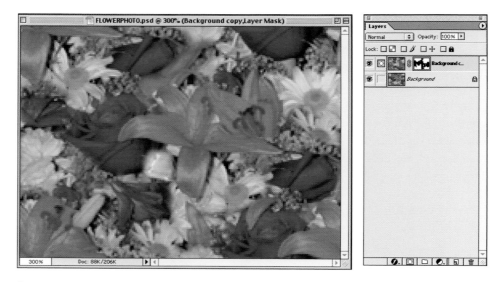

Create a layer mask that hides the center seam line and partially reveals the image beneath the top layer.

4 Add a new, empty layer at the top of the layer stack and leave the new layer active. Press Alt (Opt) and choose Layer/Merge Visible to merge the visible layers into this new layer. Reapply the Offset filter using the same settings as before. Check the image for seams.

Your image might have looked seamless at the end of Step 3, but that doesn't mean it really is seamless yet. You need to "test" it. When you press the Alt (Opt) key as you select Layer/Merge Visible or use the shortcut Shift+Alt+Ctrl+E (Shift+Cmd+Opt+E), Photoshop places a copy of the combined image into the new, empty layer that you previously created. In this example, the problem areas are at the center-top and the center-bottom seam lines.

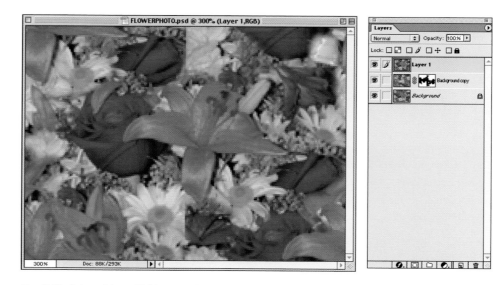

Use Alt(Opt)+Layer/Merge Visible to combine the layers into a new layer and reapply the Offset filter.

5 Create a layer mask on Layer 1. Repair the seam as you did in Step 3.

6 Define the image as a pattern. Accept the default name of FLOWERPHOTO.

Make sure the image rather than the mask is active when you define the pattern. Otherwise, you won't define the color image as the pattern. There is no need to merge your layers as Photoshop automatically defines a pattern from all of the visible layers.

Remove any remaining seams by painting in the Layer Mask.

7 In the LadyQuilt image, set a Pattern Overlay effect on the Skirt layer of the FeatherFan Lady dress. Use the FlowerPhoto pattern with the following settings:

Opacity: **100%**

Blend Mode: **Soft Light**

Scale: **50%**

Soft Light mode makes the color of the dress shine through the pattern and softens it.

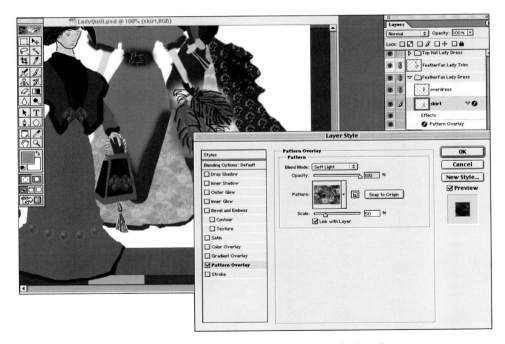

Use the FlowerPhoto pattern in Soft Light mode at 50% Scale as a Pattern Overlay effect on the Skirt layer of the FeatherFan Lady doll.

CREATING A MOSAIC REPEAT

The mosaic repeat is the easiest seamless method to learn. In this repeat system, you can make any image seamless by turning it into a four-way pattern similar to those used on tile floors. You copy the starting tile and flip it horizontally, and then flip the resulting half-tile vertically. The final repeat is twice the original height and width. You'll use a computer-generated piece of tie-dye "fabric" in this section. The complete instructions for creating a tie-dye are embedded in the starting file. To read these instructions, you need to click on the Notes icon in the image with the Marquee or Move tool selected.

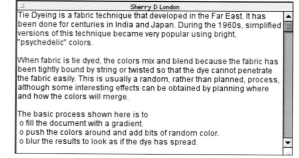

Use the Notes tools to read the tutorial embedded in the file.

1 Open the image **TIEDYE1.psd** from the accompanying CD-ROM. Read the note embedded in the image if you want, and then deselect the Annotations option on the View/Show menu.

Turning off the annotation makes the image easier to see. If you haven't tried it yet, Annotations is a cool addition to Photoshop 6. You can leave notes to yourself as you create an image so you can remember what you did.

2 Double-click the Background layer to create Layer 0. Use the Canvas Size command to change the Width and Height of the image to 200 pixels each. Set the Anchor in the top-left corner of the dialog box.

The original image is 100×100 pixels. You need to double those dimensions. Change the background into Layer 0 before you use the Canvas Size command so the area around the original tile stays transparent when you enlarge the canvas.

Double the image Width and Height in the Canvas Size dialog box.

3 Duplicate Layer 0. Choose Filter/Other/Offset. Set Horizontal to 100 pixels and Vertical to 0 pixels.

You need to duplicate your original layer and offset it into the right corner of the image. The offset amount is the original width (or one-half the current width).

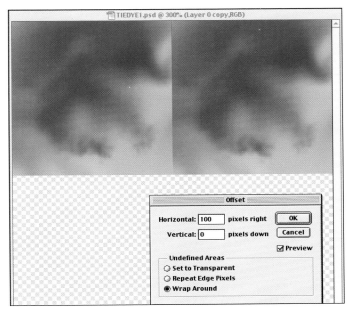
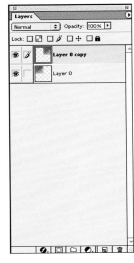

Duplicate Layer 0 and offset it 100 pixels horizontally.

4 Choose Edit/Transform/Flip Horizontal. Merge the layer into the preceding layer.

This step makes the top half of the image seamless. You might find it easier to create the bottom half of the tile if you merge the layers (Layer/Merge Visible).

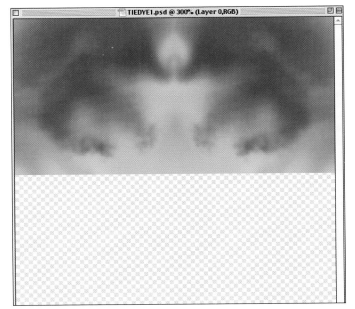

Flip the new layer horizontally and merge down to the layer below.

223

5 Duplicate Layer 0. Choose Edit/Transform/Flip Vertical. Offset Layer 0 copy 0 pixels Horizontally, and 100 pixels Vertically.

This step finishes the pattern repeat by creating the bottom half of the pattern. The offset amount is one-half the current height.

6 Define the pattern as TIEDYE1.

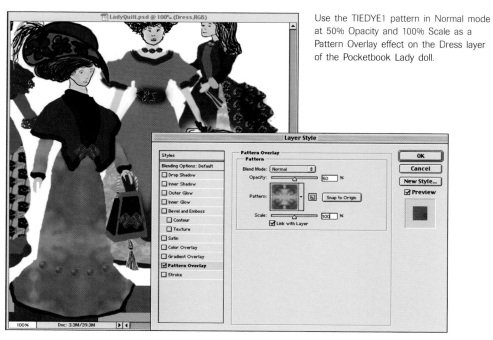

Flip a duplicate of Layer 0 vertically and offset it by 100 pixels down.

7 Add a Pattern Overlay effect to the Dress layer of the Pocketbook Lady. Use the TIEDYE1 pattern in Normal mode at 50% Opacity and 100% Scale.

Lowering the opacity of the pattern is another way to blend it into the base color of the layer. In this case, lowering the opacity makes the dress look more in tune with the 1860s than the 1960s.

Use the TIEDYE1 pattern in Normal mode at 50% Opacity and 100% Scale as a Pattern Overlay effect on the Dress layer of the Pocketbook Lady doll.

At this point, you've had a chance to create several patterns and to fill areas of the LadyQuilt.psd image with them. The PDF for this project on the CD-ROM contains instructions for creating a brick repeat, an overlapped repeat, a diamond repeat, a diaper repeat, a sateen repeat, a plaid repeat, and a kaleidoscope repeat. It also has instructions for using patterns as masks, filling the quilt squares, and painting the background. If you are enjoying this project, I urge you to work the rest of it on the CD-ROM. You can then return here for the final steps. If you just want to see how the project ends, you can continue on with a flattened version of the entire image in the next section.

ADDING THE QUILTING

You will create quilting lines as a final method of applying patterns. You'll copy an area of the image, alter its values, and emboss it. You'll then create a pattern from the embossing and fill a Hard Light layer with it. To begin, open the image **LadyQuiltFlat.psd** from the CD-ROM. This is the flattened version of the image for which you've created pieces in this project. If you have followed along in both the book and the CD-ROM to complete the entire image, you can use your working image that is still layered.

1   Set the Fixed Size of the Rectangular Marquee tool to 400×400 pixels. Drag the marquee into the image to enclose the area of interest. Choose Edit/Copy (or Edit/Copy Merge if you are using the layered version of the image).

This step grabs a random piece of the image to use as a texture.

Choose Edit/Copy Merge for a 400-pixel square selection.

2   Open a new file at the default 400-pixel square that's on the Clipboard. Paste the copied image and choose Layer/Flatten Image.

3   Choose Filter/Stylize/Find Edges.

The thin lines left by the Find Edges filter do a wonderful job of looking like quilting when you are finished.

4   Choose Image/Adjust/Threshold. Set the Threshold Level to 69 or wherever you have a small amount of detail left.

You need a mostly white image with black lines. Try to keep the main lines in the image solid black.

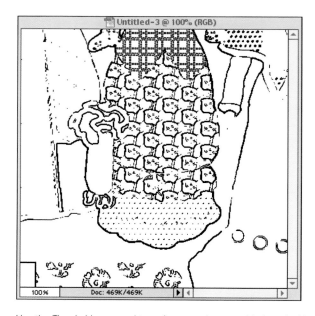

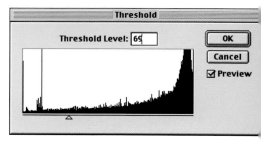

Use the Threshold command to reduce your image to black and white.

5 Choose Filter/Stylize/Emboss. Set Height to 1 pixel and Amount to 100%. Set the Angle to -61 degrees.

The embossed lines need to go in rather than out. The other settings keep the embossing from becoming too harsh.

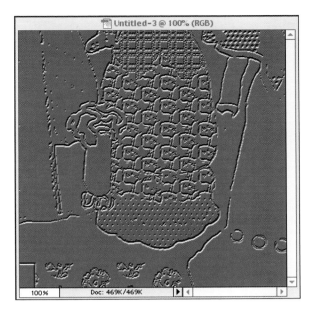

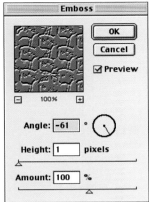

Emboss the image.

6 Choose Filter/Blur/Gaussian Blur and set a Radius of 1 pixel.

This step softens the embossing. You only need a small amount of blur.

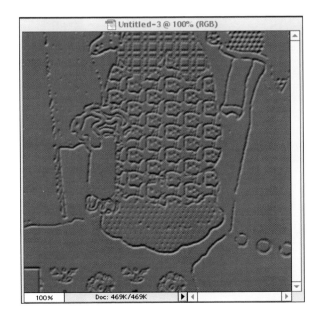

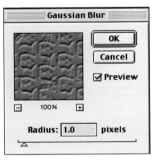

Apply a Gaussian Blur of 1 pixel.

7   Define the small image as a pattern named Quilting.

8   Create a new layer at the top of the layer stack in the LadyQuilt image. Choose Edit/Fill and fill the layer with the Quilting pattern. Change the Blend mode to Hard Light. Set Opacity to 68%.

Hard Light mode enables you to add texture to any image with an embossed layer. The neutral gray in the embossing disappears in Hard Light mode and allows only shadows and highlights to show through.

9   Add a layer mask and paint out any inconvenient areas of quilting, such as anything on the faces of the dolls.

Add a layer mask to remove undesirable areas of quilting.

MODIFICATIONS

You've learned many pattern techniques and additional ways to use patterns. You have learned how to take many different grid repeat schemes and force them into a rectangular pattern that Photoshop can apply. You have learned how to use Pattern Overlay effects and change Scale and Blend mode. You can apply patterns with the Pattern Stamp, apply patterns to a layer mask, apply patterns in a Pattern layer, or apply patterns directly to a layer.

After seeing so many different ways to modify patterns, you should have a great idea at this point how to vary patterns in almost any direction that you want.

Patterns are very useful for Web pages, so long as they are not allowed to dominate the page. You can take photographs and enhance them, and then create natural textures, such as repeating grass, bricks, stones, siding, or architectural detail. By creating seamless patterns from these textures, you can develop texture maps to bring into 3-D programs.

COLORING A SKETCH

"Cats are intended to teach us that not

everything in nature has a function."

—UNKNOWN

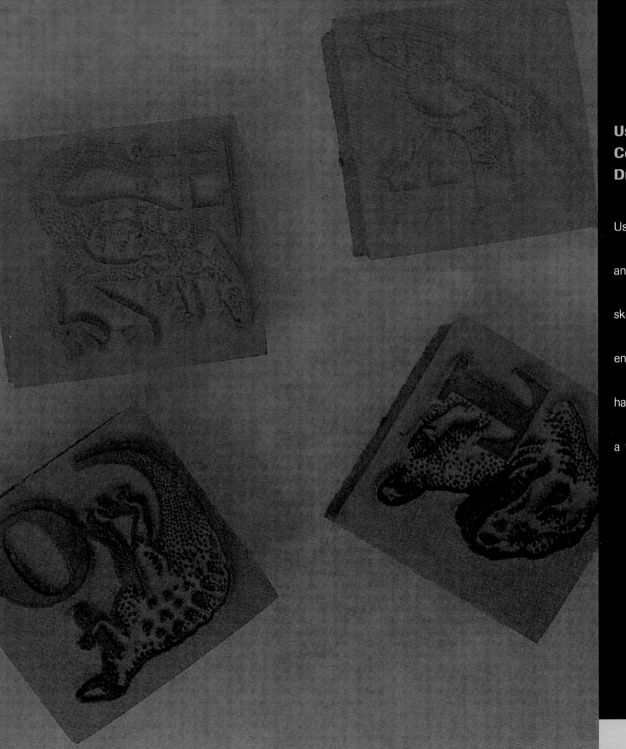

USING LAYER EFFECTS TO ADD RICH COLOR TO A BLACK-AND-WHITE DRAWING.

Use a combination of painting, layers, modes, and opacities to transform a simple monotone sketch into a colorful finished illustration. The end result retains all the qualities of the original hand drawing, but with the color and feeling of a finished illustration.

Project 16

Coloring a Sketch

by Sharon Steuer

GETTING STARTED

In this project, you take a loose sketch and create a finished drawing by using freehand painting and duplicated layers in a variety of opacities and blending modes to make the final artwork. The technique takes advantage of the Layers palette by duplicating and manipulating many layers to preserve desirable effects along the way. This approach encourages experimentation without having to worry about retracing steps or erasing through the History palette.

Note: For this example, I used a Wacom tablet with Opacity set to Stylus for pressure control. This method simulates the look and feel of the traditional painting and drawing process for both the artist and the final product.

PREPARE THE LAYERS

Before beginning the layering and coloring process, you need to prepare the image.
Because this technique depends heavily on the duplication and manipulation of layers,
you want to have the Layers palette in view throughout the process.

1   Open **CAT.psd** from the accompanying CD-ROM.

2   Choose Image/Adjust/Levels and change the center
Input Level to 1.13.

   This lightens the sketch and increases detail.

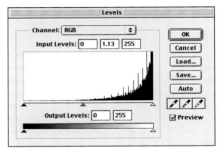

Change the Input Gamma
Point to 1.13 in the Levels
dialog box.

3   Click the New Layer icon on the Layers palette to
add a new layer. Name the layer Color 1 using
Layer/Layer Properties. Change the mode of the
Color 1 layer to Multiply and the Opacity to 90%.

   Multiply mode enables you to apply paint and have
the drawing underneath show through.

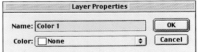

Add a new layer named
Color 1 in Multiply mode
at 90% Opacity.

BEGIN COLORING

Before proceeding, be sure that your Swatches palette is in view and use the Swatch menu to choose a color palette. An easy way to create a set of colors to use is to open a photograph that has the desired range of colors. Then choose File/Save for Web. Prepare a GIF image using the current color profile and allow Photoshop to select the 256 colors from the image that best suit the picture. Save the color table from within the Color Table menu in the Save for Web dialog box. The resulting table has an .act extension on it and can be used in the Swatches palette.

1 Load the **SPRING.act**, **SUMMER.act**, or **FALL.act** color table from the accompanying CD-ROM into the Swatches palette by choosing Replace Swatches from the drop-down menu in the Swatches palette.

You will find it easier to replace your current Swatches document with the new one. The Load Swatches option simply places the new colors at the end of your current list, which makes the new colors hard to find. Make sure you save your Swatches palette document first if you have colors there that you want to use again.

Load the Summer, Spring, or Fall color table into your Swatches palette.

Warning: Make sure you save your original Swatches palette document first if you have colors there you want to use again by choosing Save Swatches from the drop-down menu on the Swatches palette.

2 Select a 21-pixel or larger soft-edge brush from the Paintbrush menu options. Set the Brush mode to Normal and the Opacity to 100%. Choose a color from the swatches and begin coloring on the new layer.

Because the subject of the picture was my cat, Bear, on a summer outing, I chose a palette of grays and greens. The same image could also be painted using spring or autumn colors. Using the Wacom tablet, you can vary the opacity of your strokes by the pressure that you apply to the tablet. When using your own artwork, just choose the brush style, size, and color palette that are appropriate for your image and paint those colors onto the Color 1 layer.

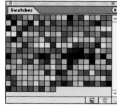

Choose colors from the Swatches palette and paint on the Color 1 layer to add the basic colors to the image.

Note: If you don't have a Wacom or other pressure-sensitive tablet, you can just dab on a variety of colors in the general location where you want them to go. Then choose Filer/Blur/Gaussian Blur. Use a large blur (perhaps even a blur of 50) to blend and subtly change the colors.

3 With Color 1 layer selected, choose Duplicate Layer from the Layers palette and name it Color 2. Change the new layer's mode to Color Dodge and Opacity to 15%.

Color Dodge mode uses the image itself to lighten and brighten the highlights of the layer underneath. You can see how this begins to build up the strength of the color through the layers, but the main intensity is still mostly in the strokes of the drawing at this point.

Note: You also might like the effect of the Color Burn mode.

Duplicate Color 1 as Color 2 and change the Blend mode to Color Dodge at 15% Opacity.

4 Create a new layer and name it Color 3. Change the Color 3 layer's mode to Multiply and Opacity to 100%.

You use this new layer to paint more depth into the shadows.

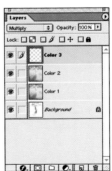

Create a new layer named Color 3 in Multiply mode at 100% Opacity.

5 With the Paintbrush active, select a soft-edge brush from the Brushes palette on the Options strip. Set the Brush mode to Normal and Opacity to 100%. Choose a color from the Swatches palette and begin coloring in the shadow area on the new layer.

I wanted to add more depth to the shadows in the image, so I chose grays, dark greens, and red violets that were complementary to the greens. I also added highlights of bright greens and yellows to the tops of the trees and bushes. This layer completes the coloring process.

Color the shadow areas of the image on the Color 3 layer.

FINISHING TOUCHES

To reveal some of the detail now getting lost under multiple layers, duplicate the Background layer and use the new layer to reinforce the original lines of the sketch.

1 Duplicate the Background layer and drag it to the top of the Layers palette. Change the mode to Color Burn and Opacity to 14%. Name the layer Background 2.

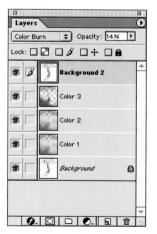

Duplicate the Background layer, change its Blend mode to Color Burn at 14% Opacity, and drag it to the top of the layer stack.

236

2 Select the Soft-Edge 21-pixel brush with Normal mode and 100% Opacity. Selectively paint with 50% grays into the shadow areas on this layer.

Color Burn acts as the opposite of Color Dodge by deepening the shadow areas of the image. This increases the contrast and depth of field in the drawing. Gray paint helps to intensify the image without altering the color balance.

At this point, the color is rich and the strokes of the drawing are clear. If you like, go on adding layers and changing blending modes and opacities to achieve different results. In the next steps, you add one last layer for touch-ups.

3 Select the New Layer icon in the Layers palette to create another layer. Name it Touch-ups.

4 Select a very small soft-edge brush with Normal mode and 100% Opacity.

A dark spot beside the cat's foot needs fixing, so use the Eyedropper tool to choose a color from right near the spot and use the color on the Touch-ups layer to paint out the spot.

5 Use the Layers palette to flatten the image and save the finished illustration in the format of your choice.

Flatten the image only after you have decided your drawing is finished and that you won't want to go back into the individual layers. Save a layered copy as well in case you want to revise the image at any point.

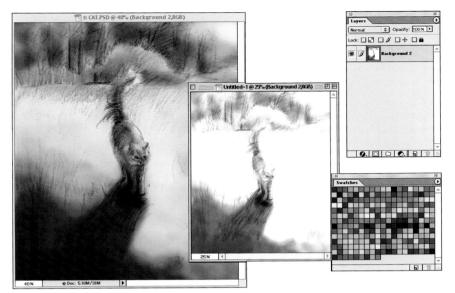

Paint on the shadow areas of the layer with shades of gray to intensify and deepen the colors.

Pick a color from the image and paint over the blotch near the cat's foot.

MODIFICATIONS

I hope this example has inspired you to experiment with or add to this technique using your own artwork. You can, of course, use many more layers than the example shown here. You also can use different Blend modes and use layer masks to localize the changes that a Blend mode makes to a layer. By changing any of these items (more layers, different Blend modes, and layer masks), you can create an infinite variety of effects.

If you prefer to begin with a photograph rather than a line drawing, you can give it a hand-drawn look by using the Find Edges, Smart Blur with Edges Only, or High Pass filters and adjusting the result with the Levels, Threshold, or Desaturate commands. To touch-up the results, erase unneeded lines and slightly blur the final outlines.

Consider the Puma image. It uses different Blend modes and also uses layer masks to keep the changes localized.

Scared Puma/Bear Kittens is an example of using multiple Blend modes with layer masks.

The example uses three Image layers and a Levels layer. Each layer has a layer mask on it.

The Background copy layer is in Normal mode at 92% Opacity, Background copy 2 is in Screen mode at 60% Opacity, and Background copy 3 is in Color Burn mode at 55% Opacity. The Levels layer is in Normal mode at 100% Opacity. As you can see in the Layers palette, the mask keeps most of the purple background from appearing. I masked the cat on the left in the Levels layer only to make the colors darker and more intense. I wanted the white cat to remain light.

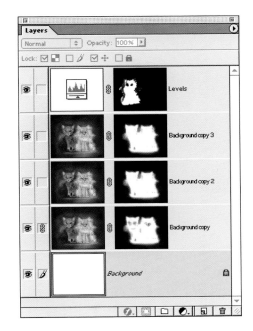

Each layer has a layer mask to isolate the effect of the layer's Blend mode.

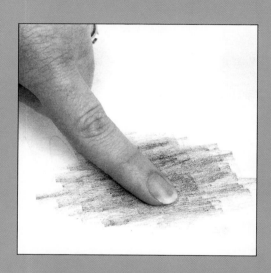

UNPAINTING

"The coldest winter I ever spent was a

summer in San Francisco."

—MARK TWAIN

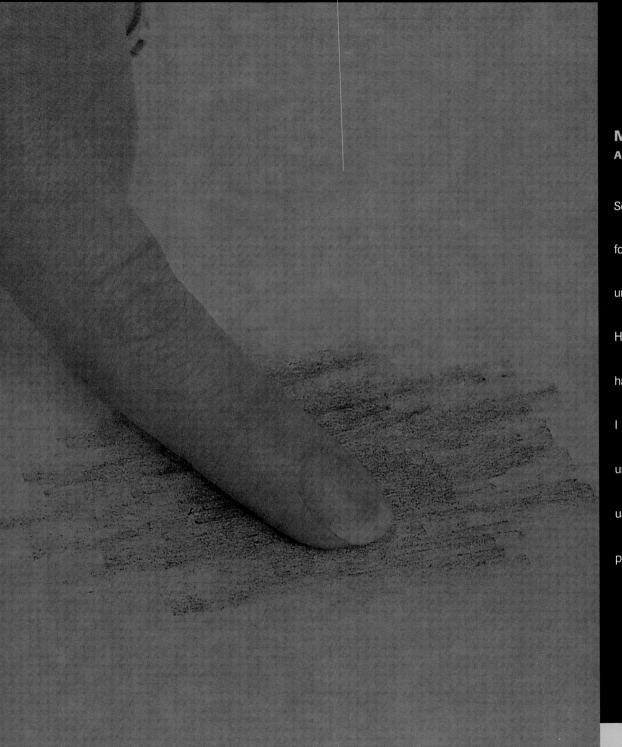

MAKING YOUR ART OR PHOTO LOOK LIKE A TRADITIONAL UNDERPAINTING

Sometimes you have to go backward to go

forward. In order to fit new ad copy, I had to

unpaint a section of a previously finished piece.

Had this been a traditional painting, I would

have taken a rag and turpentine to it; instead

I invented a digital solution that mimics the

underlayers of a traditional painting. You can

use this same technique to give your art or

photos an extra sense of artistic depth.

Project 17

Unpainting

by Michel Bohbot

Note: The original job for Robert Anthony Advertising was to paint a family picnic for a real-estate developer who was touting that his homes would have the ambiance of the south of France. Several months later I was asked to "unpaint" a section of my art to fit the ad copy "Almost finished, already a masterpiece." The original art was a 200-dpi resolution file for the newspaper ad, but you can adjust the values up for a higher-resolution file or down for a lower-resolution file.

GETTING STARTED

This project "deconstructs" part of an image to "reveal" the early stages of a traditional painting. To understand where the project is headed, it helps to know how a traditional painting develops. First, a thin layer of tone is applied to the canvas surface to eliminate any bits of white showing through. Then a pencil sketch is added to define the color forms. Over this the artist paints in brown or gray tones and then transparent glazes. After those are dry, opaque paint is applied in full color.

To mimic these layers of underpainting in a digital painting, you'll use masks, blending modes, transparent color, faux pencil, and more.

DEFINE THE AREA TO UNPAINT

1 Open the file **Painting.psd** from the accompanying CD-ROM. Make sure that the foreground color is white and the background color is black.

2 Use the Lasso tool to make an irregular selection shaped like the edge of a torn sheet of paper.

   This shape defines the area to "unpaint."

3 Click the Save Selection as Channel icon at the bottom of the Channels palette.

   This saves the selection to a new channel.

Load the image file to be "unpainted."

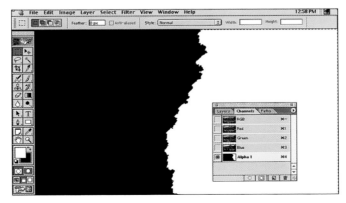

Save the selection to a new channel.

4 With the new channel active, choose Filters/Brush Strokes/Spatter, and set the Spray Radius to 8 and the Smoothness to 6.

5 With the channel still active, choose Filter/Blur/Gaussian Blur, set the Radius to 0.3, and deselect.

6 Click the RGB composite channel and turn off the Eye icon on the Alpha 1 channel. Double-click the Background layer to turn it into a floating layer and name it Original. Choose Select/Load Selection. In the Channel field, choose Alpha 1. Copy and paste. Name the new layer Sepia.

Now the area to unpaint is selected and on its own layer.

7 Activate the Sepia layer. Choose Image/Adjust/Desaturate, and then select Image/Adjust/Levels and enter the following:

Input Shadow: **0**

Midtones: **1.22**

Highlights: **235**

Output Shadow: **10**

Highlight: **255**

These settings lighten the image so that, when all the other art layers are added, the total effect is not muddy.

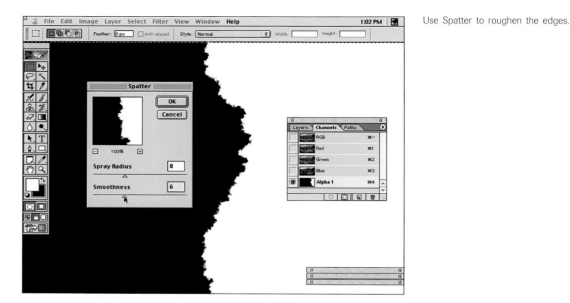

Use Spatter to roughen the edges.

Note: Spatter adds some random splotches on either side of the selection so it doesn't look like a cut paper shape. A Gaussian Blur slightly softens the edge of the spatters to give the edges a more natural look.

8 Choose Image/Adjust/Hue/Saturation. Click
Colorize; set Hue to 30 and Saturation to 23.

You now have a sepia version of the section of the
art that is unpainted. This is analogous to painting
the forms more opaquely in browns or grays before
adding the color in a traditional painting.

Make a sepia version of the
area to be unpainted.

FAUX PENCIL

To add to the feeling of a transparent underpainting, you will now add a pencil
layer. All outlines of the shapes in your painting are "penciled" in a normal
painting. Here, however, you can decide to pencil in only selected areas if you
want to draw a little more attention to that section.

1 Create a new layer and name it Pencil. Press
Ctrl+Backspace (Cmd+Delete) to fill with the
white background color. Click on the Foreground
color swatch and enter R69, G52, and B45 in
the Color Picker.

This RGB value results in a dark brown color for the
"pencil" lines you will add.

Note: The Pencil layer should always be the topmost
layer because it has to be set on the Multiply blending
mode. Adjusting the Opacity of the pencil layer controls
the amount of "snap" your art has.

2 Choose a 3-pixel paintbrush and set the Opacity at 78%. Lower the Opacity of the Pencil layer to 50%.

You should now be able to see the Sepia layer.

3 Loosely trace the major outlines of the elements of the Sepia layer. Reset the Opacity of the Pencil layer to 100%

The supposed "pencil" is still too clean looking, but the next step fixes it.

Create a "pencil" layer and lower Opacity, so you can trace the shapes.

4 Choose Filters/Brush Strokes/Spatter. Set the Spray to 1 and the Smoothness to 6. Choose Filter/Blur/Gaussian Blur and set Radius to 0.2.

The Spatter filter makes the Pencil layer look more organic whereas the Gaussian Blur slightly softens the edges.

Use the Spatter filter to give the pencil line a rougher, more organic look; then add a little Gaussian Blur to soften slightly.

ADDING TEXTURE

Add that background layer of streaky brushstrokes using the Paintbrush and Smudge tools. This emulates the strokes that cover the white board or canvas in traditional media and gives the whole piece a more dynamic feel.

1   Create a new layer, name it Brushstrokes, and drag it to the bottom in the Layers palette. Turn off the Eye icon on the other layers. Draw a rectangular selection a little wider than the unpainted part and about 2" tall. Fill with white, and make the foreground color black. Do not deselect.

2   Select the 59-pixel Spatter brush (last brush in the fourth row) and set the Opacity to 30%. Paint side-to-side strokes with a bit of overlap. Select the Smudge tool at 100% Pressure and blend side to side using the same brush. Then use the Unsharp Mask filter and enter the following settings to bring back a little crispness to the smudged strokes:

Amount: **150**

Radius: **1.1**

Threshold: **0**

Note: When you use the Smudge tool, click in the center of the canvas and brush toward the sides of the image so that you don't pull in any extra colors by accident. Use a slightly circular motion and mix the strokes until they resemble the image shown. Release the mouse after each stroke rather than painting continuously.

3   Choose Image/Adjust/Hue/Saturation. Click Colorize, and set the Hue to 30 and the Saturation to 23. Deselect

You now have a sepia version of the brushstrokes.

Note: Creating the brushstrokes traditionally gives you the quickest and best results. But if it's three o'clock in the morning and you don't already have the supplies at home, there's a way to get decent results digitally.

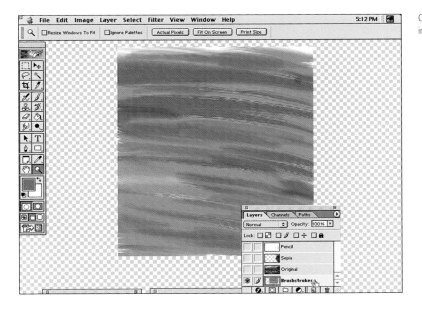

Create digital brushstrokes in black and white first.

4   Create a new layer and name it Texture, and drag it
    above the Brushstrokes layer. In the Color Picker,
    enter R117, G73, and B16 for the foreground
    color. Draw a 3/4-inch square selection and fill it
    with the foreground color. Deselect.

    This step creates a blurry mottling to give an uneven
    and more natural look to the brushstrokes.

5   Choose Filters/Noise/Add Noise, check
    Monochromatic and set the amount 30 in the
    Gaussian mode, and then choose the Gaussian Blur
    filter at 0.8 pixels. Select the Transform tool and
    enlarge the blurry noise art so it is slightly larger than
    and overlaps the brush strokes art. Set the Blending
    mode to Overlay and the Opacity to 18%.

6   Press Ctrl (Cmd)+E to merge the Texture layer into
    the Brushstrokes layer. Turn on the Eye icon on the
    Sepia layer.

    When you merge, only the name of the bottom
    layer remains, so you don't need to rename the
    merged layer.

7   Select the layer with the brushstrokes art. While
    pressing the Alt(Opt) key, use the Transform tool to
    scale the brushstrokes art to be as tall as the sepia art
    and make it wider than the sepia art.

    Because brushstrokes art is wider, it covers any
    possible gaps between the sepia and full-color art.

8   Choose Filter/Noise/Add Noise, with a setting of 12
    Monochromatic so as not to add extraneous colors.
    Choose Select/Load Selection. In the Channel tab,
    choose Alpha 1, check the invert box. After you exit
    the dialog box, press the Delete (Backspace) key.
    Deselect all.

    The Noise filter adds a little "grit" to the
    brushstrokes, though you won't be able to see the
    effect until later in the project.

Create a blurry mottling to color
the brushstrokes unevenly.

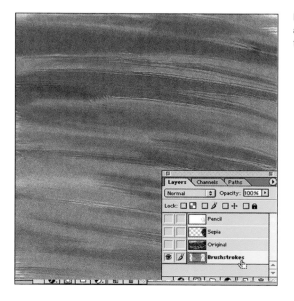

Enlarge digital brushstrokes
and add noise to approximate
traditional media.

COLOR WASH

Adding a layer of transparent color simulates the laying in of traditional color washes over brown tones to delineate the forms.

1 Create a new layer and name it Color. Place it directly under the Pencil layer. Turn on the Eye icon on the Original layer. Turn off the Eye icon on the Sepia and Brushstrokes layers so they won't distract you. Reset the Brush Opacity to 100%.

Create a new Color layer.

2 Select the Paintbrush tool and pick a soft-edged brush. Set the brush's Opacity to 75%. Use the Eyedropper tool (press Alt[Opt] to change the paintbrush into the eyedropper) to select colors from the Original layer and paint on the Color layer, directly over the counterpart.

Select a midtone from a face, for example, and then use that color to paint over the face in the Color layer. You decide which areas need to be painted in order to draw a little more attention to them. To better allow you to see the color you're painting with, turn on the Eye icon on the Sepia layer. You have to toggle the view on and off on that layer to select the colors in the Original layer. Don't try to fill in all the colors or worry about keeping perfectly within the outline of a figure.

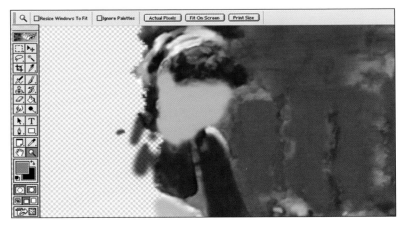

Choose colors from the Original layer and paint loosely on the Color layer.

3   Select the Paintbrush tool and pick a soft-edged brush. Then paint on the Color layer at 75% Opacity. Set the Blending mode to Color at 50%.

The example shows the results at this stage with the Original layer and the Brushstrokes layer invisible.

Change the Opacity of the Color layer to 50% and the Blend mode to Color.

FINISHING TOUCHES

You'll create the appearance of a little paint thickness using Bevel and Emboss at the right-hand edge of the original art. This shows the difference between the "finished" part and the underpainting. Finally, you'll need to adjust all the layers to their various blending modes to achieve the right balance of color, tone, and line in the "unpainted" part.

1   Click on the Original layer and drag it to the New Layer icon at the bottom of the Layers palette. Select the Original copy layer and turn off the Original layer's Eye icon.

2   Choose Select/Load Selection. In the Channel tab, choose Alpha 1, click OK, and press the Delete (Backspace) key. Deselect all.

Load Alpha 1 selection on the Original layer.

3 Choose Layers/Layer Style/Bevel and Emboss, and enter the following settings:

Structure:

Style: **Inner Bevel**

Technique: **Smooth**

Depth: **100%**

Direction: **Up**

Size: **1 pixel**

Soften: **0 pixels**

Shading:

Angle: **120°**

Use Global Light: **Checked**

Altitude: **30°**

Gross Contour: **Linear**

Anti-aliased: **Unchecked**

Highlight Mode: **Screen (white)**

Opacity: **0%**

Shadow Mode: **Multiply**

Opacity: **55%**

This step adds a little paint "thickness."

4 Choose Layer/Layer Style/Create Layers. Merge the visible layers.

This enables you to work on the Original copy layer without adding further bevel effects.

5 Choose the Eraser tool at 100% Opacity. Erase the bottom ¼-inch of the Original copy layer art, as well as randomly erasing parts of the ragged edge.

6 Choose the Original layer. Load the selection Alpha 1 and delete. Merge the Original layer with the Original copy layer.

Your ragged edge now has some areas of bevel (thickness) and some without.

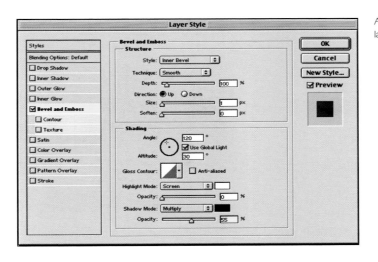

Add a Bevel and Emboss layer style.

Note: By erasing parts of the bevel effect, you ensure the thick paint effect doesn't look too even and, therefore, fake.

Add Bevel and Emboss to create paint thickness.

7 Set the following layers to their corresponding settings and turn on the Eye icon for all the layers. The order of the layers from top to bottom (and their Blending mode and Opacity) should be as follows:

Pencil: **Multiply, 58%**

Color: **Color, 50%**

Sepia: **Overlay, 50%**

Original: **Normal, 100%**

Brushstrokes: **Normal, 100%**

The Pencil layer settings are just enough to add snap. If you go any stronger on the Color layer, the colors become too dominant. The Sepia layer settings add to the richness of color in the brushstrokes without overpowering them. The Original and Brushstrokes layers settings form the left and right bases of the piece respectively.

The example shows a smaller area of the artwork unpainted, to satisfy the client's request.

Set the Blending mode and Opacity for each layer to reach the final image.

Note: There are actually several different settings that yield pleasing results. You can try placing the Sepia layer into Hard Light mode and start at 50% Opacity to find a pleasing setting. You can use Normal mode and lower the Opacity, but you will lose much of the texture.

You can also set the Sepia layer to 100% Normal mode and move it to the bottom of the Layers palette. Change the Brushstrokes layer to either Overlay mode at 50% or Hard Light mode at 50% Opacity.

MODIFICATIONS

To add an extra dimension to your unpainted image, you can composite it with a photographic layer. I was photographed by Don Corning, for example, in front of a huge blank canvas as if I was actually painting. A Quick Mask was then used to isolate both me and the dropcloth from the background, and that layer was copied over to the "Unpainting" file. The layer with the dog model was add for a little bit of humor. Finally, drop shadows were added to the dropcloth and dog, so they seemed more natural and they flattened the file.

Composite a photographic layer over your "unpainting" to make it look like a work in progress.

If you have the time, the best way to add the brushstroke texture is with traditional materials. Use a tube of medium dark acrylic paint and a one-inch painting brush on a piece of illustration board slightly larger than the dimensions of the unpainting. Add a little water to the paint and paint a series of loose horizontal strokes that overlap until the white paper isn't visible.

Scan the brushstrokes at 100% at 200 ppi in RGB. Select All and then choose Copy. Click on the unpainting file and paste. Name the layer Brushstrokes, and then Desaturate it. Finally, set Hue and Saturation as you did for the digital brushstrokes.

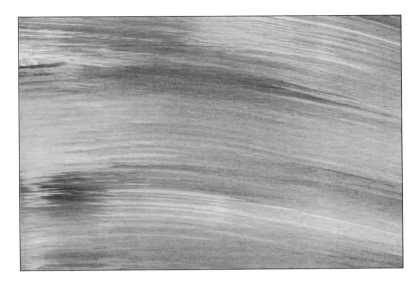

Paint brushstrokes with traditional paints.

You could use the unpainting technique on art. Use natural brushstrokes for the best effect. Also, you can give a regular photograph an artistic lift by unpainting the whole image for a total transformation. The left figure is an out-take reference shot for an illustration. As a photo, it has some drama with the strong lighting and deep shadows, but perhaps too much. Unpainting the whole shot (right) gives it a warm glowing feeling and a more artistic feel.

To make the art feel dominant, you'll need to adjust the final settings for the layers. For the Pencil layer, Multiply mode and 80% Opacity show the loose drawing more. For the Color layer, try Overlay mode and 80% Opacity. When only unpainting, the color has to be stronger to carry the piece. To show less of the photo, choose Overlay mode and 60% Opacity for the Sepia layer. Because the photo example is all unpainted, it has no Original layer. The Brushstrokes should use Normal mode and 100% Opacity to form the base of the piece.

You can transform an original photo (left) that is too contrasty and cool in color into a warm artistic feel by unpainting all of it.

253

BLENDING IMAGES

"There is nothing more fearful than

imagination without taste."

—GOETHE

USING LAYERS AND LAYER MASKS TO ADD DEPTH

Layers and layer masks impart not only visual

depth but also add conceptual depth to your

designs. They add flexibility to your work, as

well, enabling you to experiment with image

placement and size without altering your original.

In other words, you can explore several versions

of a composite image without committing to

any one of them.

Project18

Blending Images

by Aren Howell

GETTING STARTED

When beginning a project, you must first consider the
type of and decide how many elements you plan to integrate
into the final composite. It is most effective to use a mixture
of elements to make the image more visually interesting.
Consider photos, line art, type, textures, and other media
that you can scan to add personality to your collage. This
project uses a combination of US Navy memorabilia and
photos from my grandfather's service during World War II.

Some of the techniques explored in this project include
layers and the addition of layer masks, adding layer masks
to adjustment layers, which is a new feature in Photoshop
6, and experimenting with the endless possibilities of layer
modes. All of these features make the blending images
visually interesting, and can add depth to your work.

BUILDING THE BACKGROUND

Ever since Adobe added the layers feature to Photoshop, the possibilities of making complex collages became endless. The use of layer masks made the process even easier, and can give you final art that looks professional without the time that it used to take to do the same image. To build the background, use layer masks and learn the new Photoshop 6 feature of adding layer masks to Adjustment layers.

1   From the accompanying CD-ROM, open the file named **Banner.tif**, which is sized to the dimensions of the project's final image. Go to File/Save As, and save the banner background as Navy.psd.

In any collage, your first step is to determine the project's final size and main image. Here the Serving Our Country banner is the primary image and background. To prepare the original scan of the banner for use, missing areas were repaired using the Rubber Stamp tool and the red stitching at the top was cloned out.

Open Banner.tif from the CD-ROM and resave it as Navy.psd; this is your final image. Because you are scanning real objects, some clean-up work and cropping needs to be done on the banner.

2   Open the file named **portrait.tif** from the accompanying CD-ROM. Press Ctrl(Cmd)+A to select the entire image. Switch back to Navy.psd copy and paste the Navy portrait image into a new layer and name it Portrait. Reduce the Layer Opacity to about 50% so you can see the background while you scale and adjust the size of the portrait to fill the majority of the tan-colored area of the banner. Return the layer to 100% Opacity.

After sizing the portrait to the banner, you can move it slightly to the left using the Move tool. I know my secondary images are going on the right side of the final image, so bumping the portrait over a bit makes a space available for the additional images.

Scale and adjust the portrait to fit into the final image background.

3 In the Layer Modes (or Blending Modes) menu on the Layers palette, set the Layer mode to Hard Light.

The Hard Light mode makes the portrait look like it has more contrast than it had originally, and also enables the image to become partially transparent, letting the flag show through the portrait.

Note: Layer modes are excellent ways to experiment with different visual effects in a layered image. Using combinations of Layer modes and Opacity, you can add depth to an image and get virtually any effect you can dream up without taking a lot of time. You might want to take the opportunity to quickly apply each mode to see what kind of effect results, and to see which modes are applicable in different situations.

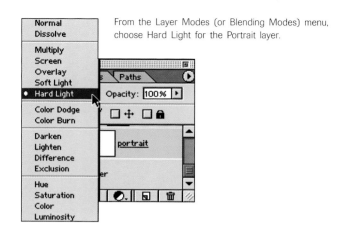

From the Layer Modes (or Blending Modes) menu, choose Hard Light for the Portrait layer.

4 Choose Layer/New Adjustment Layer/Levels for a new adjustment layer, and group it with the previous layer so it effects the portrait only.

One of the new features of Photoshop 6 enables you to apply layer masks to adjustment layers. Using this technique, you can make any adjustment that you could have previously made to a layer, and then only apply it to specific areas by using the mask. It allows you to make changes such as brightness and contrast, posterize, adjust levels, and so on to only portions of a layer. The technique of using the layer mask here is to isolate the additional contrast only in the eye area of the portrait (Steps 6 and 7).

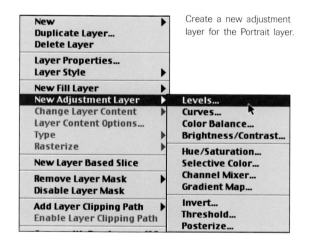

Create a new adjustment layer for the Portrait layer.

5 Change the levels so that the black slider is set at 44. When the levels are set the way you want them, click OK, and then activate the adjustment layer mask.

Setting the black slider at 44 increases the amount of contrast in the portrait layer.

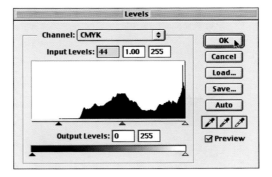

Move the black slider to the right until it reaches 44 to increase the amount of black in the portrait.

6 From the Gradient Options bar, choose a black to white radial blend, and then set it to reverse so it becomes white to black.

In this step, you are using the Gradient tool to create a mask that highlights the eye and face area by darkening that portion of the image alone. This change is very subtle, which is important to complex images.

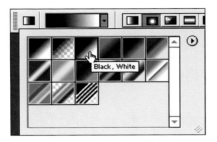

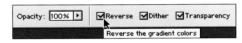

Choose the type of gradient that you want to use in the Adjustment Layer mask from the Gradient Options bar.

7 Drag the Gradient tool from a point between the eyes, pulling it out far enough to make the change subtle; stopping around the lips is a good starting point.

Because of the subtlety of the change, you need to watch carefully as Photoshop renders an updated preview. You can test different gradient lengths until you get a result that only increases the contrast in the eye and face area.

Test different lengths on the gradient to determine how dramatic an effect the adjustment layer has on the image.

8 Open the file **certificate.tif** from the CD-ROM, select all, and then copy and paste the certificate into the working file on a new layer and name it Certificate. Change the position of the new layer, so it is between the Banner and the Portrait layers.

The certificate has a tan background. In the next step, use a technique that drops the tan background out of the image.

Drop in the certificate on a new layer, make sure the Certificate layer falls between the Banner and the Portrait layers.

9 Double-click the Certificate layer. In the Layer Style dialog box, under Advanced Blending, set the This Layer white slider for this layer in the blending image range to 160. Set the Layer mode to Darken and the Opacity to 30%.

By setting the blending range to 160, only the black type will remain in the layer. Changing the Layer mode to Darken and adjusting the Opacity to 30% integrates the text into the background.

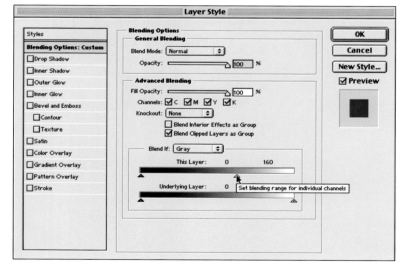

Move the white slider until you see the tan background drop out of the certificate.

10 Click the Add a Mask button to create a layer mask for the certificate and choose a 300-pixel soft brush from the Brushes option bar. Set the Opacity for the brush to around 60%. With the foreground color set to black, paint in the area of the face to fade the text out over the portrait.

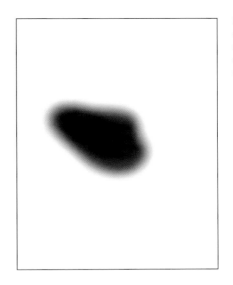

Use the paintbrush on the new layer mask to erase the certificate over the central face area.

FITTING IN THE FOREGROUND IMAGES

Now that the background has been established, you can start adding the foreground images into the working file. The foreground images are the images in the collage that tell the majority of the story or the ones that are the most important to the overall message of the piece. The techniques that are used in these steps are similar to ones that you used in the background, such as layer masks and Blending modes, they just need a bit more attention to detail since they are at the front of the image.

1 Open the file named **wedding.tif** from the CD-ROM, copy and paste the entire image onto a new layer in the working file and call it Wedding. Size the wedding photo so it fits into the bottom-right corner of the image.

One way to see the relationship of the new layer to the background is to adjust the Opacity to around 50% so the wedding photo becomes temporarily transparent. When you have the wedding photo sized, change the Opacity back to 100%.

Paste the wedding portrait on a new layer, and use the Opacity to temporarily see the size relationship between the wedding photo and the background.

2 Click the Add a Mask button to add a mask to the Wedding layer. Using the Gradient tool, choose a black-to-white linear blend and pull a blend that stretches from the bottom of the photo up to cover the bottom third of the wedding photo.

To keep the gradient straight, hold down the Shift key. The gradient makes the bottom of the photo disappear and blend into the background. At the top of the photo, the mask should be more freeform, outlining the silhouettes in the photo. You can fix this in the next step.

3 Using the Soft Round 300-pixel brush with the foreground color set to black, paint around the outside of the heads and continue up until all the background is gone at the top of the image. Adjust the Opacity to around 80% if you want the blend to look softer as you get close to the heads.

Because the paintbrush is so large, you might erase some of the portrait itself. You can replace it in the next step.

4 Change the foreground color to white and choose the Soft Round 65-pixel brush from the Brushes option bar.

You can view just the layer mask by clicking the Channel palette and turning on only the wedding mask channel.

Add a mask to the Wedding layer, then add a black-to-white gradient on the bottom third of the wedding portrait.

Use the Soft Round 300-pixel brush on the layer mask to paint around the silhouettes in the photo.

5 Zoom in on the image, and draw over the portions that you want to bring back. Paint over the top of each hat, for example, to restore their detail.

Note: One of the most appealing features of layer masks is their flexibility. If you don't like what is happening to your image, just select all and delete the mask or switch from a black brush to a white brush, and go back over the areas that you did not mean to erase. There is no need to revert and you have not made any permanent alterations to the actual pieces of art. Using combinations of gradients and brushes on single mask gives you complete control over what areas of the image are transparent and opaque.

Use a foreground color of white and a smaller brush to paint back over the top of the hat and bring the detail back into the image. You can view just the layer mask by clicking the Channel palette, and turning on just the wedding mask channel.

6 Set the Wedding layer's Opacity to 80% by adjusting the Opacity slider.

This allows the background to become slightly visible and further integrates the wedding portrait into the image.

Adjust the Opacity of the Wedding layer to 80% so the background starts to show through the image.

ADDING DEPTH

Now that the primary image has been created, you can tell more of the story by adding smaller detail images into the foreground to support the main image. Adding snapshots into the image creates yet another set of layers that add to the overall effect of the composite image.

1 Open the file **lagoon.tif** from the CD-ROM, select the entire image, paste it into a new layer, and call it Lagoon. Scale the lagoon to a size that is about an inch and a half wide and fits into the lower-left corner of the collage.

Paste the lagoon photo into a new layer, and adjust the size and placement of the image.

2 Adjust the layer's Opacity to 65%. Change the Layer mode to Hard Light to add depth to the image.

If you prefer another percentage, just be sure it lets the background show through while still keeping the lagoon recognizable.

Change the Opacity of the lagoon layer to 65% and the Layer mode to Hard Light.

3 Add a new layer to add in the drop shadow. With the new layer active, hold down the Ctrl (Cmd) key and click on the Lagoon layer to get the exact selection of that layer. With the Selection tool active, nudge the selection to the right and down. Press Alt+Backspace (Opt+Delete) to fill it with black.

Now you have a box that is the same size as the lagoon photo, but it is filled with black.

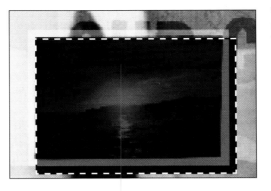

With a selection that is identical to the Lagoon layer, nudge it to the right and down and fill it with black to begin creating the drop shadow.

4 Choose Filter/Blur/Gausian Blur and set Radius to 10 pixels to blur the shadow. Change the Layer mode to Multiply and Opacity 45%.

Because the Opacity of the Lagoon layer is at 65%, the image looks muddy because the black drop shadow is showing through the Lagoon layer. You can fix this in the next step.

With the Gausian Blur, blur the shadow by 10 pixels. Change the Layer mode to Multiply and Opacity to 45%.

5 While holding down the Alt (Opt) key, click the Lagoon layer in the Layers palette.

You now have the same selection active as when you started the shadow.

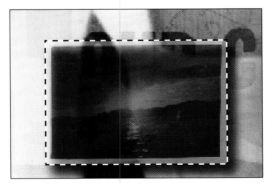

With the lagoon shadow layer active, hold down the Alt (Opt) key and click the Lagoon layer.

6 Press Delete (Backspace).

Photoshop deletes all the black from behind the layer and lets the other art show through again. This time, however, the newly revealed art looks like a drop shadow under the photo.

Press the Backspace (Delete) key to remove all of the black that is directly behind the Lagoon layer.

MODIFICATIONS

As you can tell from the project's opening image, there are several more layers of photos, art, and type added in using all of the techniques that you have just learned. In the background, I added additional layers of text and line art in various sizes, opacities, and layer modes. In the upper-right corner is another photo of my grandfather on his boat, and it is masked out similarly to the Wedding layer. On top of that was added several other snapshots with shadows. Use Layer modes and layer masks to let your imagination run wild. If you get too wild, remember you haven't made any changes to the images themselves, so you can keep adjusting them until you get exactly what you want.

To add a different effect to type in the background, paste in a new layer with a portion of the certificate type and enlarge it so it is visibly larger than the other type. Rather than making it look dark, lighten it by setting the mode to Overlay and the Opacity to 75%. Overlay mode makes the dark portion of layer blend in, similar to Multiply mode, and it makes the light areas act more like the Screen mode without being as extreme as those individual modes.

Use the Overlay Layer mode to add variety to the type in the background.

Another option that you can experiment with is colorizing line art or photos to make them blend in with the colors of the image. To colorize the boat image only, select its thumbnail in the Layers palette. The Layer mode of the boat art in the bottom-right corner is set to Color Burn with Opacity at 65%. Add an adjustment layer and alter the Hue and Saturation. Click the Colorize button and move the Hue sliders around until the boat becomes a shade of blue. Try different colors to make the art stand out or recede into the back. You can find the boat line art on the CD-ROM. It is called **boat.tif**.

Add a Hue and Saturation Adjustment layer to the line art and select Colorize to change the color in the layer.

One last modification that I used in the image was multiplying layers and adjusting their modes for different effects. Drag the Lagoon layer down to the Layer Copy icon so you have an identical copy of the layer. Change the Layer mode to Hard Light to add the burned-out glow to the photo. You can adjust the opacity as needed to keep the image transparent.

Placing layers in different Layer modes on top of each other can give you different results. Experiment with several combinations.

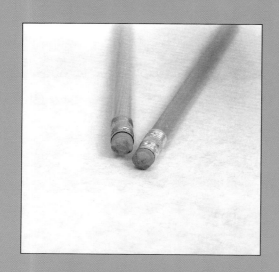

A DIFFERENT COMPOSITE

"Opportunities are usually disguised

as hard work, so most people don't

recognize them."

—ANN LANDERS

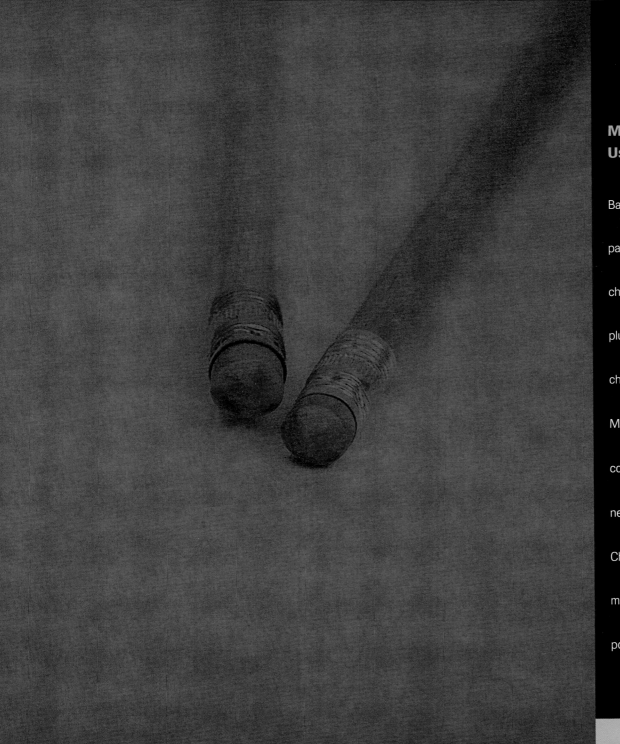

MULTIPLE IMAGE EFFECTS WITHOUT THE USE OF LAYERS

Back in the early days of Photoshop, a third-party filter enabled you to exchange the channels in the image for startling results. The plug-in serves no purpose now. You can split channels and recombine them with Photoshop's Merge Channels command. You can build a composite image from multiple sources without needing layers or laboring over mask making. Channel swapping can produce either a mess or very exciting graphics that are only possible digitally.

Project 19

A Different Composite

by Rhoda Grossman

GETTING STARTED

Working with channels in Photoshop can seem difficult and mysterious. This project presents an opportunity to demystify the process. As for difficulty, the hardest thing you have to do is decide among a wide array of possibilities.

The source images provided are the same pixel dimensions. That is the only prerequisite to combining channels across different images.

CHANNEL CHANGING: RGB

Begin with two RGB images, a Renaissance painting and a view of present day Rome.
Use the Split Channels and Merge Channels commands to create a composite image.
Then adjust the colors in the new image with the Channel Mixer.

1 Open **PAINTrgb.tif** and **ROMErgb.tif** from the accompanying CD-ROM.

Begin with two RGB images that are the same pixel dimensions.

2 Use the Split Channels command in the pop-up menu on the Channels palette. Use it on both images.

When you split channels, the image is replaced by three grayscale images, one for each of the color channels. So, you should have six such images, three for the painting and three for the Rome scene. Shown here from left to right are the images corresponding to the Red, Green, and Blue channels of the painting.

Split the channels for the painting.

3 Use the Merge Channels command in the Channel menu, and set the mode to RGB. Assign the Green channel of the painting to the Red channel of the new image you are creating. Choose the Blue channel of the Rome image for the new Green channel. Use the Red channel of the Rome image for the new Blue channel.

You have access to all six of the grayscale images you created in Step 2. You can assign any one of them to any of the three channels that make up your new image. You are not permitted, however, to assign the same image to more than one channel. Even with that restriction, you still have lots of choices.

The choices made here produce a new image with a saturated blue-green sky, due to the absence of red. (Notice that the Red channel is very dark in the sky area.) That blue-green is so saturated that it is out of the CMYK gamut for printing, so the sky in your screen image will be more intense than the figure shown here.

Merge the channels.

272

The face and body of the woman (Red channel) allow large amounts of red, which combine with the sky to lighten it. (Recall that equal amounts of red, green, and blue light combine to produce white.) Wherever lighter pixels from the Red channel overlap the darker areas of the buildings, the result is a strong red color.

4 Use Channel Mixer in the Image/Adjust menu to manipulate color. The following settings are suggested for the results shown:

Output channel: **Red**

Source channels: RGB +**74**, +**42**, +**21**

Output channel: **Green**

Source channels: RGB +**30**, +**87**, +**2**

Output channel: **Blue**

Source channels: RGB −**2**, +**23**, +**79**

The result is more pleasing in several ways. The figure of the woman was strengthened and her skin is a creamy ivory color. A warm brown replaces the harsh red where she overlaps the building, and the sky is now a softer and more realistic blue. Examine the settings and the new (output) channels to see how those changes were accomplished.

Mix the channels to improve color.

For example, compare the Red channel you had in Step 3 to your new Red channel. The mixed channel has a much lighter sky, indicating that some red will be present to dilute the strong blue-green. Conversely, the woman's garment is now darker in several places (where the architecture from the Blue and Green channels were added), so the amount of red in the current mix is reduced.

Note: You do not have to calculate settings beforehand, because the image updates as you move the sliders for each channel. Trial and error is just fine; the more you know about how color channels combine, however, the more you will experience "trial and success."

Compare the Red channel before and after mixing.

MODE MERGING

The images you combine using these techniques do not have to be in the same color mode. You can merge channels from an RGB source with those of a CMYK, Lab color, or even a grayscale image.

1   Open the CMYK version of the painting, **PAINTcmy.tif**, and **ROMErgb.tif**.

2   Use the Split Channels command on both images, resulting in seven separate grayscale images.

Before you merge any channels, examine them with the intent of making some choices based on a desired outcome. I was intrigued in this case with the Yellow channel, which gives the woman a moody, mysterious quality. I thought it would be effective in the Black channel of a new composite.

Consider using the Yellow channel of the painting as the Black channel for a CMYK composite.

3   Use the Merge Channels command to make a new CMYK image, using the Yellow channel of the painting in the new Black channel and the following other choices:

Green channel of the Rome image for Cyan

Blue channel of the Rome image for Yellow

Magenta channel of the painting for Magenta

The decision to make the new composite CMYK rather than RGB was determined in part by my desire to use the painting's Yellow channel for Black. I also wanted the two source images to have equal visual weight in the composite, so I needed to assign two channels to each of them. The result certainly gives the woman a moody quality, but the entire image is too dark and there is not enough contrast between the buildings and the sky. The Channel Mixer will fix that.

Merge two channels from the RGB scene with two channels from the CMYK painting for a new CMYK image.

4   Use the Channel Mixer with these settings:

Output channel: **Cyan**

Source channels: CMYK **−11, 0, −30, −21**

Output channel: **Magenta**

Source channels: CMYK **0, +49, −74, +30**

Output channel: **Yellow**

Source channels: CMYK **−30, +77, +32, −60**

Output channel: **Black**

Source channels: CMYK **−21, −11, +4, +77**

Mix channels to lighten the image and increase the contrast between buildings and sky.

The resulting image has inverted (negative) yellow buildings against a low saturation red sky. A comparison of the Magenta and Black channels before and after the mixing reveals how that was achieved. Just make the Cyan and Yellow channels invisible.

Compare the Magenta and Black channel combination before and after mixing.

> **Note:** The mixed image has no data at all in the Cyan channel. (That channel is pure white.) Resist the temptation to drag the Cyan channel to the trash. Your image will look the same, but it will no longer be a CMYK document. It converts to Multichannel mode and cannot be saved in TIFF, PICT, JPEG, or other useful file formats.

5   Enrich the colors by using Image/Adjust/Levels. For the Magenta channel, move the left input slider (black triangle) to 113 and the middle slider to 1.46. For the Yellow channel, drag the left slider to 135 and leave the others unchanged.

The outcome, shown at the beginning of this project, has an opulent golden yellow for the buildings, a crimson sky, and more definition in the woman's face. If you prefer the more delicate coloration in the preceding state, undo the Levels adjustments. In either case, the image is finished. You created a composite without layers, masks, or blending modes.

MODIFICATIONS

Multichannel mode, previously mentioned, is useful for saving channels from several images in one place. When you split channels and merge them into a multichannel image, you create a document with only Alpha channels—channels that are not associated with a color. Recall that saving a selection creates an Alpha channel. In effect, you have a collection of masks that you can use with any open image of exactly the same size.

Merging and mixing color channels from different images gives you many possible effects. When using image data that has been converted to Alpha channels, you have even more choices! You can use the Load Selection command and fill with any color at any opacity. You have access to blending modes as well. I made a multichannel image consisting of the Red channel from the Rome image; the Cyan, Magenta, and Yellow channels from the painting; and the single (Black) channel from a grayscale image **DUOMO.tif**. (The photo of the Duomo cathedral in Florence is available in the source folder for this project on the *Photoshop 6 Effects Magic* CD-ROM.)

With the new multichannel document available, open the original painting. (You may use either the RGB or CMYK version.) Load the Duomo channel as a selection. I used a chocolate brown color and filled the selection with the foreground color at 100% Opacity in Color Dodge mode. The result was too harsh, so I used the Fade command and switched to Screen mode at 100%. Now the painting has a subtle background of the Florentine cathedral.

> **Tip:** If your prediction about the outcome of a blending mode is a bit off (or way off), don't bother to undo. Use the Fade command to explore other blending modes.

Create a multichannel document to include as many Alpha channels as you want from the same size images.

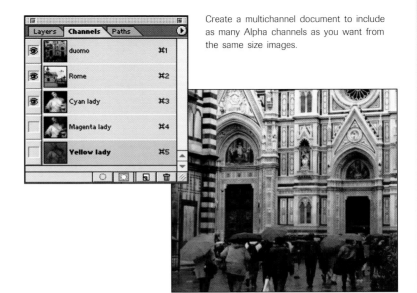

Fill the selection with brown in Color Dodge mode, and then switch to Screen mode with the Fade command.

277

You can build a composite from scratch on a blank image (same pixel dimensions, of course). For the first stage, I loaded the Rome scene as a selection, with the Invert box checked, and then filled it with brown.

Then the white background was selected with the Magic Wand tool. I loaded the Duomo channel, also inverted, choosing the Intersect option in the Load Selection dialog box. This restricted the Duomo selection to the background. I used a slate blue for the fill.

I could not resist adding some elements of the painting to the mix, so I loaded the Alpha channel that had been the Magenta component of the original painting. This time the fill color was a low-saturation purple. I used Multiply mode to ensure that the darker areas would not fade.

Load the inverted Alpha channel for the Rome scene and fill with brown.

Load the Duomo channel to intersect with the background and fill with grayish blue.

Load and fill the former Magenta channel of the painting with grayish purple in Multiply mode.

Wanting to strengthen the figure of the woman a bit, I loaded the original Cyan channel from the painting and filled it with a flesh tone. I used 100% Normal mode, anticipating that I might need to change the mode or the opacity with the Fade command.

Sure enough, a change of mode was desirable and I finally settled on Hard Light. That mode brought back the architecture of the Rome scene with the additional benefit of a warm Sienna brown.

If you want to continue working with images of the art and architecture of Renaissance Italy, go to Project 21, "Designing with Type."

Load and fill the former Cyan channel of the painting with flesh color in Normal mode.

Use Edit/Fade to change the fill mode to Hard Light.

CLEAR BEVELED TYPE

"Human beings are 70% water, and

with some the rest is collagen."

—MARTIN MULL

CUSTOMIZING LIVE LAYER EFFECTS FOR TITLE TYPE

With Photoshop 6's new Styles and Layer Effect options, you can create cool graphic effects for type and logos much easier than ever before, without the use of multiple channels and masks. Because the effects are "live," you can quickly change the look of the effect as you develop it by making choices in the live Layer Effects dialog boxes.

Project 20

Clear Beveled Type

by Cher Threinen-Pendarvis

GETTING STARTED

Photoshop 6 offers robust live effects, such as Drop Shadow, Bevel and Emboss, Glow, and Pattern Overlay. You can customize these effects and save them as Styles, and then apply them to type and logos.

Created as color comprehensives for a surfing-industry client, the type treatments that follow demonstrate these effects. To learn how the effects work, and work together, you re-create some of my comp variations; including a complicated custom bevel, a glow, and drop shadows.

You begin with an image of a sandy tidepool photographed in San Diego on a warm, sunny day. This image is used as the basis for both type effects.

SETTING THE TYPE

Sample a color from the tidepool image. Then choose the typeface you want. The text
you create automatically fills with your foreground color.

1   Open the image **Cleanwater.tif** from the
    accompanying CD-ROM.

2   Use the Eyedropper tool to sample a medium aqua
    color from the image.

    The example uses R0, G154, B175.

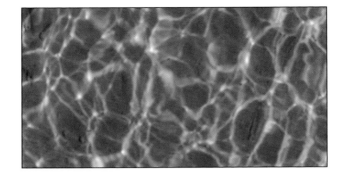

Open the tidepool photo
from the CD-ROM.

3   Choose the Type tool and click the Palettes button
    on the Options bar to open the Character palette.
    Choose a bold font with even strokes from the Font
    menu. Type **Clean Water Classic**.

    The type automatically fills with the foreground
    color and occupies its own new layer. The example
    font, Monoline MT, has flowing lines and strokes
    with even thickness that complement the freeform
    shapes in the water reflections. I set the type at 62.2
    point using the controls in the Options bar. If you set
    the type smaller or larger, the effect will look different.
    However, you can scale the effect to suit your typeface.

Choose a font and type the text (shown
here without the background).

4   Make any adjustments needed for kerning and align-
    ment in the Options bar and Character palette. To
    tighten the spacing between two letters by a small
    increment, highlight both letters with the Type tool,
    and then press the modifier key (Alt[Opt]) and the
    left-arrow key. Increase spacing between two letters
    with the right-arrow key.

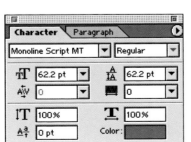

Adjust kerning or other text attributes
in the Character palette.

283

When I typed the Monoline script letters without any kerning adjustment, noticeable gaps could be seen. In this script font, the letters in each word are meant to be connected, but not overlapping. To make it pleasing to the eye, I applied custom kerning (tightening spaces between each letter, where a gap was noticeable). Before the custom kerning, I attempted a global tracking setting, but the result was not acceptable.

Note: The Character palette for Photoshop 6 offers sophisticated text-editing controls. These include kerning (adjusting the space between two letters), tracking (spacing between all letters), leading (space between lines of type), baseline shift (adjusting the vertical position of selected letters), and independent controls for vertical and horizontal scaling. Many of these features were available in the Type dialog box in Photoshop 5 and 5.5. The type controls have been moved to the Options bar in Photoshop 6, and some of them have been made easier to use. The features that a designer would use on a daily bases are tracking and kerning. For a special logo type solution—where a larger initial cap might drop down a bit—baseline shift is indispensable. The cool thing is that all the choices you make are "live" until you decide to render the type into pixels.

COMBINING TYPE WITH THE BACKGROUND

Lighten the background image to create more contrast with the type, and then put the water photo inside the type.

1 Click the Create New Fill or Adjustment Layer icon in the Layers palette and choose Hue/Saturation. In the dialog box, move the Lightness slider to 64%. Position the Adjustment layer directly above the Background layer.

By using the Adjustment layer to lighten the Background layer, you make the type stand out from the background. Unlike applying the change directly to the Background layer, using an Adjustment layer keeps your options open. If you or your client changes your mind, you can alter or eliminate it at any time before flattening the final image.

Place the Adjustment layer directly above the background.

Lighten the background with a Hue/Saturation Adjustment layer.

2   Select the background. Ctrl(Cmd)+click the type
layer to load a selection from its Transparency mask.
Press Ctrl(Cmd)+J to make a new layer via a copy.
Drag the new layer to the top of the layer hierarchy.

This step places the original background photo inside
the type. Clicking a layer with the modifier key held
down is the keyboard equivalent of Load Selection
using the transparency data from the layer as the
channel source. Transparent pixels are not selected,
but everything else is. In this case, the type is selected.
The New Layer Via Copy command converts the
selection you just made to its own layer. I left the
name of this layer as Layer 1. You could name it
Type with Texture from Photo.

Select the type and make a new
layer via copy.

ADDING BEVEL AND SHADOW TO THE TYPE

Use the Layer Styles feature to add bevels and drop-shadow effects to your type.

1   Target the layer you made in the preceding section.
Click the Add a Layer Style icon at the bottom of
the Layers palette and choose Bevel and Emboss
in the drop-down menu. The entire Layer Styles
dialog box displays.

You can also access the Layer Styles dialog box by
double-clicking the target layer. Bevel and Emboss
appear in the Styles list on the left.

2   Highlight Blending Options: Default in the Styles
list. In the Bevel and Emboss dialog box's Advanced
Blending options, set Fill Opacity to 48% and turn
on Blend Clipped Layers as a Group.

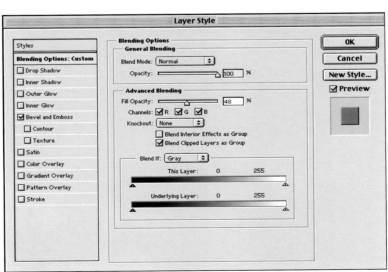

Create the custom Bevel
effects with the settings
in the Bevel and Emboss
dialog box.

3 Highlight Bevel and Emboss in the Styles list to get access to controls that are specific to this style. Under Structure, set the following:

Style: **Inner Bevel**

Technique: **Smooth**

Depth: **100%**

Direction: **Up**

Size: **21 pixels**

Soften: **0**

4 Under Shading, set the following:

Angle: **138°**

Global Light: **Checked**

Altitude: **39**

Gloss Contour: **Ring**

Highlight Mode: **Screen**

Opacity: **75%**

Shadow Mode: **Multiply**

Opacity: **75%**

5 Highlight Contour under the main Bevel and Emboss entry in the Styles list to access the Contour dialog box. Choose the Gaussian profile, turn on Anti-alias, and set Range to 50%.

6 In the Drop Shadow dialog box, set the following:

Blend Mode: **Multiply**

Opacity: **55%**

Angle of Lighting: **138°**

Use Global Light: **Checked**

Distance: **21 pixels**

Spread: **0**

Size: **21 pixels**

Contour: **Linear**

Anti-alias: **Checked**

Noise: **0%**

Note: Check boxes in the Layer Styles dialog box enable you to turn effects off or on. To access the settings for an effect, you must highlight the item. Because you have so many choices, you should save a combination of settings as a new style so that you won't have to reconstruct it again from scratch on another project. To save a setting as a new style, click the New Style button in the Layer Style dialog box. When the dialog box appears, name your style and click OK. This process adds your custom effect to the current Styles library.

The Styles menu operates just like the Brushes menu. Alternative libraries are available for loading. You can choose whether to display them as thumbnails, lists, or both. Shown here is the Buttons library displayed as a Large List. The styles are "live," so you can modify them to suit your needs.

There does not seem to be a direct way to create a new (empty) library to receive your custom layer styles as you create them. If you want to make one, you must drag one of the existing Styles libraries from the Presets folder to another location, rename it, and load it (after quitting and relaunching Photoshop). Then delete each of the styles one at a time.

Note: When you select a specific preset such as the Gloss Contour, you need to click on the menu to see the list. The default is to show image thumbnails with no names. You can see the preset's name by moving your cursor on top of the preset and waiting for the cursor tips to show the name, or you can view the presets as text only, Small List, or Large List by selecting that option from the drop-down Preset menu to the right of the thumbnails.

Finish your custom style by adding a drop shadow to the text.

This final group of settings adds a drop shadow to the text. Also shown is the result of turning off the Contour and Drop Shadow elements. Compare it to the completed Bevel and Emboss effect. It is useful to be able to turn on or off each component of a style, to see exactly what it contributes to the final effect.

Turn off Contour and Drop Shadow and compare the result to the completed style.

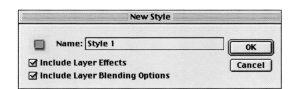

Save your custom settings as a new Style.

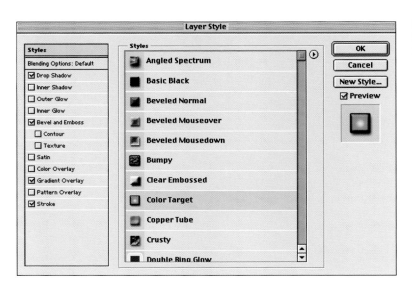

Load alternative Layer Styles libraries and modify them as needed.

MODIFICATIONS

If you follow my settings and apply them to a different font and they do not look similar, consider scaling the effect to fit the width of your letterforms. Choose Layer/Layer Style/ Scale Effects. In the dialog box, turn on the Preview box and type a larger or smaller percentage into the field to scale the effect.

Other minor variations include altering the contrast between the type and the background or changing the Opacity of the type layer. Here the font "Sand" was used, a good choice not only for its name, but also because the irregular edges of the letters give you a head start on creating watery effects. The custom style was applied at 125% Scaling, the type layer Opacity was reduced to 75%, and the lightness of the Background layer was reduced in the Hue/Saturation Adjustment layer.

Use a different font, adjust the opacity of the type, and darken the background.

To achieve a more metallic look, just switch from the Gaussian profile to the Linear Contour profile in the Bevel and Emboss Contour section.

Switch to the Linear Contour profile for a more metallic effect.

A variation that looks as if the type is made of glass was more complicated. It required three layers for type and separate Layer Effects on two of them.

The lowest type layer is the type filled with the water photo, just as you created it earlier.

Make the glass effect with three type layers.

288

The middle type layer is offset a few pixels to the right and filled with the aqua color sampled from the photo. The drop shadow is the same color as the type. Also in the Structure section for the Drop Shadow dialog box, Blend mode is Multiply, Opacity is 100%, Angle is 138°, Distance is 8 pixels, Spread is 0, and Size is 5 pixels. The Contour chosen in the Quality section is Linear. Anti-alias is turned off, and Layer Knocks Out Drop Shadow is turned on.

Use the following settings for the upper type layer and the Layers palette after all effects are in place; settings omitted are all 0:

Outer Glow: **Structure**

Blend mode: **Screen**, Opacity: **75%**

Color: **Pale yellow** (R255, G255, B190)

Elements

Technique: **Softer**

Size: **5 pixels**

Quality

Contour: **Linear**

Range: **50%**

Bevel and Emboss: **Structure**

Style: **Inner Bevel**

Technique: **Smooth**

Depth: **151%**

Direction: **Up**

Size: **13 pixels**

Shading

Angle: **138°**

Use Global Light: **Checked**

Altitude: **34°**

Gloss Contour: **Ring**

Anti-alias: **Checked**

Highlight mode: **Normal**, Opacity: **75%**

Shadow mode: **Color Burn**, Opacity: **75%**

Make a drop shadow the same color as the type fill.

Give the top type layer an outer glow and an inner bevel.

DESIGNING WITH TYPE

"'See Venice and die,' is that what they say?

Or is it Rome?"

—DICKIE GREENLEAF, IN *THE TALENTED MR. RIPLEY*

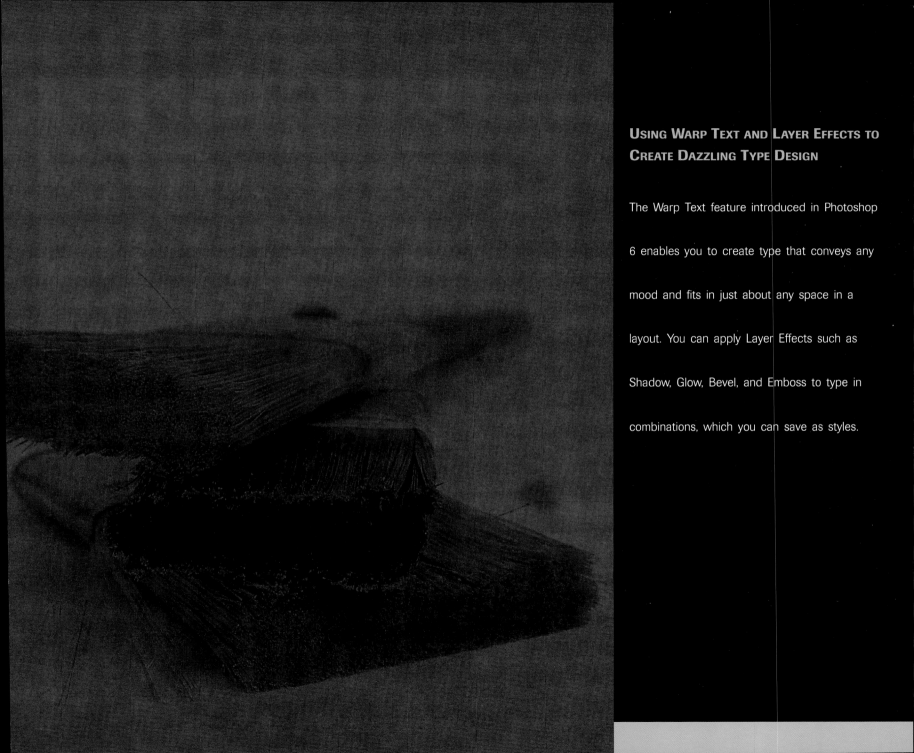

USING WARP TEXT AND LAYER EFFECTS TO CREATE DAZZLING TYPE DESIGN

The Warp Text feature introduced in Photoshop

6 enables you to create type that conveys any

mood and fits in just about any space in a

layout. You can apply Layer Effects such as

Shadow, Glow, Bevel, and Emboss to type in

combinations, which you can save as styles.

Project 21

Designing with Type

by Rhoda Grossman

GETTING STARTED

In the first exercise, you'll create an image consisting
primarily of Warp Text effects. Following that are two
projects for adding type to a background image. They
combine Warp Text and Layer Effects, as well as some
alterations to the background image, to enhance the type.

WARPING TYPE

Graphic design limited to type need not be limited at all. In this tribute, to my favorite
Italian cities, several kinds of text warps are used.

1   Start with an image filled with black.

    The size used here is 7×5 inches at a resolution
    of 200 ppi.

2 Choose a bold sans-serif font and type **Italia**.

Shown here is the font "Hot Coffee" at 120 points. There appears to be too much space between the "t" and the "a" and a little too much between the "i" and the final "a." There's not quite enough space between the "a" and "l." Kerning is needed.

> **Note:** The settings provided in these projects might need to be altered to accommodate the fonts you work with, if they are different from those used here.

3 Select the Type tool and click between any letters that need adjustment. Open the Character palette and choose the amount of increased or decreased space you want.

A value of −50 was used to kern the space between the letter pairs "t" and "a."

4 Apply Warp Text using the Squeeze style and these settings:

Vertical button: **On**

Bend: **+56%**

Horizontal Distortion: **−72%**

Vertical Distortion: **0%**

Type **Italia** in a bold sans-serif typeface.

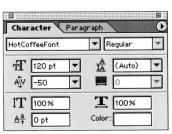

Adjust kerning between letter pairs in the Character palette.

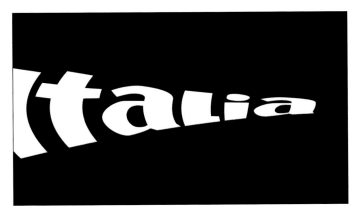

Apply a Squeeze style from the Warp Text menu.

5 Use Free Transform to stretch the type vertically and rotate it counterclockwise.

Stretch and rotate the type with Transform commands.

6 Type **Venetzia** in a contrasting font. Fill the type with golden yellow.

"Vivaldi" is used here, an elegant script that just happens to be named after an illustrious son of Venice.

Use an elegant script for your text.

7 Apply Warp Text to the new type, using the Rise style with these settings:

Horizontal button: **On**

Bend: **+63%**

Horizontal Distortion: **−39%**

Vertical Distortion: **−34%**

8 Move the Venetzia text to the top of the Italia text. Rotate it if needed for a bit of overlap. Change the Blending mode for this new layer to Difference. Reduce the Opacity of the Italia text to 60%.

Difference mode has no effect when the underlying pixels are black. Against white pixels the complementary color appears. So, blue (the complement of yellow) is the result where pixels overlap the white type. Fading the white type has two benefits: the Italia text is less overpowering, and the bright blue of the overlapping pixels becomes deep purple.

Warp and reposition the "Venetzia" type. Use Difference mode.

9 Add a type layer for the city of Florence (Firenze, in Italian).

The font used here is "Wide Latin," filled with a reddish brown or burnt sienna, to stay with the theme of the Tuscany region.

Create the "Firenze" type layer.

10 Apply the Arc style of Warp Text with these settings and move the Firenze layer to the bottom of the stack:

Vertical button: **On**

Bend: **−28%**

Horizontal Distortion: **+19%**

Vertical Distortion: **−55%**

Apply Warp Text, using the Arc style. Place the Firenze layer below the others.

Relationships among the type layers are developing. Venetzia now shows a rich green where it overlaps the reddish brown type, and the reduced opacity of the original Italia layer allows for a pleasing interaction with the new text.

11 Type **Roma** in a Roman typeface, such as Times New Roman or Trajan. Use the Arc Upper Warp style with these settings and then move the layer to a position below Italia:

Horizontal button: **On**

Bend: **+74%**

Horizontal Distortion: **−25%**

Vertical Distortion: **+24%**

The Arc Upper style suggests the ancient architecture of Rome's Forum and Coliseum. The color used here is a warm, medium brown similar to raw umber, once again keeping with the subject matter. Where the 60% white of Italia overlaps Roma, the color is similar to café latte.

FITTING TEXT TO A FLORENTINE ARCH

In this section and those that follow, you will design a cover for a book called *Impressions of Italy*. You'll create two designs using that text, each with a photograph of Italian Renaissance art as the background image. Both designs use the Warp Text feature and Layer Effects.

You'll begin with a background image of a building in Florence showing a bit of sculpture, the symbol of the Medici family, and an arch. Using Warp Text you will fit the book title into the arch shape. Type effects give the letters a 3D volume and the patina of old silver.

1   Open the source image **FLORARCH.tif**.

Begin with the source image of Italian Renaissance architecture.

2 Type the words **Impressions of Italy** in white. Make any adjustments needed for leading, tracking, and alignment in the Options strip for the Text tool.

This example uses the typeface "Raphael" for the word Impressions. "Charlemagne" is used for the second line of type, adding a bit of variation within the Italian Renaissance theme. "Trajan" is an appropriate choice also, due to its classic Roman letterforms.

Use white for typing the title, with appropriate fonts.

3 Click the Create Warped Text button, choose the Arc Upper style, and apply a Bend of +84%. Vertical and Horizontal Distortion should remain at 0%.

Arc Upper seems the obvious style choice, because you can fit the type to the shape of the arch in the background image.

None
⌒ **Arc**
⌒ **Arc Lower**
✓ ⌒ **Arc Upper**
⌒ **Arch**
⊖ **Bulge**
⌒ **Shell Lower**
⌒ **Shell Upper**
≋ **Flag**
≋ **Wave**
⌒ **Fish**
⊟ **Rise**
▥ **Fisheye**
○ **Inflate**
⌇ **Squeeze**
▨ **Twist**

Choose Arc Upper from the Warp Text Style menu.

Note: Options for the Type tool include more than just font, size, style, and alignment. You can specify tracking, leading, kerning, and both vertical and horizontal scaling numerically in the Character palette. A set of choices is also available for the degree of anti-aliasing of text.

4 Choose the new Layer Style feature from the Layer menu. To reproduce the effect shown here, use these styles and settings:

Drop Shadow: Use defaults

Inner Glow: Light orange picked up
      from the upper part of the
      background image

Bevel and Emboss: Check the Contour box

Satin: Use defaults

Pattern Overlay: Use the Metal Landscape
      pattern in the pop-up menu

This combination of effects gives your text the look of slightly raised metallic letters. You can access Layer Styles at any time by clicking the "f" icon at the bottom of the Layer palette. Selecting any item in the list brings up the entire array of styles and settings in one large dialog box.

In the example, changing Inner Glow's default color from pale yellow to an orange tone gives the type a warmer look. Pattern Overlay's Metal Landscape preset adds a distressed look to the type.

Tip: When you are happy with the combination of settings, you can save it as a new preset by clicking the New Style button and giving it a name. Each effect you enabled is then listed in the Layers palette, where you can toggle visibility in order to have instant feedback on the look resulting from turning one or more of them on or off.

Finish by adding a combination of Layer Effects to the warped type.

Tip: Click the triangle button next to the pattern swatch to see all patterns currently loaded. Another triangle button is now available, giving you access to alternate pattern libraries and a number of commands, including options for displaying the current patterns. Choose a list display if you want to see the names of the patterns along with sample swatches.

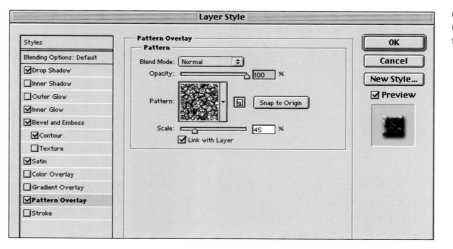

Choose a Pattern Overlay to give the type a distressed look.

TYPE ON THE SISTINE CEILING

For this design, you'll use a scanned photo of Michelangelo's (recently cleaned) painting on the ceiling of the Vatican's Sistine Chapel. Using the same book title, you'll create text effects using Blend modes and requiring alterations be made to the background image as you work.

1   Open the image **Sistine1.tif**.

2   Type **Italy** in a font that works with the style of this Renaissance painting.

    Here is the Raphael font once again, trusting that the real-life rivalry between Michelangelo and Raphael would not create too much tension!

3   Fill the type with a flesh tone sampled from the background image, or use R206, G183, and B176.

    If you prefer CMYK, the equivalents are C16, M24, Y24, and K0.

Begin with a section of the Sistine Chapel ceiling.

4   Click the Warp Text button and choose the Rise style with these settings:

    Horizontal Button: **On**

    Bend: **+20%**

    Distortion: **0%**

    A detail of the image at this stage shows the text is not legible enough and needs more manipulation to be distinguished from the background.

Warp the text and fill it with a sampled flesh tone.

5 Add an Outer Glow from the Layer Styles. Change the spread to 9% and the Size to 25 pixels; use the defaults for all other settings. Replace the default yellow color for the glow with a deeper golden ochre sampled from the cushion.

6 Change the Blend mode for the Type layer from Normal to Color Burn. Reduce the Opacity of the Type layer to 70%.

This combination of effects works to reveal some of the image through the type and to create enough contrast for easy readability.

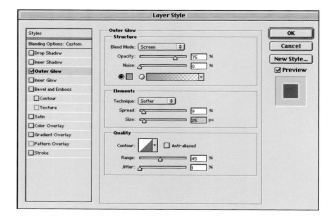

Add the Outer Glow effect.

CHANGING THE BACKGROUND

Before tackling the other two words in the title, let's improve the background image (with apologies to Michelangelo). You'll simplify and darken the image enough to enhance the type later in the project.

1 Apply the Cutout filter in the Artistic group with the following settings, but do not click Save just yet:

Number of Levels: **5**

Edge Simplicity: **4**

Edge Fidelity: **2**

Cutout has the effect of simplifying the image in a way that looks similar to a serigraph (silkscreen print).

2 Use the Fade command to change the Blend mode of the Cutout filter from Normal to Multiply.

Apply the Cutout filter to the background and switch to Multiply mode with the Fade command.

You have kept the Cutout effect at 100%, so you haven't really faded it. By switching to Multiply mode, you brought back some of the detail of the original background and darkened the image to emphasize the glow around the type.

Note: In Photoshop 6, the Fade command has been moved to the Edit menu (it was formerly part of the Filter menu). Actually, it makes sense to move it to the Edit menu because fades can be used for more than just filters and it can do more than just fade.

You can use an Opacity slider to fade the last command, and you can combine them with Blend mode changes for a wide variety of effects. It's practically as good as having two layers with identical images, applying an effect to the upper layer, and then altering the Opacity and Blend mode of that layer. The advantage is you don't have the extra pixels required for an additional layer. The downside, if any, is that you are committed to the opacity and mode you choose.

3   Use the History Brush to lighten the area of the image under the word Italy. Establish the state prior to the Cutout filter as the History source. Use a large brush with a low opacity, so you can control the amount of change.

At this point you might want to alter or tweak the settings for your text layer. I changed to Darken mode at 100%.

Use the History Brush on the background and alter the text layer settings as needed.

4   Add the text **Impressions of**.

The example uses the typeface "Sand" filled with white.

5   Apply Text Warp, using the Flag style, and these settings:

Horizontal Button: **On**

Bend: **+36%**

Horizontal Distortion: **18%**

Vertical Distortion: **1%**

Create white type for the text.

301

6 Add the Layer Style Bevel and Emboss with these settings, leaving all others at their defaults:

Style: **Pillow Emboss**

Technique: **Chisel Soft**

Size: **11 pixels**

Soften: **6 pixels**

Highlight Mode: **Soft Light**

Highlight Opacity: **80%**

Shadow Opacity: **50%**

Apply the Bevel and Emboss Layer style (background visibility is turned off).

When the Sistine Chapel ceiling background is made visible again, your new type should give the illusion of tooled leather embossing. Adjust the Opacity of the type layer if needed. The example is at 70% in Normal mode.

Turn background visibility on again and you're done.

Note: If you want to warp individual letters into some of the shapes in the vault of the Florentine arch, using vector outline type, available in Adobe Illustrator, would be more appropriate. Moving individual anchor points and direction lines gives considerably more control to letter shaping than Photoshop's Text Warp feature. Illustrator's Type on a Path tool is a better way for text to follow a specific or complex line. For shaping whole words or phrases, however, Warp Text is a powerful and welcomed addition to Photoshop's text handling capability.

If you need to use Illustrator for some tasks, such as distorting individual letter outlines or Type on a Path, use the Place command to create a rasterized version of the vector type for your Photoshop image.

MODIFICATIONS

Filter effects, which have been available in Photoshop as far back as I can recall, can manipulate type. Here's a list of Italian cities created in Wide Latin type that have been duplicated several times. The layers were flattened into the background and the Copper gradient was applied to produce several variations of brown and orange.

The remaining effects are applied with filters from the Distort category. First, a Twirl at 50%, and then a Pinch at 75%.

Immediately after applying the Pinch, use Edit/Fade to reduce the distortion to 75% and switch to Screen mode. This adds texture and complexity, and increases the lightness of some letters.

The final effect pushes the complex layered look even more. It was made by taking snapshots of the Twirl and Pinch states from the History palette and then dragging each of them to the image. The Twirl layer uses Screen mode and the Pinch layer is in Difference mode.

Type a line and duplicate it several times. Create color variations with a gradient fill.

Apply a Twirl distortion followed by a Pinch effect.

Fade the Pinch and switch to Screen mode.

Add previous states made from snapshots in the History palette. Change Blend modes to maximize the layered look.

DIFFERENCE PAINTING

"I hate quotations. Tell me what you know."

—RALPH WALDO EMERSON (1803-1882)

A NEON-PAINT TECHNIQUE

Difference painting creates images with strong

color against a black background. It's great for

those die-hard '60s fans who have never grown

up. It brings back the days (and nights) of

black-light viewing and the smell of incense.

(It's also a great way to take a photograph

and turn it into a very powerful graphic image.)

Difference Painting

by Sherry London

GETTING STARTED

Difference painting is a trick I developed by accident. It produces strong colors on a black background because it depends on comparing two very similar layers placed in Difference mode. If there is no difference between pixels on the two layers, the resulting color is black. In this project, you'll learn how to filter images so the filter produces only a slight change, to create a basic difference painting, and then to control the technique so it is not a totally random experience. You'll learn how to apply the Lens Flare filter to an empty layer, so you can light an image non-destructively. You'll also learn several different methods of creating outline drawings from photographs.

Note: If you want to read some tips on designing composites to use in Difference Painting, be sure to check out the file **22_extras.pdf** on the accompanying CD.

ON DESIGNING

You're going to begin your exploration of difference painting with a ready-made composite image. So that you gain a better idea of ways to approach your own designs for this technique, however, I first want to show you the parentage of the image you'll use.

1 Select your base image.

The goal was to create a Halloween scene, and so I chose this image taken at a farmer's market.

Choose an image that you want to use.

2 Select the other images for the composite.

I also found an image of a witch and a ghost, but they were taken against parked cars (which was not very attractive).

Choose other images that you want to composite.

3 Create your composite.

The image composite was created adding another pumpkin and some dried corn stalks.

> **Note:** If you want to learn about building image composites, check out Project 18, "Blending Images," and Project B, "Compositing," on the CD-ROM.

4 Evaluate your creation.

I tried difference painting using the image composite, and discovered it was exceedingly busy and seemed to lack focus. Sometimes, you need to try the image and see how it turns out. Then you can begin to alter it to simplify the composition. In the next section, you'll see the simplification—and, because you have now seen the original, you can compare the results. The original composite is called **ghosts.psd** and is on the accompanying CD-ROM, so you can play with it if you want.

For the original finished image, combine the two images shown previously plus another pumpkin and some corn stalks.

BASIC DIFFERENCE PAINTING

The basic difference painting technique is quite simple: You duplicate the background image of a layer, change the mode to Difference, and filter the new layer. You then create a duplicate copy with merged layers and apply the Auto Levels command.

1   Open the image **halloween.psd** from the
accompanying CD-ROM.

This image is the simplification of the previous
section's composite.

Select an image with a focal
point or main area of interest.

2   Duplicate the Background layer by dragging it to the
New Layer icon at the bottom of the Layers palette.

This is the fastest way to duplicate a layer within the
same image. Because this technique requires a very
small difference between layers, you need to start by
duplicating your base layer.

Make two layers in your
image: the Background and
the Background copy.

3 Change the Layer Blend mode to Difference.

Because there is no difference between the two layers yet, the image looks as if it is solid black. Changing the Layer mode before applying filters enables you to preview the result of the filter on the composite as you apply the filter, saving time and reducing steps.

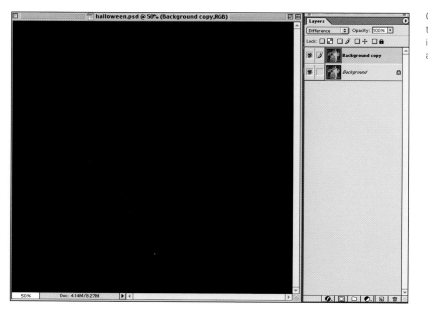

Change the Blend mode to Difference, and the identical layers produce a solid black image.

4 Choose Filter/Sharpen/Unsharp Mask. Use the following settings:

Amount: **100%**

Radius: **1.5 pixels**

Threshold: **0 levels**

The Unsharp Mask filter changes the image data along the areas of the image where Photoshop sees a sharp change in color. Here you aren't using this filter for sharpening—you're using it to make only a *small* change in your image. Because you put the top layer into Difference mode, when you try this technique on your own images, you can "push" the filter settings until you see differences in the image "develop" on the blackness of the top layer. The smaller the change you select, the more black will remain in your final image.

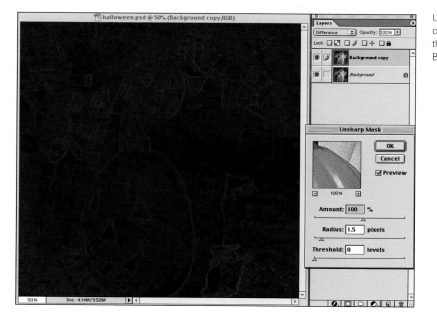

Use the Unsharp Mask filter to create a small change between the Background and the Background copy layers.

5 Choose Image/Duplicate/Merged Layers Only.

This step creates a new image from the two layers in the original.

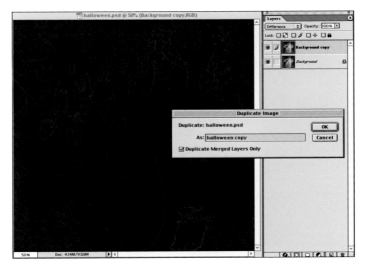

Use the Image/Duplicate command to prepare a flattened version of the image.

6 Choose Image/Adjust/AutoLevels (Shift+Ctrl[Cmd]+L).

This step adds the "magic" to the technique, and makes tiny differences that are almost invisible pop out. In this case, however, a bit too much pops out. The image is very noisy.

Use AutoLevels to bring out bright color in the image.

Note: How would you know an image is too noisy? In most cases, it's personal choice. The technique is supposed to produce a black background in the image. If you have applied the AutoLevels command and almost all of the image is fuzzy and you see very few areas of solid black, you might want to consider filtering the image to remove some of the noise first. The base technique is fast enough that you don't lose much by trying the original image first. If you don't like your results, simply back off and filter the image before you start. You can always use the History palette to get back to any point in the process.

Note: The **22_extras.pdf** file on the CD contains instructions on how to prefilter images to remove excess noise. You'll also learn to apply a woodcut look to the image and how to brighten it. The next section in the book picks up with those steps already applied to the image.

CREATING A FOCAL LAYER

The image as you've created it so far could be complete, but you can create additional layers that highlight the key focal elements in the image. Taking the time to create an area of emphasis changes the project from something that could be automatically generated by an Action to one that really requires thought and planning.

Note: The instructions for creating the first focal layer are in the **22_extras.pdf** file on the CD. The second focal layer, "Decorating the Pumpkin," uses most of the same techniques; however, you might find it more fun to work through. If you want to continue along in the book, you can pick up by using the file **HALLOW7.psd**.

Note: For those of you who are not yet familiar with the tips written by Kai Krause, you can find them online at **http://www.pixelfoundry.com/Tips**. These are the classic tips on channel operations and high level Photoshop work that formed the bedrock of Photoshop techniques for the program's early adopters. Kai Krause (the creator of the Kai's Power Tools filters) is an absolute genius. Although his tips are for Photoshop 2.0 and the command names have changed, the tips are brilliant and should still be in everyone's library. They are free for downloading. The tips were originally released on AOL, and Kai has given the Photoshop community a gift of immense value.

DECORATING THE PUMPKIN

This section shows how you can use filters other than Unsharp Mask to add a slightly different contour to your difference painting. Although this section is basically a repeat of the "Creating a Focal Image" section on the CD, it has several key differences: the Threshold amount is higher, which gives you more image to filter, and the filter used for the difference painting is the Crystallize filter. In addition, you can control exactly where the added detail appears by using a layer mask. You can start here with **HALLOW7.psd** on the CD-ROM if you want.

1 Open **HALLOW7.psd** from the CD.

Open HALLOW7.psd from the accompanying CD-ROM.

312

2 Change the Layer Blend mode to Screen. Choose Image/Adjust/Threshold and accept the default of 128.

The larger Threshold setting makes the image stronger.

3 Apply a Gaussian Blur of 3 pixels.

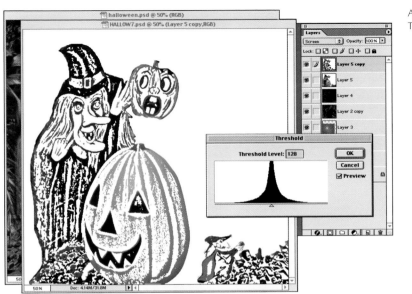

Accept the default Threshold value.

4 Choose Image/Adjust/Levels ands use these settings:

Input Level Black: **121%**

Input Level Gamma: **1.00**

Input Level White: **148%**

5 Merge Down and then duplicate Layer 5 as Layer 5 copy.

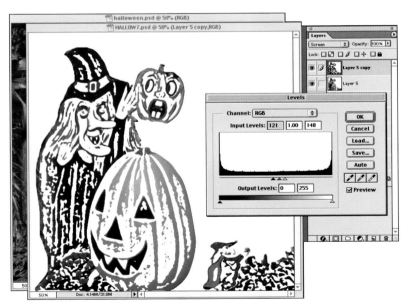

Place the three sliders in the Levels command near the center of the Histogram.

6 Change the Blend mode to Difference. Set the Cell Size of Filter/Pixelate/Crystallize to 21.

Unfortunately, the Crystallize filter lacks a full-screen preview. You can create an enormous difference with this filter. The smallest Cell Size produces the smallest differences.

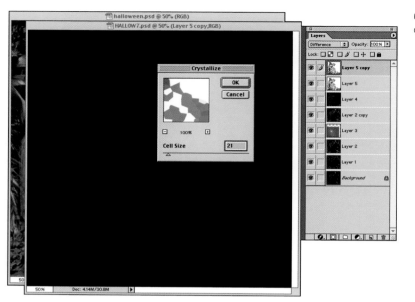

Choose Cell size of 21% on the Crystallize filter.

7 Merge down. Use the AutoLevels command.

You almost don't need to use AutoLevels here. The difference between the images is so great you can clearly see an image "develop" without the AutoLevels command. You also could use Image/Adjust/Levels and control the values that way.

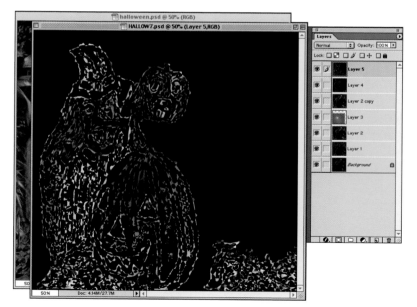

Merge down and use the AutoLevels command.

314

8 Change the Blend mode to Lighten.

Lighten mode displays the lightest values in the combined layers, but doesn't move the image toward white the way that Screen mode does. Therefore, you get a slightly more subtle composite in Lighten mode.

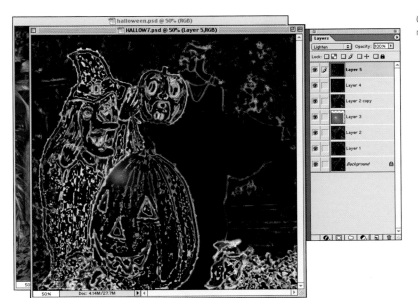

9 Add a layer mask to Layer 5. Working in the mask, using black, paint out the all the enhanced areas except for the pumpkin and the flowers to the left of it. In the pumpkin, hide the image area that overlaps the Lens Flare.

The drizzled detail from the Layer 5 image looks good on the pumpkin but is, perhaps, a bit of overkill on the witch and the mask face. You can paint out as much or as little of the image as you want, or lower the Opacity of Layer 5. I left some of the image in the witch's face as well.

10 Save the image as **HALLOW8.psd**.

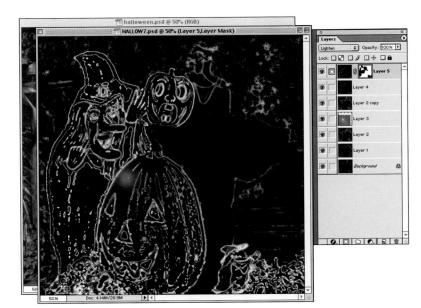

Create a layer mask that hides most of Layer 5 except for the pumpkin.

CHANGING COLORS

You don't need to settle for the colors in the image at this point. You can easily recolor the image by adding a Gradient overlay. You can start with **HALLOW8.psd** on the CD-ROM.

1 Open the image **GRADOVRLAY.psd** from the accompanying CD-ROM.

   This image is a Gradient Overlay layer already set to 55% Opacity. You also could create your own custom gradient in any colors you like.

2 Drag the Gradient layer from the GRADOVRLAY.psd image and drop it onto the HALLOW8.psd image.

   You have an instant color change, and your image is complete.

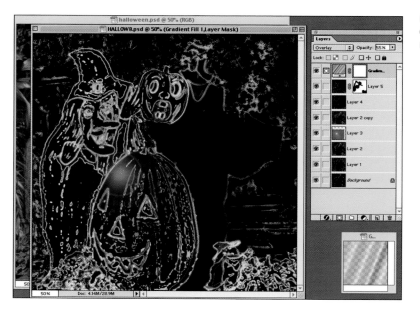

Drag the Gradient Overlay into the HALLOW8.psd image.

> **Note:** You can save the gradient if you like it as a Gradient preset. I also could have sent a Gradient palette instead of a PSD image. Notice also that the Gradient Overlay layer resizes automatically to match the size of the document that it's stored in. That makes it easy to include a tiny PSD file that grows as large as needed when you use it.

HOW IT WORKS

The basic difference painting technique is quite simple. It compares two versions of the same image—an original and one with a filter applied. Areas that are the same in both images appear as black in the combined image. The closer the two images are, the more black you'll see. The AutoLevels command, used on the merged image, can make the tiny levels that aren't black pop out and develop very strong color. You can add to your image by combining various versions of the merged images and changing Blend modes. You can reorganize and recombine in an infinite number of ways.

MODIFICATIONS

You could have changed this project at many different points along the way. You might, for example, want to move the Lens Flare layer to just under the Gradient Overlay layer. You could then remove Layer 2 copy without any effect on your image.

Brighten the flare by moving the Lens Flare layer to just under the Gradient Overlay.

You also might want to further emphasize the witch, mask, and pumpkin by fading back the rest of the layer. One cool way to fade the layer is to create a solid layer of black at the top of the image and apply an inverted copy of the **HALLOWEEN.psd** Alpha 1 channel to it. This blacks out everything in the image except for the Alpha 1 channel. You can then put back some detail by changing the Blend mode to Dissolve at 77% Opacity. I further changed the image by expanding the canvas with black to add a 100-pixel border along each edge.

Mask the image with black in Dissolve mode to make the foreground of the image pop out.

You've learned a large number of techniques that you can extract from this lesson and apply to totally different images. Included on the CD-ROM is the action **Woodcut.atn**. Load the Action and try it on one of your own images. Here's what it did to a still life of onions. The original image, **ONIONS.psd**, is on the CD-ROM as well.

The Woodcut Action changes the mode of the top layer to Multiply, and adds a High Pass of 1.6% and a Threshold of 128%. It blurs the background layer and then blurs and levels the woodcut layer.

You can dramatically change the result simply by putting the top layer into Screen mode.

Try out a variety of different filters when you do a difference painting. The one shown here uses the Colored Pencil filter instead of the Unsharp Mask. Sharpen Edges also works well.

Change the top layer to Screen mode to make the woodcut more of a line drawing.

The Colored Pencil filter makes a big change in the look of the difference painting.

Not all difference paintings have to scream at you. Patricia Uffelman, a student in my online Photoshop class, created this image, called "Celebration." Patricia is a photographer who prefers photographing people and likes to look for small, interesting details that others might overlook. She used only the basic difference painting technique but colorized her original black-and-white image before creating the difference painting. As you can see, the look and feel is quite different from the Halloween image.

Note: Patricia Uffelman is a photographer from Napa Valley, California, where she lives with her husband and photography partner, Mark. Patricia specializes in portraits, weddings, and events, devoting her time and attention to giving the viewer a different perspective, carefully capturing what is often overlooked.

Choose an unaltered photograph.

Colorize or manipulate it.

Then follow the directions for the basic difference painting technique.

SPOT COLOR

"So I says, 'Blue M&M, they all

wind up the same color in the end.'"

—HOMER SIMPSON

USING PANTONE COLOR IN PHOTOSHOP

CMYK printing is expensive. Because it uses

four inks, it requires four printing passes.

Using spot color can add color to a document

without breaking the budget.

Project 23

Spot Color

by Sherry London

GETTING STARTED

Spot color files consist of special Spot Color channels. Each channel represents a single printing plate for (usually) a Pantone or other custom color. Custom colors are inks that are not mixed the same as process colors (CMYK inks). They are used for coverage and are generally thicker and more opaque than process inks. If you want a hot pink, for example, you get a Pantone ink and print in hot pink—you do not try to mix it on different printing plates from component inks.

The problem with building spot color files in Photoshop is that many techniques won't work on the individual files. You usually need to build the image in layers and then convert to channels. The process is not hard, but it is complex and time-consuming.

In this project, you build a fish image that works very well as a four-color spot design. You construct this image in several pieces:

- You build black-and-white image layers that will eventually become the Spot Color channels.

- You construct the image in layers and add color to these layers so that you can preview the effect. This preview also enables you to convert a starting photograph into spot color in your own examples.

■ After your image has been constructed in color, merge the individual color layers so that each color occupies only one layer.

> **Note:** The preceding instructions are in the **23_extras.pdf** file on the accompanying CD. You can work them from the CD before finishing this project, or you can begin from a prepared file and follow along to convert a layered file into spot color.

■ You create the Spot Color channels and convert your color layers into the Spot Color channels.

■ You trap the channels, compensate for dot gain, and save them as a DCS2 file.

> **Note:** The images used as "starters" here—the **TWINFISH.psd** image and the pattern that you create—are traditional African patterns taken from *A Treasury of Design for Artists and Craftsmen* by Gregory Mirow, Dover Books (1969).

From Channel to Plate: A Brief Printing Primer

In traditional four-color printing, your image is separated into four printing plates: Cyan, Magenta, Yellow, and Black (CMYK). Each plate is placed on the press and one of the four inks is used to print the image on the plate. Where does this color separation information come from? It comes from the CMYK channels of your Photoshop image.

You need to either create in or convert your image to Photoshop's CMYK mode if you want to send the finished image to a service bureau for printing. When the image is output, the data in the Cyan channel is written to a plate to be printed with cyan ink. Each plate has its own color ink; each channel becomes a plate. To create the illusion of full-color printing, the four process inks (CMYK) are overlapped.

When you print with spot colors, however, you use inks that do not get mixed with another ink to produce a new color. The most common of the spot color inks is from Pantone. When you separate an image designed to print with Pantone colors, each color becomes its own channel and, therefore, its own printing plate.

CMYK inks mix on the paper to give the illusion of color, but spot color inks, such as the Pantone inks, are meant to be printed as independent colors. You cannot select a spot color in Photoshop and just paint with it in the regular color space and expect to have it print in the ink that you have selected. If you use a Pantone custom color on your image, Photoshop converts it into whatever color mode you are currently using (RGB, LAB, CMYK). You don't want this to happen. As soon as a color has been separated into Photoshop's "normal" color channels, it loses its capability to be output as a spot color plate.

Instead, you need to add Spot Color channels to your image. Because spot colors generally don't overlap one another, you need to trap these Spot Color channels very carefully before you print the image. In this project, you learn how to create layers, preview their colors, organize the layers so that each color is on a single layer, and trap the final channels.

CREATING CHANNELS

Open the **FishLayers.psd** image from the CD. This starting image contains the end result of the preparation steps that are included in the **23_extras.pdf** file in the accompanying CD's Projects/23 directory. At this point, you have an image that consists of four layers, and each layer contains only one color. So long as you create images that are set up in this manner (one color per layer and areas that are not of that color on the layer are transparent), you can prepare any image for spot color printing.

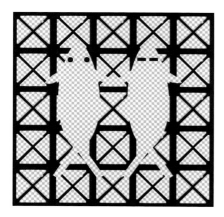  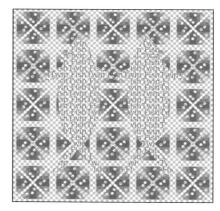 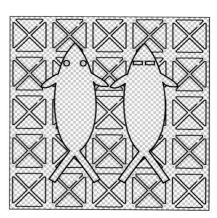

Start with your image in layers that contain only a single color per layer.

1   Choose Image/Calculations. Use the following
settings:

Source 1: **FishLayers.psd** (your current image)

Layer: **Black**

Channel: **Transparency**

Invert: **Checked**

Source 2: **FishLayers.psd** (your current image)

Layer: **Background**

Channel: **(gray)**

Invert: **Not checked**

Blending: **Multiply**

Opacity: **100%**

Mask: **Not checked**

Result: **New Channel**

Name your new channel Spot Black.

This is the fastest, most efficient way to create the
channels. You can also load the layer transparency,
save the result to a new channel, and invert the new
channel. After you have set up the Calculations
dialog box, however, the other three channels will
fly. Calculations is an expanded form of the Apply
Image command and enables you to combine the
grayscale values of layers and channels. It is the only
command that can combine into a new channel.

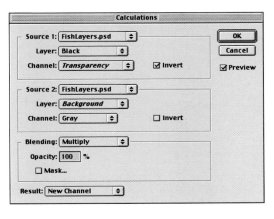

Use the Calculations command to multiply
the transparency of the Black layer with
the gray values of the Background layer
and place the result into a new channel.

325

2 Activate the Rust layer. Choose Image/Calculations. Change Source 1 to Rust and click OK. Name the new channel Rust.

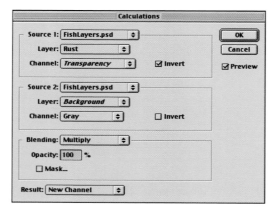

Multiply the Rust layer's inverted transparency with the Background layer's gray values and put the result in a channel and name it Rust.

3 Activate the Yellow layer. Choose Image/Calculations. Change Source 1 to Yellow, click OK, and name the new channel Yellow.

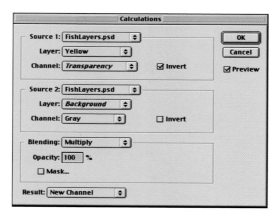

Create the Yellow channel by multiplying the inverted transparency of the Yellow layer with the gray values of the Background layer.

4 Activate the Green layer. Choose Image/Calculations. Change Source 1 to Green, click OK, and name the new channel Green.

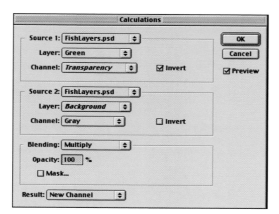

Create the Green channel by multiplying the Green layer's inverted transparency with the Background layer.

CONVERTING TO SPOT COLOR

Now that you have built the channels, it's time to turn them into Spot Color channels. The process is quite simple. To be safe, however, save your image and make a duplicate to use for the next steps. You probably won't need to revert back to your saved image, but saving your work at this point and finishing on the duplicate gives you an easy way to edit your image if a client changes requirements or if you need an audit of how you created the channels.

1   In the duplicate, drag each of the image layers (not the background) to the Layers palette trashcan.

    If you have any layers in your image, they print. You do not want that to happen; therefore, you need to delete them all.

2   Change the order of your channels as follows:

    Yellow: **Channel 5**

    Green: **Channel 6**

    Rust: **Channel 7**

    Spot Black: **Channel 8**

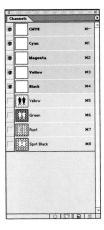

Rearrange the order of your channels.

3 Double-click the Spot Black alpha channel. In the Channel Properties dialog box, click the Spot Color option button. Change the Solidity setting to 100%. Click the color swatch. In the Color Picker, click Custom and choose the Pantone Process Black ink. Click OK. Photoshop should rename the channel PANTONE Process Black CVC.

Photoshop automatically enters a new channel name when you select a custom color.

4 Change the other three channels to spot color with 100% solidity. Use these Pantone colors:

Rust: **PANTONE 167CVC**

Yellow: **PANTONE 108CVC**

Green: **PANTONE 350CVC**

5 Turn off the Eye icon next to the CMYK channel and turn on the Eye icons next to all four spot printing plates.

Notice that just as if you were working in CMYK, the areas that are black in any channel are the areas that will print in color.

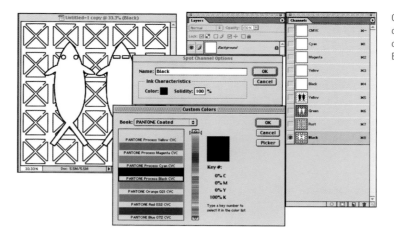

Change the Spot Black alpha channel into a Spot Color channel and select Process Black as the spot color.

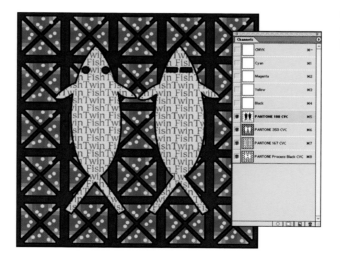

Turn on all the Eye icons next to the Spot Color channels and preview the printing plates.

TRAPPING

Spot Color channels can (and usually do) require trapping. Trapping is a process that introduces a deliberate flaw in the print process in the hopes of preventing a worse one. When paper goes through a printing press, some mis-registration is almost bound to occur. The paper stretches or gets too wet on press, and the plates then misalign. When two colors that were supposed to touch one another don't, and leave a tiny gap instead, the white paper stock shows through. This is quite ugly. One way to try to hide this is to make sure that any areas that touch one another contain either a percentage of the same color, or that one color slightly overprints another. Spot colors never contain common percentages because they are all single colors. Therefore, you need to trap to achieve overprinting.

David Xenakis (the talented publisher of *Knitter's* magazine and a true Photoshop color expert) developed some techniques to make the trapping process more controllable.

The trapping trick uses Difference mode on a before-and-after trapping version of the channel to isolate only the changed pixels. You can then control how much of a trap you actually multiply back into the original plate. Although 40% is sufficient for a good trap, the very opaque Pantone inks could require less, whereas light colors such as yellow could require much more.

1   Activate the Cyan layer in the CMYK channels. Choose Image/Apply Image. Set Source 1 to the current document, PANTONE 167CVC channel. Set the Blend mode to Normal at 100% and click OK.

To create a trap that is less strong than the Photoshop default, you need to copy the Spot Color channels temporarily into the CMYK images. You can trap only two channels at a time using this technique. The darker of the colors being trapped needs to go into the Cyan plate. The most obvious place where two colors touch is the Rust and Yellow plates.

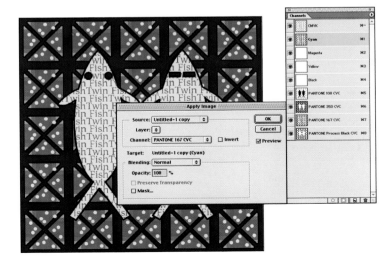

Use the Apply Image command to place the Rust channel into the Cyan plate.

2 Repeat Step 1 for the Yellow layer using the PANTONE 108CVC channel.

The lighter spot color goes into the lighter channel (Yellow). When you trap the Cyan and Yellow plates, the trap is only in the Yellow plate.

3 Activate the PANTONE Process Black channel. Using the Magic Wand with the Add to Selection icon selected, click inside of both fish to select the interior areas. Activate the Yellow channel. Shift+click the Cyan channel to activate it. Choose Image/Trap and enter a value of 1 pixel. Click OK.

You can see the trap in the changed color of the text. Only the Yellow plate should have changed. You need a smaller trap on the text than you do on the pattern circles.

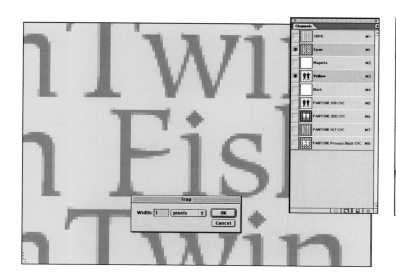

Choose Image/Trap to create a spread of yellow into the Blue channel.

4   Choose Select/Inverse, and then select Image/Trap
and enter a value of 2 pixels. Click OK. Deselect.

5   Right(Ctrl)+click the Yellow channel and choose
Duplicate Channel from the pop-out menu.
Duplicate the channel as Trapped into a new
document, also named Trapped.

This step makes no sense right now. You need to
compare the before-and-after trapping Yellow plates
and, from this comparison, you create an image that
has *only* the changed pixels.

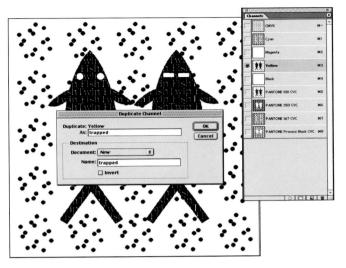

Duplicate the Yellow channel
into its own document.

6   In the History palette, click back until you have
reverted the image to the last state *before* you applied
the first Trap command. Deselect if you get a
selection back in the image.

If you have your History setting to the default of
Linear History only, the steps after the one to which
you revert back are grayed out (but still recoverable
until you perform another command, such as
deselection).

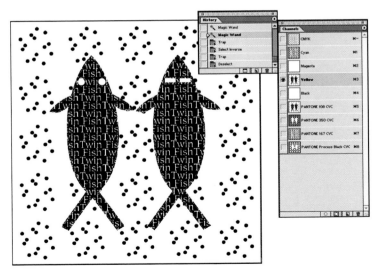

Revert back to the last
History step before you
applied the Trap command.

7 Right(Ctrl)+click the Yellow channel and choose Duplicate Channel from the pop-out menu. Duplicate the channel (and rename it Before) into the document named Trapped that you created in Step 5.

By comparing the Before and Trapped channels, you can find only the changed pixels.

8 Activate the trapped image. Choose Image/Calculations. Create a new channel using the following settings:

Source 1:   **Trapped**

Layer: **n/a**

Channel: **Before**

Invert: **Unchecked**

Source 2:   **Trapped**

Layer: **n/a**

Channel: **Trapped**

Invert: **Unchecked**

Blending: **Difference**

Opacity: **100%**

Mask: **Unchecked**

Result: **New Channel**

Photoshop names the channel Alpha 1. Activate Alpha 1 and invert it [Ctrl(Cmd)+I].

The new channel contains only the changed pixels, but the values are inverted. You need to invert the channel to get back to the original color (value) of the pixels.

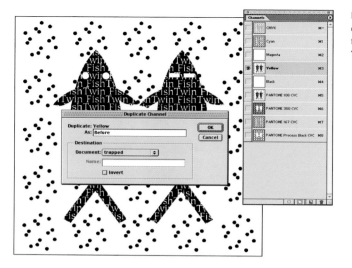

Duplicate the untrapped Yellow channel into the same document that you created for the trapped Yellow channel.

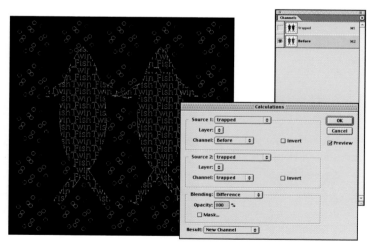

Create a new channel that shows the difference between the before-and-after channels.

9 Activate your main image (probably Untitled-1 copy). Activate the PANTONE 108CVC channel and make sure it is the only active channel. Choose Image/Apply Image.

Source: **Trapped**

Channel: **Alpha 1**

Blending: **Multiply**

Opacity: **40%**

Mask: **Unchecked**

Using Multiply mode, you are adding the changed pixels back to the Spot Color channel where they belong. However, you are adding them back at only 40%. The lighter amount means that you get a more delicate (but still effective) trap. The difference is that you won't see the color change as much on your printed image—which is good!

10 Activate the CMYK composite channel, choose Select/All, and delete.

This clears the channels so that you can trap the PANTONE 108CVC and PANTONE 350CVC channels to each other.

11 Repeat Steps 1–9, placing the PANTONE 350CVC channel into the Cyan channel and the PANTONE 108CVC into the Yellow channel. Either change the name of the "holding" document, or close the trapped document and re-create a new one.

12 Activate the CMYK composite channel, choose Select/All, and delete.

This clears all the CMYK channels. No other trapping is required. The center line strokes that created the Black channel already overprint the rest of the places where the colors touch.

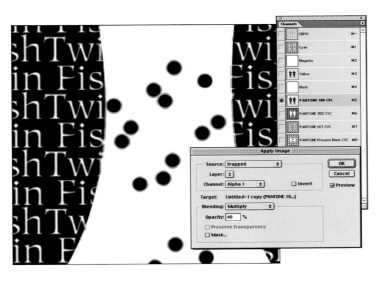

Multiply back 40% of the changes to the Yellow channel onto the PANTONE 108CVC channel.

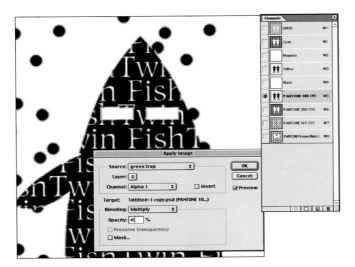

Multiply back 40% of the changes to the Yellow channel that represent the trapping with the dark green spot color onto the PANTONE 108CVC channel.

333

COMPENSATING FOR DOT GAIN

Dot gain occurs on press when the ink spreads on paper. You need to get the specific dot gain amounts from your printer for your print job, but this section shows you how to adjust the PANTONE 167CVC channel for dot gain.

You need only to adjust for dot gain if you have areas that are neither solid white nor solid black in the channel. PANTONE 167CVC is the only channel in this image that has gray values in it. Dot gain is usually measured in terms of the movement of the 50% value when it is printed. A 20% dot gain (which is what the example uses) means that values that are supposed to be 50% gray will print as 70% gray. This section demonstrates David Xenakis's technique for compensating for dot gain. This technique also works with any grayscale image.

Note: The dot gain curve trick enables you to see and compensate for the dot gain on press. Photoshop's grayscale gains have never worked as well as they could; and with this trick, you don't need to hassle with using profiles as compensation. Just make sure that you turn off Photoshop's color management so that you get what you actually asked for.

1 Right(Ctrl)+click on the PANTONE 167CVC channel and select Duplicate from the pop-out menu. Duplicate the channel into a new image and name it DOT GAIN. Choose Image/ Mode/Grayscale.

2 Create a new Curves Adjustment layer (Layer/New Adjustment Layer/Curves). Move the 50% point to 70%. Click OK. Name the new layer Dot Gain Curve.

This is the correction that shows you how your channel would print with a 20% dot gain. If you have a different dot gain amount in your own work, you add it to the baseline of 50% here. If you were doing a job on newsprint and the dot gain figure was 35%, for example, you would change the 50% input to 85% output.

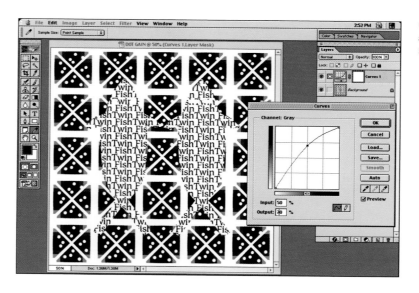

Create a dot gain curve as an adjustment layer and change the 50% point to 70%.

3 Choose the Color Sampler tool. Place Point 1 on a 25% gray area, Point 2 on a 50% gray area, and Point 3 on the 75% gray area.

These points help you to create your compensation curve.

4 Create another Curves Adjustment layer at the top of the layer stack. In the Curves Adjustment Layer box, place the Eyedropper tool on Point 1. Make sure the Input and Output boxes read 39%. Click on the curve to leave a point, and edit the Input box to read 39% and the Output box to read 25%—the desired value for that 39% pixel. Repeat for Points 2 and 3 and edit them so they are set back to 50% and 75%, respectively.

The dot gain curve shows you how the pixels change on printing, and the second curve enables you to lighten the pixels of the original image so they lighten up enough to still print at the desired densities.

Use the Color Sampler tool to identify the 25%, 50%, and 75% values in the image.

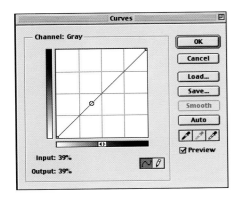
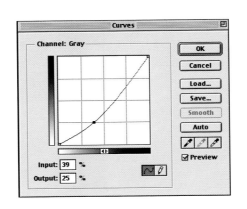
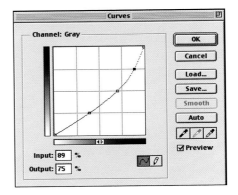

Create a new Curves Adjustment layer that lightens the image back to the original densities.

5 Drag the dot gain curve to the Layers palette trashcan. Activate the Curves 1 layer and merge down (Ctrl[Cmd]+E).

Now you have applied the compensation curve so that the channel will print to your desired values (as long as the press holds to a 20% dot gain).

6 Activate the PANTONE 167CVC channel in the working document. Choose Image/Apply Image. Change the source to the dot gain image and the channel defaults to gray (your only choice). Change the Blend mode to 100% Normal to replace the entire channel with the tone-compensated one.

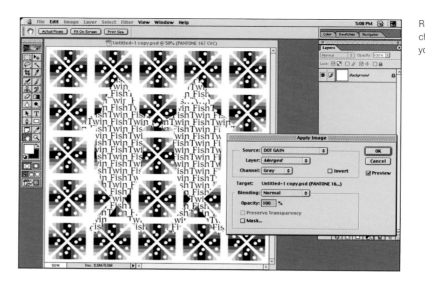

Replace the PANTONE 167CVC channel with the new channel you created.

SAVING THE FILE

You need to save the image in DCS2 format to be able to place the image into QuarkXPress or InDesign to print spot plates.

1 Choose Image/Mode/Multichannel.

2 Activate the Channels palette. Drag the Cyan, Magenta, Yellow, and Black channels to the Trashcan on the Channels palette. Leave only the four Spot Color channels.

If you save your file with the empty CMYK channels in them, you produce blank plates. That's wasteful, and if you burn film for the empty channels, it's expensive.

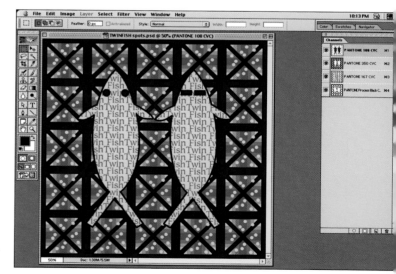

Select the CMYK channels, leaving only the Spot Color channels.

3 Choose File/Save As. In the dialog box, select
Photoshop DCS 2.0. In the second dialog box,
select the options that you want.

My favorite options appear in the figure.

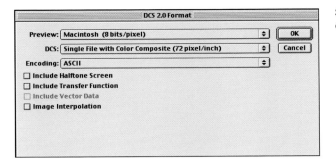

Select the options you need or the
options your printer requests.

MODIFICATIONS

The easiest way to modify this project is to select different colors for it. You can also build the trap in the Cyan
and Magenta plates. However, the trapping in the Cyan to Magenta always generates changes to *both* plates.
Photoshop splits the trap in half and places half the amount in each channel. Therefore, you need to do twice
as much work, or you need to use the CMYK Background layer for both the Difference image and to multiply
the desired trap back onto the spot channels.

In this project, you began with a project that you built from the ground up. You could have also started with a
photograph you wanted to turn into spot color. You would need to separate the image into the layer that you
need to build the channels. If you cannot use layer transparency, you need to work in grayscale and be sure
Photoshop is not adding profile transforms to your values (tell Photoshop to *not* color manage). If you have an
image on a layer and that layer is the only visible layer, you can load the values in the layer as a channel (load the
composite channel in the Channels palette) and save these values as a new channel. This process is equivalent to
saving the layer transparency (but you must work in grayscale).

Another common use of spot color is to create a bump plate. A bump plate is an overprinting plate that adds
additional emphasis to another plate, usually by using an ink that is out-of-gamut for CMYK printing. If you
were printing an image of a circus performer and needed to make the poison yellow satin of her costume stand
out, for example, you could duplicate the Yellow channel as a Spot Color channel. Select the portion of the
channel you want to use as the bump plate and then you need to tone it down. You can preview the image
to determine how much ink you need by first selecting the Pantone color you want to add and then view
the image with the fifth channel turned on. Adjust the solidity value of the channel until the color looks right.
Pretend that when the solidity value in the Channel Options dialog box gets to 25%, the costume jumps fairly
off the page. To fix the bump channel so that it produces that value, fill that channel with white in the amount
that is the solidity value subtracted from 100. Therefore, if you find that 25% percent solidity looks right, you
need to fill the bump plate channel with 75% white in Normal mode.

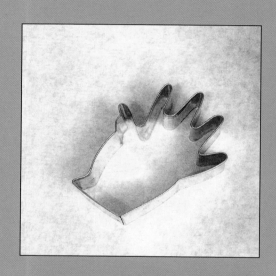

APPENDIX A

"If it keeps up, man will atrophy all his

limbs, but the push-button finger."

—FRANK LLOYD WRIGHT

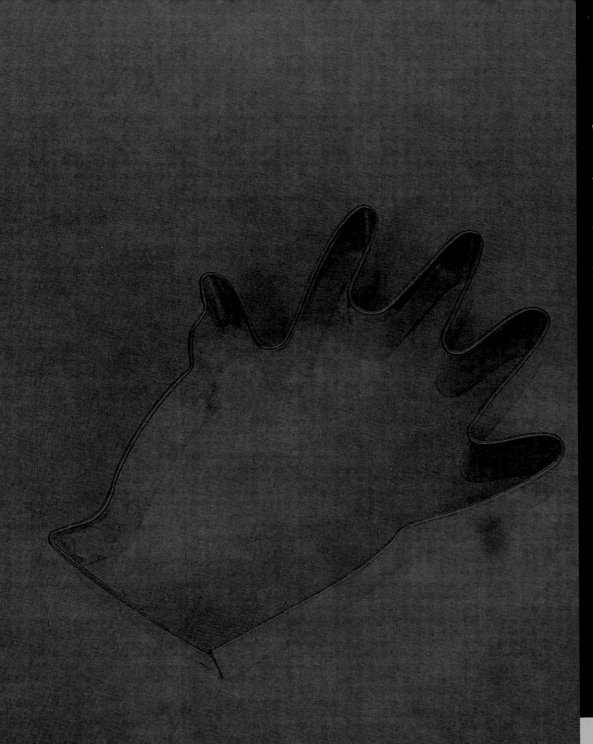

WHAT'S ON THE CD-ROM

The accompanying CD-ROM is packed with all sorts of exercise files and products to help you work with this book and with Adobe Photoshop 6. The following sections contain detailed descriptions of the CD's contents.

For more information about the use of this CD, please review the ReadMe.txt file in the root directory. This file includes important disclaimer information as well as information about installation, system requirements, troubleshooting, and technical support.

SYSTEM REQUIREMENTS

This CD-ROM was configured for use on systems running Windows 9X/NT and Macintosh.

PC:

Processor: 486DX or higher.

OS: Microsoft Windows 95/98/NT or higher.

Memory (RAM): 24 MB.

Monitor: VGA, 640x480 or higher with 256 color or higher.

Storage Space: 10 MB Minimum (will vary depending on installation).

Other: Mouse or compatible pointing device.

Optional: Internet connection and Web browser.

MAC:

Memory (RAM): 24 MB.

Monitor: VGA, 640x480 or higher with 256 color or higher.

Storage Space: 10 MB Minimum (will vary depending on installation).

Other: Mouse or compatible pointing device.

Optional: Internet connection and Web browser.

LOADING THE CD FILES

To load the files from the CD, insert the disc into your CD-ROM drive. If auto-play is enabled on your machine, the CD-ROM setup program starts automatically the first time you insert the disc. You may copy the files to your hard drive, or use them right off the disc.

Note: This CD-ROM uses long and mixed-case filenames, requiring the use of a protected mode CD-ROM driver.

EXERCISE FILES

This CD contains all the files you'll need to complete the exercises in *Photohop 6 Effects Magic*. These files can be found in the root directory's Projects folder. Please note, however, that you'll not find any folder for Project 4; this project contains exercises for which you do not need to access any project files.

Note: In order to access the exercise files for each project, you will need to decompress them. Evaluation copies of WinZip (PC) and Expander (Mac) have been included on this CD so that you can easily extract them to your hard drive.

THIRD-PARTY PROGRAMS

This CD also contains several third-party programs and demos from leading industry companies. These programs have been carefully selected to help you strengthen your professional skills in Photoshop.

Please note that some of the programs included on this CD-ROM are shareware-"try-before-you-buy"-software. Please support these independent vendors by purchasing or registering any shareware software that you use for more than 30 days. Check with the documentation provided with the software on where and how to register the product.

■ **WinZip 8.0 Evaluation Version (for PC only).** WinZip brings the convenience of Windows to the use of Zip files and other archive and compression formats. The optional wizard interface makes unzipping easier than ever. WinZip features built-in support for popular Internet file formats, including TAR, gzip, Unix compress, UUencode, BinHex, and MIME. ARJ, LZH, and ARC files are supported through external programs. WinZip interfaces to most virus scanners. (By WinZip Computing, Inc.)

Expander Evaluation Version (For MAC only). Aladdin Systems' Expander freeware for Mac is the easiest way to expand and decode all those files you download from the Web or receive in your email. Just drag, drop, and you're done! Expander works seamlessly with Web browsers such as Internet Explorer and Netscape Navigator. From BinHex to Zip, StuffIt to MIME, Expander accesses more formats, in less time, with zero hassles. (By Aladdin Systems.)

Acrobat Reader 4.05. The free Adobe Acrobat Reader allows you to view, navigate, and print PDF files across all major-computing platforms. Acrobat Reader is the free viewing companion to Acrobat and to Acrobat Capture software. You'll need to use Acrobat Reader to view the Bonus Projects on this CD.

BONUS PROJECTS

In the Bonus Projects directory, you'll find two extra chapters. We have included them (in PDF format) as a bonus to you:

Bonus Project A: Camouflaging Photographic Flaws by Felix Nelson

At one time or another, all of us have seen a torn, scratched, or ripped image that we might have used on a project—if it weren't for those useless flaws or imperfections. The thing is, however, if you look close enough, there is usually something in the image that you can use to repair it—a silver lining, as it were. In this project, you learn to use the most powerful retouching tool that you have at your disposal: the original image itself.

Bonus Project B: Compositing
by Aren Howell

Photoshop users often need to combine two or more photos into one professional-looking image. Placing objects into backgrounds other than those the objects were originally photographed against requires techniques that separate the "men from the boys" in Photoshop users. The right selections make or break the success of your image. This project looks at compositing from a man's (or woman's, in my case) point of view—no kid stuff.

Additional Bonus Sections

In the project directories for Projects 6, 9, 11, 15, 22, and 23, you'll find bonus sections (in PDF format) for each of these projects. These were designed to allow you to further expand upon the art and techniques you created and learned in these six projects. Be sure to see the individual projects in this book for more information about these bonus sections.

READ THIS BEFORE OPENING THE SOFTWARE

By opening the CD package, you agree to be bound by the following agreement:

INDEX

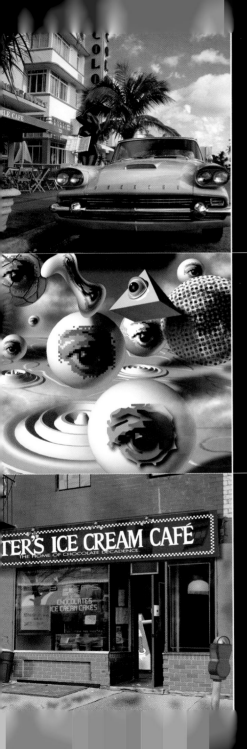

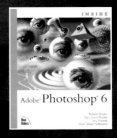
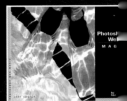

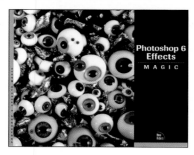

Photoshop® 6 Effects Magic

Each New Riders Magic book uses Intellistation systems to output and test all media contained within the book. New Riders Magic books and Intellistation systems have been created with you, the computer graphics professional, in mind.

Photoshop Graphics Workstation

Build your own Photoshop graphics workstation online and choose from a wide selection of the ultimate in processors, RAM, monitors, and graphics cards including Nvidia, Elsa, IBM, and 3DFX Voodoo.

Adobe® Photoshop® 6.0

Adobe Photoshop 6.0 software introduces the next generation of image editing with powerful new features that offer something for every user. Delivering the broadest and most productive tool set available, Photoshop helps you explore your creativity, work at peak efficiency, and achieve the highest quality results across all media. Try version 6.0 and see why Adobe Photoshop continues to be the world-standard image-editing solution.

Scanners, Tablets, and Printers

Check out IntelliStations.com for all of the latest tablets, printers, scanners, and enhancement plug-ins for Photoshop.

Intellistations.com

The Ultimate Internet Resource for Video, Film, 3D, and Creative Graphics Professionals.

Buy Online via our secure ordering system for VISA, MC, and AMEX

Build your video/3D dream machine with our **Online Configu**

3D — design your 3D object

process with your favorite software

graphics

output to DVD, CD-ROM, Web/Streaming media, or any other tape format

video

IntelliStations.com is your sou digital content creation tools will allow your projects to be on time, every time. The one really want for video editing, animation, Web design/grap and more.

Our knowledgeable technical production engineers will also ASSIST you with INTEGRATIO of your IntelliStations.com sys with your professional produc equipment.

If you have questions while b your dream system, you can us 24x7x365 at 1-800-501-0 for assistance from one of ou IntelliStations.com DCC specie Ask about our no money dow creative financing programs.

Check out CGchannel.com, o content provider for 3D reviev demos, and more!

 channel.com

THE PHOTOSHOP 6 EFFECTS MAGIC CD

The CD that accompanies this book contains valuable resources for anyone using Photoshop 6. All files needed to complete the tutorials are included, as are before-and-after images, actions, and textures.

Note: For a complete list of the CD-ROM contents, please see Appendix A, "What's on the CD-ROM."

ACCESSING THE PROJECT FILES FROM THE CD

The majority of projects in this book use pre-built Photoshop files that contain preset parameters, artwork, or other important information you need to work through and build the final project.

All the project files are conveniently located in the CD's Projects directory. To access the project files for the Coloring a Sketch project (Project 16), for example, locate the following directory on the accompanying CD: Projects\16. In order to access the exercise files for each project, you will need to decompress them. Evaluation copies of WinZip (PC) and Expander (Mac) have been included on this CD so that you can easily extract them to your hard drive.

COLOPHON

Photoshop 6 Effects Magic was laid out and produced with the help of Microsoft Word, Adobe Acrobat, Adobe Photoshop, Collage Complete, and QuarkXpress a variety of systems, including a Macintosh G4. With the exception of pages that were printed out for proofreading, all files—text, images, and project files—were transferred via email or ftp and edited on-screen.

All body text was set in the Bergamo family. All headings, figure captions, and co text were set in the Imago family. The Symbol and Sean's Symbol typefaces were used throughout for special symbols and bullets.

Photoshop 6 Effects Magic was printed on 60# Mead Web Dull at GAC (Graphic Arts Center) in Indianapolis, IN. Prepress consisted of PostScript computer-to-pl technology (filmless process). The cover was printed on 12-pt. Carolina, coated o one side.